THE COMPLETE LYRICS OF AVTAR SIMRIT

ALSO BY AVTAR SIMRIT

True Fiction (Volume One)
A Dream of True Time

Break Every Chain
Shackled to Creation

The Complete Lyrics of Avtar Simrit

NILOTIC YEARS

Avtar Simrit

Apocalyptic Rhymes

Copyright © 2022 by Avtar Simrit

All rights reserved. No part of this book may be reproduced in any manner whatsoever without written permission except in the case of brief quotations embodied in critical articles and reviews.

First Printing, 2022

These songs are for Everyone, Everywhere, All At Once

Contents

Introduction   xix

Messiah Complex (2009)   1

Seven	3
Skin Like You	6
The Antichrist Scenario	8
Destroyer	13
Hanging on a Twisted Cross	16
VisionLand	20
The Sound	23
Fever Dream	24
I Kill With My Cunt	28
Killer of Last Things	30
GODDAMNIT	40
Humanimal	42

Opposite Man	47
Outbound Train	52

CNT (2010) — 57

Intro: Them Hollow	59
See Media	61
I Rep for the Darkness	65
My Mother	69
Join Hands in the Sands	75
I Am One of Them, I Am All of Them	80
Gettin Paid	82
If I Killed You	86
Jiz and Rainbows	92
We Are Not the Living	94
Sacagewaea	98
B-CUM	102
HOO	103

The Girls in My Screams EP (2010) — 107

The Girls in My Screams (Part 1)	109
The Girls in My Screams (Part 2)	121
The Girls in My Screams (Part 3)	132

Contents | ix

Alice	142
The Screams in My Girls	145
The Sky Is Falling	150
Suffering	153

net.art (2011) — 161

Cellar Door	164
She's So Heavy	169
The Rock Without Roll	174
Another Brick in the Wall	177
Alt Gangsta	181
ar	186
This Is Hell	192
Hate Love	196
Her Body	200
Cocaine (No Pain)	204
Not So Fucked Up	208
Where Are We Going?	213
Who Are You?	217
Intercision	219
The World Is Yours	223
Freedom of Leave	229

x | Contents

AOC	234
Out of Sight	239
This Is Where It's At	243
Trick Tock Tick	248
On the Journey Toward the Infinite	252

Lullabies for a Lifestyle (2011) — 259

Apology	263
EDEN	265
Fuck Chicago	268
Hourglass	272
Create My Pain	276
Play Party In Hell	280
The Heartbeat Mile	283
Fame & Fucking	287
My Heroin	293
VisionLand	299
False Reality	303
Fall With Me	309
Girl with a Gun	315
Hollow Woman	321
Soul(less) Electric	326

Bates Motel	335
Nothing Is Private	340
Child's Pose	344
Headcase	348
Goodbye Lifestyle Lullaby Soliloquy	354
No Gandhi	360
Open Your Eyes	366

Emotional Ghetto (2011) — 371

Opening Sequence	374
Cracked Lips	378
With Sunglasses On	381
Build a Forest	386
Monster	389
Get Off Dat Nigga's Nuttz	395
Suicide Eyes	399
Emotional Ghetto	403
Bloodstained Treehouse	409
Keep It Real	414
Finding the Audience	418
Steal Your Fans	424
Wigger	428

Like Water	432
Beauty/Sexy	437
To You Bitch	441
Portrait of Distania	445
Ambivalent Narcissism	450
Negative Seven	454

Pornographic Childhood (2011) — 461

Dear Listener	463
Born with an Erection	465
Seven Years Young	467
Penetration	470
Family Ties	472
Not Allowed	475
Your Little Girl	478
Run Lolita Run	481
Let the Past Be Past	483
Was it Really Rape? (skit)	488
Child Be Still	489

The Threshold EP (2011) — 495

Introspeculation	497

Suspenseful Pencils	499
Past the Point of Distortion	502
(IV)y	506
Light	510
Dark	515
Threshold	519

That's Not Me - Single (2013) — 527

That's Not Me	529
Free & Accepted Type	533
In Our Flesh (Demo)	539

Psychoactive (2013) — 545

Dreaming of Water	547
Trans-Mute	551
Psychoactive	555
Tangled	560
N7 6666	565
What It Really Is	569
The Dark Prince Speaks	574
manIcure	577
Kush Push	582

Twinkle Twinkle	588
ARR Radio Interlude	593
Queen of Da Nile	596

antiSwag EP (2013) — 605

antiSwag	607
InI	612
Keep Ya Mouth Shut	616
Lightbulb	622
Suck a Deep Dick	625
Chi-Town Queen	630

The L Test (2015) — 635

451	637
Earth Spins	640
Double Murder	647
Fuck the Industry	652
Sex Mouth	657
Curse of the Empath	660
New Creature	665
Soon the Union Cometh	672
Metamorphosis	677

Bonus Tracks — 685

Away From Here	687
Sea Lion	691
East Coast Figures	694
God's Gift	695
Murder-Suicide	699
Psycho Dick	704
Apocalyptic Rhymes Chicago Cypher	708
Shout Outs	715

Note:

The majority of these albums can be streamed and downloaded at mcpan.bandcamp.com

Thanks for coming on this journey with me! I love you all!

Introduction

Apocalyptic Rhymes
We write about the End Times

Every being in existence is a unique expression of God-Source. Some beings have gone so far out that they have forgotten this; separation is the experience that they've chosen to explore with their own free will. However, you can never be separated from God-Source, not really, because everything is contained within the body of God-Source. The negative forces are still part of God even if they have lost all memory of that reality. The whole experience I've explored through art and music is the separation of the Shadow Self, then coming back into the wholeness of divine sovereignty.

When I was growing up, I experienced sexual abuse, physical abuse, and emotional abuse. This creates soul-fragments; which it does to any being who goes through something like that. Within me was created a lot of rage at first. And I was conscious enough to realize that if I didn't explore that darkness through art and writing, then it would destroy me. That being said, some of what you read in these lyrics may shock you—but other times they may take you to the heights of Oneness. I do not condone actions that bring harm to others. What I've always tried to show is the reality of this distortion, this negative mutation within us all. Do not repress your Shadow, you can explore it in a creative way that won't hurt anyone. This is psychological and spiritual exploration.

I do admit that some of the perspectives that I connect to are somewhat... Drakonian. But I am also a mirror of the world I find myself in. That is what artists do: we observe and then we comment on what we see. Groundbreaking art does this in a way that is thought-provoking and courageous enough to ask the tough questions. Through writing, I can explore all perspectives within consciousness—the divine, the horrific, and the grotesque. This process helps to transform consciousness, and expand awareness.

Performance art is very near and dear to my heart. So when I construct concept albums and themes for songs, what I pull through is meant to tell a story. And I play every part as if it was a drama played out on the stage of your mind. Sometimes we must play the villain. If an actor plays the 'bad guy' in a movie, does that mean he is evil in real life? Of course not. Music can be cinematic just like films. I enjoy playing all these roles. However, not one of them defines me. The essence of consciousness is beyond classification—yet all pieces are present within. So love your enemies. Have no enemies.

We do not fight against anyone or anything. We stand in the Kryst.

In the name of the Ultimate Reality which is Love, I thank you for sharing this human experience with me. I Love you more than I can say.

    Avtar
    June 9, 2022

Messiah Complex (2009)

1. Seven
2. Skin Like You
3. The Antichrist Scenario
4. Destroyer
5. Hanging on a Twisted Cross
6. VisionLand
7. The Sound
8. Fever Dream
9. I Kill With My Cunt
10. Killer of Last Things
11. Goddamnit
12. Humanimal
13. Opposite Man
14. Outbound Train

The concept of this album is pretty simple actually. Track by track it describes the journey of a man who believes he will single-handedly bring about the destruction of mankind and the world. It is similar to the concept for Marilyn Manson's *Antichrist Superstar*; however, where his character destroys himself at the end, mine decides to go another way.

This is an exploration of my darkest and most destructive nature.

Seven

I am the daughter of Finality.
The sister of Apocalypse.
The wife of Extinction.
The priestess of Rape.
The mother of Despair.
And the seductress of Deception.

There seem to be no buttons to control this life.
So I've taken it upon myself to manipulate the spirit.
And I understand now what it means
      to hope for the desperation.
I have followed my path toward divinity,
And discovered femininity, and absent virginity.
Speak to me in hushed whispers
      as you create the substance.
This substance of emptiness in Tantra.
I live by nothingness,
And my only god is Zero.
Emptiness is an easy concept,
Infinity flushes away our consciousness and leaves us
In a flooded desert drowning in our ignorance.

I am here to put out the fire with flames.
I am here to warm the cold women with ice.
And if you bother to love me,
I'll share with you what has become single
    inside our constellations.
How we find hope.

The box that I keep under my bed
    is filled with chipped teeth,
Neglected by the tooth fairy of my desires.
I covet her dress and her powers,
And what she stirs up in the young.
If there is a way to undress the lies,
What then will we find to put behind bars?
My conscience goes backwards.
My desire is to unmake,
But in hopes of rebuilding.
There is still beauty in the dilapidated,
So why aren't we happy with the rubble
    we are scattered in?
And the pain we feel is only a temporary pleasure,
Holding on to it is an art that is learned.

Scars given to butterflies
Lie down in daffodils of blood.
As we smell the perfume of factories,
We strip paintings of gravel ceilings holding up our hands
Into the dry air as we crack, crumble,
    and embrace our lungs.
I haven't got time to grow another pair of hands,

And I certainly can cremate with my own two feet.
Paint me up, make me certain, then I'll be free.

I haven't even begun,
But this is your finale.
My overture will start momentarily.
But for now,
Wait for me, my darlings.
You won't live for much longer.

Skin Like You

I came down from heaven
Can't you see I'm hurting just like you?
Am I just a human?
Or something less of kin?

You made me beg
But I have skin like you
You made me beg
I have sickness just like you

Feed me to the monster of fame
It's what's on our dinner plate
We devour this land
And when we are done
We find another man

Put me on a high platform
I'll find a way to court the norm
And she will hold my breathing heart
When I'm watering these slander roots

You made me beg
But I have skin like you
You made me beg
Cause I don't think like you

Dismiss my pleadings
Standing on my head
I must look ridiculous
With my court jester face
Why must I run
To escape your moist embrace

You made me beg for forgiveness
Cut off my old skin
You made me beg for salvation
You'll all see my point of view

The Antichrist Scenario

People never see what is really in front of them.
It's a world corrupted with sin.
We are only fed what the media wants us to see.
What is wrong with a society that gets pleasure
    from the grotesque?
We only see the world through this mist of blood.

We all bow to Satan.
We don't love Jesus or the Cross.
We only see our personal pain.
So it's time to lay down our arms
    and give in to the Darkness.
Evil is the only thing that lives.
Evil is the only thing worth fighting for.
It is so easy to see Lucifer
But where has our Lord gone?
Has he forsaken his children?

The only thing left is to blow out my brains.

Let the blood spray like cleansing rains.
My skull fills
My skull fills with blood
Blood of the Raven
Of the Time
Of the Crime
We all committed against our Creator.
Can we fuck Jesus?
If we can,
We already have.

Why can't you see
That the only one worth worshipping is the Fallen One?
To tie a woman to a bed is ceremonial.
To insert the blade into the chamber of life
Is what has to be done to
Be accepted by the Prince of Darkness.
Draw blood from every orifice and
Bask in the acceptance of Sin.

Why must we kill God?
Because without him, it's all about
Us
And our selfishness.
But it's not about us
It's about
The Prince of Darkness
And how to bow.

I fucked the cross and

Raped the tomb
And pissed on the spot where
He was buried.
We have
We all
We know
We have
Done that.
We need to know
The cross is burning.

All this time we live in
The wastelands of our souls.
As I trek on through the dark spirals of forgotteness
The only comfort I get is from these Demons.
The only pleasure I get is from these Demons.
They rake my skin with their jagged claws.
I cum as my naked body is whipped by bone tipped leather.
The crown of thorns is pressed into my scalp.
Until all I can see is blood.

As I walk through this world with my crown of thorns,
Dragging a splintered cross over my own grave
Which is boiling with sewage and monsters of my mind.
But when the crucifix is on the ground,
I lay nailed in the wood by screws out my spine.
Blown by a vampire maiden as my lumbar bleeds
    on my holy wood.
I am the Antichrist.
We are the Antichrist.

We need to know that.

Is the harvest here?
All the corn,
All the Christians to slaughter.
America,
Where Jesus Freaks are scorned and
Triple Six Mafia is worshipped.
To eat my own heart and bile from the intestines of Truth.
It is Time.
It is always Time
To Rape everything.
We constantly rape the name of God.
The Bible becomes laughable
When society views Christians as crazy.
God must be just lazy.
All this violence.
All this sadness.
God doesn't give a fuck.
He can get on his knees
And suck.

Blasphemy.
This is blasphemy.
But I don't give a shit
Because the hooks of rusty demon chains
    are imbedded in my ankles.
Pulling me around.
Controlling.
Because I like it.

Because I like to rebel.
Because I like to scream "FUCK GOD!"
Before my tongue is cut out by gremlins.
So I walk through life
Dragging chains.
Raping.
Torturing.
Fucking mutilated skulls dug up
    from the graves of the saved.
This is evil.
This is the Antichrist.
America is the Antichrist.

And I love it...

Destroyer

I have to live with the fact that I'm a snake
And not a dragon
Transformation of soul is greater
Than to take and start braggin'
Maybe I haven't become Nothing but I can still hope
I've written ten million memoirs
And papier-mâchéd them into a rope
To hang myself
To dream about destruction
I can't be part of my own film's construction
Destruction of consciousness,
Nonsense of fluorescent ascension
Pull me into the clouds
So I can see what it's about
We all have something to say
Living is learning how to speak it
Some of us choose not to preach it
From pulpit into the mouths of geese
All I ask is that if you don't cease
Become disciples of this land of ours
Know that we cause these damage showers

Of fire driven through the spire tires
Rolling over our demise
Just look up into the skies
I'll help you undress the lies

[CHORUS]
I can't be your superman
To save this world is not my plan
We will spin forever hopeless
But I'm not separate from the madness

Masonic unconscious clouded in our righteous judgment
Forgive me not for images on film stock ultra-violent
Pulled, ripped, and bent
Our world is doomed by our gray matter tent
Watch me as I bring it there
Fire reflected by your blank stare
STOP!
Was that a sub drop?
Consumes the entire human race
It's not Creation, but Destruction you chase
Should I continue to bring the sky to its knees
I fail to reach its light, undress me please
Transformational soul has nothing but to seize me
From complacency and hurl me into the darkness
Don't think I don't see you
Swimming blind with the sharks
But watch me as I slow it down
To commune with hourless sunlight
I'll stand as I see it bleed into open mouths

That nonetheless shut tight
Shut tight, shut tight…
Behind the transformation shedding skin into the air!
How does god pick the ones worthy to be spared?
Behind the white horse galloping into the metallic horizon
If our time has come we must choose nothing as we rise on
Into the dark rays of sunset that lets us die
As everything gone
Become one with me as dragons take flight
And then we run
Then we run…

[CHORUS]
I can't be your superman
To save this world is not my plan
We will spin forever hopeless
But I'm not separate from the madness

Hanging on a Twisted Cross

Shoot me into the sun
Watch me burn to ashes
Then watch me rise then out the dirt
I cannot die till I am god

Tell me what it means to be
All the things that I can be
And all the things that are not me
I am on your crooked tree

Tell me what it means to be
All the things that I can be
And all the things that are not me
I am on your crooked tree

Superficial existence
I have no use for that
And I know I have a statement
If I felt that it's worth saying

Come away from all your fears
I'll cover up all of your tears
Tie me down and then they'll shoot me
But trust me, then come we'll see
The world that now I will destroy
Will crumble now so like a toy

Tell me what it means to be
All the things that I can be
And all the things that are not me
I am on your crooked tree

Tell me what it means to be
All the things that I can be
And all the things that are not me
I am on your crooked tree

I'll scream it till my throat is bleeding
This is all I think I'm needing
Hear me in my all-forgotten
You say He gave his only begotten
Son for this dying world
Why save what's already damned?

What's my competition?
You confirmed my speculation
I don't need more information
From your female masturbation

The only reason that I'm here
Is to make you all my puppets
Subjection is an art
And soon you'll know my face

Tell me what it means to be
All the things that I can be
And all the things that are not me
I am on your crooked tree

Tell me what it means to be
All the things that I can be
And all the things that are not me
I am on your crooked tree

We rejected him
As they rejected me
But from the alter of sin
This is what I see

Can you stop me before
I crack the life support
Suffer broadcast system
Will be the brand decision

I was born and now we end
Don't try to stall or to mend
I was born and now we end
Don't try to stall or to mend
I was born and now we end

Don't try to stall or to mend
I was born and now we end
Don't try to stall or to mend…

VisionLand

[VERSE 1]
Tell me what you see when you look in my face
Does it make you want to cringe and shake
But your eyes have gone and I just know
That you're blind and caught in my undertow

I know that I can see
Because starlight makes you flee
Into a shelter for the cursed
Holy water can't quench your thirst
But wait on me, wait on me
And I'll make all your dreams be free
Into this land of things to be
I can only see through my eyes of calloused stones
I rake my broken claws cause I cannot save your bones

[CHORUS]
This is all I see from you
Why save what's already dead
We fall into our crimson blue
With our eyes, the beasts are fed

[VERSE 2]
Maggots fall from blinking holes
Betwixt, be waxed in our souls
Pray to god to give you sight
With real eyes the truth is bright
Blinded by the bitter things
I cannot seem to spread these wings

[BRIDGE]
Show me now the believers dead
Into slow matchbox sand
Our lives have gone and now they end
Into this waistcoat patched-up land

[CHORUS]
This is all I see from you
Why save what's already dead
We fall into our crimson blue
With our eyes, the beasts are fed

[VERSE 3]
And I'm sick of these dreams
That never seem to come true
And I see the only thing in this world is me
But the only me in this time is dead
For you I will see these visions
But I cough up some filthy verses
The world isn't cleansing of the dirty
Feàrless merciless scars on our minds

[BRIDGE]
Show me now the believers dead
Into slow matchbox sand
Our lives have gone and now they end
Into this waistcoat patched-up land

What can you see with those empty eye sockets
What can you see with those empty eye sockets
What can you see with those empty eye sockets
And what can you think with that empty fuckin' head

[CHORUS]
This is all I see from you
Why save what's already dead
We fall into our crimson blue
With our eyes, the beasts are fed

The Sound

the Sound of a Dying Fetus

Fever Dream

I wake to the sound of a buzzing sensation
And remember that REM is just masturbation
Seeing reality in the still born images
Aborted truth closes my kill porn pages

Come with me into the apartment's wild
Jungle room with one tree hiding a child
She's naked inside the needle-sharp branches
Invaded by the wooden man holding his haunches
Peeking through the cracks will become my downfall
The man pulls the hand of the girl as if drowning a call
Razor-cuts and flesh peeling hands in the air water
A pedophile's dream starts now, one down, he's caught her
I cannot tell time because
Violence to the innocent stimulates
My lobes vibrate in the calm as the shriek-rape calculates

Walk inside my fever dreams
Talk beside my ever seams
Walk inside my fever dreams
Stalk beside my never beams

I'm a prisoner inside my factory of distortion
Looking out on corn fields,
Contemplating penis contortion
Even if I escaped, the wolves would rape my gaping ass
Getting sliced and ravaged by inadequacies in the grass
But I remain the king of this and everything bleeding
The problem is I don't know you, or what you're needing
So I sink into the semen, knowing only how to fuck
Making love eludes me in your bed of curdled luck
And I dream of absent depression
Where we know how to love
Watching your beautiful sleeping face,
Looking tranquil as a dove
Sink into me and scream
Until your vagina bleeds dead sand
I'll pull away as you're blinded in violence
And grasp for my hand
Shaking head and hands
I wait for you in the land I created
It's not alive, not dead, not wanting,
Because your clit is castrated
Not towers, not powers, not showers of dogs
And I finally know
That it takes more than holding you in nightmares
Boom! Let's go!

Walk inside my fever dreams
Talk beside my ever seams
Walk inside my fever dreams

Stalk beside my never beams

Still infected by the fetus
Always circling back to this
Distorting abortion contortion fornication
Resulting in still birth abomination
The monster continues to find new victims
Destruction of relationships become the symptoms
As I cradle your dead head, your eyes won't stick
You search my face in silence
Waiting for something to click
But it won't
Because it's empty except for the visions
And I know nothing except your circumcisions
Still waiting forever in the Territory of the Seed
Blinded by the throne of penises
And impeded by the Valley of Entrails
I'm still a failure for this, I can't see what you need
I feel useless when I see you cry
The best dreams seem to be where I die
To tell you the truth,
I really don't give a fuck if you kill yourself
The most it would do is make me a better artist
So take that DVD back to Vision Forum, I am a Marxist

Walk inside my fever dreams
Talk beside my ever seams
Walk inside my fever dreams
Stalk beside my never beams

"Death is a pussy!"

I Kill With My Cunt

"You wanted to know who and what I am? I'm a killer. I kill with my cunt. You can write about it in Midnight Magazine or National Enquirer. It's gonna be the new sensation. You wanted to know where I'm from? I'm from Connecticut, Mayflower stock. I was taught that my prince would come, and he would be a lawyer, and I would have his children. And on the weekends we would barbecue. And all the other princes and their princesses would come, and they would say, 'Delicious, delicious.' Oh, how boring. So I was taught that I should come to New York, become an independent woman. And my prince would come, and he would be an agent, and he would get me a role, and I would make my living waiting on tables. I would wait—till thirty, till forty, till fifty. And I was taught that to be an actress, one should be fashionable, and to be fashionable is to be androgynous. And I am androgynous not less than David Bowie himself. And they call me beautiful, and I kill with my cunt. Isn't it fashionable? Come on, who's next? I'll take lessons. How to get into show business: be nice to your professor. Be nice to your agent. Be nice to your audience, be nice. How to be

a woman: want them when I want you. How to be free and equal: fuck women instead of men, and you'll discover a whole kingdom of freedom. Men won't step on you anymore, women will. So come on, who's next? Who wants to teach me? Come on, teach me. Are you afraid? You're right, because they're all dead. All my teachers."

- Anne Carlisle, *Liquid Sky*

Killer of Last Things

"Don't go."
"Listen!"

"Will could hear the noise Steep was referring to. It wasn't a singular sound, it was a thousand, a thousand thousands, coming at him from every direction at once. It wasn't strident, nor was it sweet or musical. It was simply insistent. And its source? That was coming too, from all directions. Tidal multitudes of pale, indistinguishable forms, crawling toward him. No, not crawling: being born. *Creatures spreading their limbs and purging themselves of infants that, even in the moment of their birth, were ungluing their legs to be fertilized and, before their partners had rolled off them, were spreading their limbs to expel another generation. And on and on, in sickening multitudes, their mingled mewlings and sighings and sobs the din that Steep had said drowned out God."*

"It wasn't hard for Will to fathom what he was witnessing. This was what Steep saw when he looked at living things. Not their beauty, not their particularity, just their smothering, deafening

fecundity. Flesh begetting flesh, din begetting din. It wasn't hard to fathom, because he'd thought it himself, in his darkest times. Seen the human tide advancing on species he'd loved—beasts too wild or too wise to compromise with the invader—and wished for a plague to wither every human womb. Heard the din and longed for a gentle death to silence every throat. Sometimes not even gentle. He understood. Oh Lord, he understood."

- Clive Barker, *Sacrament*

Step into the heart of my secret world,
Where I dream all your dreams
The courthouse of visions,
Where nothing that is is ever what it seems
Touching the hand of Jacob Steep,
You feed the fire of the living
But dying for one last kiss of ice, this storm is never giving
We know you, we love you, we'll never disown you
And today will not be our last day,
For we are the immortal two
Come true what you seek in me, but what be my purpose?
What would you do if the flames and the fire
Were always at your service?
My realm, where everything is love and fire, fire and love
I used to be a knife, now I'm a man running with blood
Handing you a fluttering moth to burn
I wait as the choice is now in your turn
Burn what you see, burn what you love,
Burn what you dream

Burn the world away from your eyes,
Burn the entire stream
Of thoughts in your mind, just burn, burn, burn

Living and dying, we feed the fire
Living and dying, we feed the fire
Living and dying, we feed the fire

Rosa McGee, the seductress, the temptress
Part Creation, part deception, my lovely mistress
My pet ropes, cavorting around my arms like vipers
Would you rage war against me, being loving snipers
Free to do as we wish, no day of forgiveness,
No purpose we're alone
Come home to me, Jacob, I miss your warm touch,
Couldn't cope with a clone
The book has burned
And I will be a different woman from now on
I will have pleasure wherever I can take it,
And when you're gone
And I become pregnant,
I'll cut it out with a sharpened stick
You prick, you would have killed me,
I take your balls but keep your dick
We're sick, I know, but I'll always love you as my own
We are one but separate, as our forever bond has grown
You're with me, in me, against me,
But running where the wind has blown

[CHORUS]
Who is the Nilotic?
The psychotic, the demonic?
The girlboi that sings,
The extinctor, the creator,
Or the Killer of Last Things?

Have you read the book I have written?
But it is coded and all the words have bitten
Your face into fragments of confusion
However understanding will leave a contusion
The fusion is us, male and female in one
And we are a bomb, we are a gun
But we come from the sun,
The Nile, and maybe you'll split us
Into two beings, but will you be a witness?
Will we be forgiven, chapter and verse?
But are you our God, and is this a curse?
I still believe there is purpose to our lives
But I weep for myself
My work still so monumental and the sky so wide
Where can I hide to escape from the noise
The only way I have is to become what destroys

"'Make it go away.'"
"'That's what I've been trying to do all these years,' Steep replied."
"The rising tide of life was almost upon them, forms being born and being born, spilling around Will's feet."

"'Enough,' Will said."

"'You understand my point of view?'"

"'Yes—'"

"'Louder.'"

"'Yes! I understand. Perfectly.'"

"The admission was enough to banish the horror. The tide retreated and a moment later was gone entirely, leaving Will hanging in the darkness again."

"'Isn't this a finer place?' Steep said. 'In a hush like this we might have a hope of knowing who we are. There's no error here. No imperfection. Nothing to distract us from God.'"

"'This is the way you want the world?' Will murmured. 'Empty?'"

"'Not empty. Cleansed.'"

- Clive Barker, *Sacrament*

I spit into the ashes
This is for all that crashes
There's for your book, and there's for forgiveness
There's for what you too, there's for your meekness
And there's for your god, he'll have nothing more from me
But we'll see how we turn out, maybe let me be,
Then I'll be free
Do you understand who we are,
Where we've been, and where we will go?
But no, you don't, for we don't understand who we are,
I am, and so
We live as two in one, shifting one to another,

Lovers and siblings
Again, we are immortal, living through the ages,
Gaining our wings
Who sings, is it Steep or McGee,
We both have a voice to free
I feel you would have cut us apart,
Do you wish to wage war against me
I don't know a thing about myself, Jacob,
Anymore than you do
I learned it all watching women do as women always do
If only just a few more kisses could keep us from killing her
But you've started the battle,
Perhaps I'd be a very fine soldier
We'd have such a war,
That it would be like love, only bloodier
Lovelier, lovelier,
I want one of your balls, Jacob, it's that or an eye
I handed him the knife, holding it tight,
I told him to make up his mind
Saying, "unbutton yourself and cut it off,"
He almost began to cry
I made him do it himself,
And I walked away singing a soft lullaby

[CHORUS]
Who is the Nilotic?
The psychotic, the demonic?
The girlboi that sings,
The extinctor, the creator,
Or the Killer of Last Things?

There are a pair of birds I need you to kill for me
Enveloped in silence so profound
It made him hold his breath for fear of breaking it
They see me
See them back
I do
Fix them with your eyes
I am
Then finish it, go on
Lunge! Slash!
Wasn't that quick? Wasn't that beautiful?
Isn't it so easy to kill?
Suppose they were the last?
I would have changed the world

The bonfire had living fuel
I'm a killer, so what is my tool?
What have we lost, what have we gained?
Smelled like cold fire, embers left in the rain
I came out here without even knowing why
Now I see as I look up at the sky
I was looking for you
Will, you were sent to me
After tonight,
I won't be traveling with Mrs. McGee, you see
We've decided to part company
I hate her and she hates me
Then we'd have us a fire, wouldn't we

I raised my hand into the light. It was gummy with what looked like blood, but mixed with silvery paint. "This is mine," I said. "Shed because I failed to shed hers. Yes, I would have killed her. But I would have regretted it, I think. She and I are intertwined in some fashion I've never understood. If I'd done harm to her—" "You'd have hurt yourself?" Will said. "You understand this?" I said. "Lord, what have I found?"

> When I've looked, looked as deep as I dare
> Wishing for it to come crystal clear as I stare
> Sometimes I think I can get a little taste of it
> A moment of epiphany, then it's gone and I'm hit
> By only a little piece of bliss, thought I heard a hiss
> A moment you seem to understand everything
> Or know that it's there for you, but nothing
> Is there because they taunt you mercilessly
> Fuck you! I will never fall away passively
> Cause there's something worth listening for
> Watching for
> Leave me to meditate on what I've lost
> For extinction I live, but what is the cost?
> Kill them for me, Rosa,
> The perfect way to demonstrate your love
> Is to kill those fuckers, commit murder for me,
> Life flies like a dove
> Into the sky away from my eyes,
> Blood running down my knife
> Changing the world one death at a time,
> Destroy every past life
> I'll be in every part of it, Jacob in the bird,

Jacob in the tree, Jacob in the wolf
Making truth from the lies
We have no secrets, you and I

Death: it's what I live for!

[CHORUS]
Who is the Nilotic?
The psychotic, the demonic?
The girlboi that sings,
The extinctor, the creator,
Or the Killer of Last Things?

Be careful, cause I kill all who fuck me
Is it withering yet, is it growing to a tree
In me, in you, we're making love to each other
Locking in love making, one body, cum to another
We love and we hate, needing to be soothed with a fuck
Again I fall into black, and seeing the visions,
I become stuck
Untuck from your stories, I don't mean this as slander
Alexander! Come back! Do you hear me, Alexander!

This world is God's delusion
So free me from the confusion
Of noise making me deaf
Kill all the screams leaving me bereft
"If you desert me, you'll never know what you are
    or how you came to be"
So I walk into the world as I am,

This is how I'll be, entering the Domus Mundi
God is a coward and a show-off,
Hiding behind a gaudy show of forms
Are these the norms, I don't understand the signs,
The vision that transforms
God is boasting how fine his workings are
This is all I have, even though you will discard
All my words for naught, but this is what you need
But greed overclouds, and never fail to heed
What I say as I declare: I am wiser than God

You're part of the madness now…

GODDAMNIT

Ow, fuck, the sun burns my eyes as
I stare straight into the fire.
I can just feel it as my retina melts away.
I cannot determine why
I inflict this self mutilation on myself.
Oh, God, No!
Why must it happen this way when the sun
Is setting beyond the mist?
I can't fucking finish if the sun leaves
And the moon comes up.
I will be left with these horrible, steaming,
Half-fried orbs in my skull.
I gotta finish, where's my blowtorch.
Ahh, ahh, why, it burns, aww my brain, I can't, no.
I pull the flame away as
I feel boiling liquid drip down my cheeks.
I can't see… but the fire… and the burning… and
Oh FUCK OH MY GOD IT BURNS
WHY GOD WHY
It's all gone
My world has been swallowed by

The herpes infested cancerous whore I can't see
But, maybe, when I burn the world from in front of me,
The tick of time will slow,
And I can make my own fire.

Humanimal

So you're dead now, shit
And you're going to hell
Straight from your marijuana jungles
Straight from your lies, your lies, your lies
You dropped dead fuckin'
Suits you well, you go to hell
We'll go to hell, I'll go to hell too
But I know I'm damned and you never knew
So you weren't ready to toll the bell
For me it's easy, from hell to hell
I'm not dancing in marijuana jungles
I live in concrete mazes stone and glass
Hard like my heart, sharp and clean
With no romantic illusions to changing the world
I don't lie to myself that love can cure
'Cause i know I'm alone and you fought that every day you lived
You lied, you died, you lied
You go to hell, suits you well

Shit

- Liquid Sky

I do damage to the sentiment of love
When less is deserved from me, give it a shove
Living inside something that refuses to feel
Increases the pain without willingness to heal
For now I won't submit, I'm not choosing to kneel
So I'll just watch you die, life wasted, inside the snake peel
Free fast
Freedom won't last
What's deserved is a lock and a cage
Because the only thing lasting is the rage
Vicious and rabid, sink teeth into throat
I want your blood, the only sound you can make is a croak
The killing comes back, your hammer-smashed face
But I feel your love, my lips with your finger you trace
Remember, I know what self-loathing means
I have it too, even my face shows what it seems
Cut! Cut! Cut!
Rip! Rip! Rip!
Fuck! Fuck! Fuck!
Stab it with your dick
Which girl do I pick?

You know, I always dreamt to fuck a dead man. Here's my chance... Sure I am, baby, that's why you like me, so let's fuck him.

[CHORUS]
You're just a humanimal
A sick little puppy trying to become something
Being devolved and remaining an animal
But you remain in the dog pound as nothing
Discover that it's mine, lost in the cranium
Losing control and becoming the lycanthrope
Skin pop poison, red vision infected delirium
Don't sleep with me because I infect less hope

Don't get moral with me, whore. You had to fuck him, didn't you?

Don't want any, cause you've been fucked twice today already?

Take the collar from around my neck
Tie me up, strap me down, and make me watch *Star Trek*
Watch my eyes bleed into the infinite, I know one thing
Stagnant furnaces feel like ice on my back
Cutting the wings
Riddled with stings, it's my own death making you scream
Into the dream, I'm a hyena snarling into your crotch
Smelling like rot but I eat it hungrily like butterscotch
One notch into my belt, you're done and finally caught
In my trap I laid especially for you, but I taught
You not to yell as I rape your bloody child
With my talons raking into her back, I'm not mild
I'm wild like a canine that drools to fuck you to death
One breath left in your body and I laugh for the last

I'm not a pirate, I'm the parrot, perched on the blood mast

You goddamn whore...
Don't call me that, you low-class freaking monster! Monster!
I'm a monster? You let these guys walk on your bones, bitch!
You're gonna kill me with syphilis one day, you dirty cunt!

[CHORUS]
You're just a humanimal
A sick little puppy trying to become something
Being devolved and remaining an animal
But you remain in the dog pound as nothing
Discover that it's mine, lost in the cranium
Losing control and becoming the lycanthrope
Skin pop poison, red vision infected delirium
Don't sleep with me because I infect less hope

Don't get moral with me, whore. You had to fuck him, didn't you?

Don't talk to me like that. Your mother was nuts. Your father was a bum. You'll never go anywhere, but to the bottom where you belong with the bums.
You better watch your mouth or I'll cut your face and nobody will fuck your ugly cunt!

I know that I'll always be less than human
I fail to be a girl, boy, man, or woman
Always succumbing to my violent tendencies

Like a dog to its master, cumming to tragedies
Moan like a wildebeest, mount like a bitch in heat
So look for any hole to stop up and fuck to the beat
I'll embrace this as inevitable and unparalleled
Like a compass pointing south toward Cair Paravel
I'll never make it there because I'm sunk in the swamp
Of vicious cycles, packs of wolves,
What can I do with a cracked map?
I can head toward the caves
And live where Gollum is trapped
My Precious is the world that I circle and cap
Then tap the threshold of pain for every living creature
We all die alone, shedding our fur wholeheartedly
Listen to me, for I'll be your teacher...

[CHORUS]
You're just a humanimal
A sick little puppy trying to become something
Being devolved and remaining an animal
But you remain in the dog pound as nothing
Discover that it's mine, lost in the cranium
Losing control and becoming the lycanthrope
Skin pop poison, red vision infected delirium
Don't sleep with me because I infect less hope

Don't get moral with me, whore. You had to fuck him, didn't you?
If you don't like it baby, you don't have to watch.
I told you not to fuck him...

Opposite Man

When y'all know nothing, I know everything

Remember that I created everything
But I created myself to be different
And that going against the grain is just a front
I drift as I'm bent
When you express your opinion
Just know I'll be against
Showing how to play it
I vehemently disagree with you
But I'll fight to the death for your right to say it
So lynch a nigger
Gas a Jew
Lawn-mower a spic
And alcohol-poison a Mick
I haven't said anything for shock
But now strip off my pants and cut off my dick

The Sound

Dislove me or hate me

I'm still on my tree
Onslaught the enemy with walnuts to the dome
But who's my enemy if the whole world is my home?
I guess we differ because the movies I love
Leave emotional disturbances
Put *Mysterious Skin* on repeat in the DVD
My viewings are accordances
With the childhood that's ingrained in the libido
That's why I love—-
Well I dunno, ask me later, kiddo
Ted says I'm the opposite man
Nah I'm not
Gravity couldn't keep me on the land
I'm the best at not being you
So don't try to compete
I'm the opposite of a man
But still incomplete

I'm the Dead King
The Killer of Last Things
The Maker of Breakers
I am Seven
And apparently the Opposite Man
I'm the Opposite Man
Opposite Man
Opposite Man

I miss Sarcasm but he tends to send me letters
I'm four years behind

At nine I was still a bed-wetter
Thinking that I can read you when I can't
Guess you should do a little dance
And give me a chant
To show me if you're in the mood to fuck
It does suck when communication's stuck
Inside the prison of my mind
Remaining this way, becoming blind
Goo dripping down my cheeks as I burn
The world away from my eyes, then I turn
Into the sun and decide that nothing's worth
What hasn't become fact into the sky
My road goes down and I'm headed toward a dive
Spiral, spiral, spiral, spiral, spiral, spiral, SPIRAL!
GET ME THROUGH THIS FUCKING TRIAL!
I'm so sure of myself
But what I'm sure of is the uncertainty
Inside my HIV parade, with pride in eternity
For my sexuality lasts a lifetime longer than my body
Is that so much different from you, boy
I dunno, probably
What's more true
What I hear from you?
Or the way I've created myself?

I'm the Dead King
The Killer of Last Things
The Maker of Breakers
I am Seven

And apparently the Opposite Man
I'm the Opposite Man
Opposite Man
Opposite Man

Should my lifestyle be deserving of death?
Am I losing my mind and losing my breath?
Blinded and suffocated well below the ground
I can't make a sound
But I'm shaking the mounds
That built up this world
Seems it is my calling
Who's coming to rescue me
No one, I'm stalling
My life on this road into the stars
It's hard to see where the road ends without a car
But I've found that I can fly
With wings that are bleeding
I'm seeing everything that you can't
The difference is bespeaking
Authority as I talk with this noose around my throat
I discovered that you failed me
I'll put on my coat
And leave this land forever and trek through the snow
This is the journey I must plow
And the path I must follow
We've finally met
But then you reject and suspect
Me of being a sham, a fake, a flake
Just a speck of dust

But underestimating is the downfall of our species
I'll show you more
Than you're ready to comprehend or foresee

I'm the Dead King
The Killer of Last Things
The Maker of Breakers
I am Seven
And apparently the Opposite Man
I'm the Opposite Man
Opposite Man
Opposite Man

Outbound Train

Speaking sincerely on this railroad no-bound
My mother listens, but says everything with no sound
I said I wouldn't make apologies for myself
But I'm sorry for the tears to which I offer no help
Just melt
Into the platform aimed for heaven
You don't understand why I'm becoming Seven
Heaven leaves your face as leaven
Rises to the skies in mountainous lies
Defeat my insignificance
And mask my utter ignorance
As I film the world we don't see
All of it! All of it! All of it is me!
But the mirrors through your cheeks flee
From the fact that what we see
Is only half the picture
This is not a power lecture
That fills as a spade does with hair
The incessant speech spit damping your stare
I'll make apologies for my sister
We don't speak, look, I haven't kissed her

Shut your lips
Suppress your hips
Pull off the clips
She sinks into the mother's teeth
That's the one to decide to keep
Reject a deluded son
He's become a bomb

[CHORUS]
Outbound train from Millennium Station
Chest Death kills in anticipation
Fuck my life, I live in cremation
I thought I dropped it, but stay temptation

Why would I want to save a world that rejects me?
Anger injects, then slowly infects me
Scarring the land and ejecting the free
So I suffer in noise
With no secret I'm into boys
Or that I enjoy these kind of toys
But you only think the world is dark
Because your eyes are shut
I am the Dead King and the Killer of Last Things
Becoming stuck
Becoming Seven
But walking backwards through the muck
Life's not a rehearsal
It's the whole fucking show
I throw myself at a world with no eyes for me
The empty sockets of popularity bend to ignore me

I give you my body so you can play with my breath
I give you my life so you can play with my death
Sex isn't everything, but everything is sex
Please help me discard this Messiah Complex

[CHORUS]
Outbound train from Millennium Station
Chest Death kills in anticipation
Fuck my life, I live in cremation
I thought I dropped it, but stay temptation

She never had the heart to point out my delusions
I wallow in prehistory experiencing cry illusions
Why didn't you tell me my life
Wasn't the edge of a knife
Babbling, dabbling candlestick betwixt
One realm of hate broken through the gate
And I finally come to grips before I board into infinity
I have failed you, plugged up Earth's sewer
I'm no Trinity
The struggle isn't between destroying
Or saving the world
It's between destroying or saving
Myself

CNT (2010)

1. Intro (Them Hollow) 2. See Media
3. I Rep for the Darkness 4. My Mother
5. Join Hands in the Sands
6. I Am One of Them, I Am All of Them
7. Gettin' Paid
8. If I Killed You 9. Jiz and Rainbows
10. We Are Not the Living 11. Sacagewaea
12. B-CUM 13. HOO

This is the second spoken word/experimental album from Nilotic. CNT is a mixture of acapella poetry as well as some early hip-hop rhymes. Beware of Them Hollow! There's nothing behind the eyes!

At times nightmarishly dark, and other times spiritually reflective, but always truthful. This is early Nilotic at their best. It's still a CNT without U.

Intro: Them Hollow

I only see the women through the filter
I can never let them through
Keep away from me
They are the gas masks of intranquility
I hate them in everything other than nudity

Forget me
Because all I want to do is
Hurt you
Stir the behind the eyes
It's blank
Let
me
shake it

I'll make it start inside your bar-face
That's continually red

I don't care

They haven't become hollow

They always were
From the beginning of time
They've been cut open
And emptied
But what else are they good for?

Exactlyness

It's definitely not tragic
Because they don't have
The mental capacity
To contemplate this

CNT isn't in this
It's about this

Walk with me

But please know that even though I feel love
I can't

Don't forgive me
This is just how it is

No hope for Them Hollow

See Media

CNN slices and kills my face
Instilling fear
And void of any trace of logic
Or ingrained with sympathy
For the people that it speaks to
Empathy is absent
And for now we See Media
As somewhat of a necessity of Arcadia
But arcane
And understood only by a few
We knew nothing as we're attacked
On every front by ads and stacked fliers
To buy shit we never needed
But this is a warning that goes unheeded
We've been implored and entreated
And challenged to go for two days
With no media
But unbalanced goes the weasel
And down down goes the eyelids
With nothing to watch
We can't run away from ourselves

Don't leave me alone with my thoughts
They're just empty shelves

See Media
See Media
See Media

With nothing but reality TV to watch
We're left to die
As intelligence is botched
And communist stations make us subservient
Docile and ignorant
Searching for a way to prevent
The constant dulling of our minds
Unbind from the machine that's unkind
To our growth of consciousness
And remind us that we're sheep
Ready to be raped and dissected
Because we agreed to it
And willingly became infected
By the media tyrants
Brainwash air giants
And sin spinners
Let us die or be free into the atmosphere
Let me be a bringer of truth
To audiences not prepared
LISTEN
But I'm no singer
I'M A KILLER
Your minds are what I aim for

Your lives are what I strive for
Through observation I became sore
Same form
Color chloroform onto vacant eyelids
They can't see me
Till television stations
Buy kids...

See Media
See Media
See Media

Crack open the lens
And see what cums out
Pus pouch
I see it bleed raw footage
And shout out
For substance more than what is given
Images void of thought
Corporations driven
By nothing beyond money
Life isn't sunny
And this ain't funny
There remains a drought of
Conscious decision-making
Come watch us
As we sit in front of the god-box
For eternity
As the infinite locks us into our chairs
Making us stare into the void

But you don't care
About the children of the empty laugh…
Metal clap resonates art with no craft

KILL YOUR GOD
KILL YOUR GOD
KILL YOUR…

TV!!!!!!!!

I'm screaming for you
But you still don't see me…

See Media…
See Media…
See Media…

I Rep for the Darkness

Blindfolded men
Suffocated in the den
of infertility
Desperately trying to pen
a story in the works
On par with Clive Barker

Sink into hell
Dismiss the shell
This is my Bone Charter

I rep for the darkness

Stepping forth from the cave
of fluorescents
I crave brutality
And pave the road
that you all will sink through
I play through the pain
Rape through the rain
Perform all this without being slain

I rep for the darkness

I was the one who wrote
The Book of the Dead
The head rolled down the stairs
into the bed
Steep(ed) in fornication
seduction, manipulation
Stay back
Stay dead
No need for castration
Anton LaVey is still my Christ
Taking your heart
and it's a heist

I rep for the darkness

Breaking it down
I have my crown
Suck it now
Then you'll bow
I walked into the light
but came back
Cause it's way too fuckin bright

I rep for the darkness

According to nothing I live
According to everything I die

Being anything other than this
feels like a lie
I emerge out of the Purple Fog
And slowly make my way toward
the Black Mist
Take one step forward
I wage war by raising my fist
To heaven and yell SEVEN
But no one acknowledges my
presence
They wish me to die in the slow
abuse of substance
Pull back
Then enhance the Death Trap Lullaby
But I drop the collar
Bow
And bid you goodbye

I have no master
For I am the master
My dick inside you scream
"faster, faster"
I don't need protection or glove
over the head
Cause after I fuck you,
you'll most likely be dead

I rep for the darkness
I rep for the darkness
I rep for the dark—

I rep for the—
What?

What?

I rep for the what?

I rep…for what?
Fuck…you
I'll rep…for myself

Why would I rep for what
doesn't help me grow?
That never lets me know
anything beyond pain
Hate's not a trophy
All I want is for you to fucking hold me…

Hate's not a trophy…
All I want is for you to fucking hold me…
Hate is not a trophy…
All I want is for you to fucking hold me…
Hate's…
not a trophy…

My Mother

"I can't be your mother," she said.
"Emotionally you're dead, and in bed you have issues."
Save your 'I miss yous' and let your tears find their way into
Some other girl's tissues."

Your name is my name
And even though I don't blame
You for how I am, it's still a shame
That I can't break away from this game
Of broken intimacy

But I'm complaining again
Whining to the ones who don't really
Want to hear about it
But then again, I'll fucking shout it out
I might just sit on this stage and pout

The first said she wasn't going to baby me anymore
The second said she couldn't be my mother
But I still clung to her breast
And couldn't bring myself to leave the nest

Or put to rest my best effort
To force you to cradle my head
With thumb in mouth and puppy eyes
I don't know why you call my lies

When I was on top of you, you said, "Yes, Daddy. I need it."
Then I cut open my hands,
And tried to stitch your scars as I bleed it
My intimacy distress, I confess,
Runs deeper than where they get Fiji water
And I know that cutting your belly is not Forever
Or the way that I taught her
To love me, I guess I am that baby crying for milk
But your tit is sour and I scream for soft silk
And receiving nothing but delayed abortions
Kill me 20 years later because you don't like my alterations
That I've made to myself
Because I guess that untidy shelf
Holds the books of my selfish ways

And I bring it back to the fetus
Tearing it out in order to feed us
I've blocked the sun with the dead babies piled
High to the sky, you killed your own child
But it feels like it was my dick that you cut out of yourself
But I, I know what I am
And I know what you are not
I'm still four years behind

With an undeveloped mind

The Eden, the Forever, the rape victim
The one who said she loved me after we fucked
Is no longer near me, but with luck
She won't forget me the way I'm forgetting her
In every way except how she fucked like a hooker
And squeezed my arms as she came
I remember how she loved brother-sister incest play
And I still think of her name every fucking day

I thought that cross dressing
Would make me feel closer to females
But I guess it makes it seem like
I'm just on sale to old males
And they think that I can be
Their new mother fucking toy
I'm not something you can crush under your belly,
I'm still a boy
A little boy just searching for his mother

I know now I can't get what I need from a man
And in this dimension I will forever stand
The realization happened in that moment
When I had my hand on your penis,
You turned to me and said,
"You ever heard of the second coming?"
I sink and continuously feel like
A gooey piece of afterbirth running

Down my leg to come to rest
On the brink of enlightenment
However, that will not come through
Orgasm or excitement
Astral Penis Projection into the universe's uterus
I can feel myself dying, how come god won't remember us

God is my mother
God is my mother
God is my mother
We are God's failed experiment
I've been going down
Spiraling down
You let the girls pound me into the ground
And the answers for me still remain unfound
Bam I hit the ground!
Making craters and cavities riddling through expanses
Of polluted air, making me impotent
And sequentially pensive
And I live, still live,
Even if you won't help me open the seventh chakra
I'm still searching for that explorer
Who will aid me on the road to tantra
To help me dig deeper into the earth
In order to hold my hand as we shoot
Into the celestial universe together,
But she's gone and in my hand is a boot
A boot that falls into ashes
And leaves my dreams for love-making dry
And my mother lands next to me,

But I don't want her to touch me even if she tried
To love me, I reject but suspect her of something deeper
Some spirituality that I don't wish to be a keeper
Of, I'm a sleeper, a dreamer, a philosopher
Of sexual fluidity, but I remain alone
With no one to become one with, I'm still as a stone

What will happen to our sexual identity
When we are blind in the mixture of purple and black?
Fallen trap, I'll drink the sun sap,
Till I know how the weather speaks, then I fly and fall back
Into nothingness and I become sexless,
Unsex me here, and fill me from the crown
To the toe, top-full of direst understanding,
Because I am that slave bound
But with roots of energy
Striping and penetrating the ground
I have found what it really means to be inside of the spirit
Soul love, soul sex, souls weaving together,
And I don't wish to tear it
Apart and tear the heart,
The chakra that eludes my touch the most
But I guess, I'm still that failure,
And can't seem to become more than a parasitic host

I am the only one who put these motherfucking scars
On my motherfucking chest
Please tell me why I still can't figure out
How to put these thoughts to rest
My sex is just a mess, and again I confess,

About my intimacy distress
And why I cum less than you wish for me to
But this is nothing new, and I always knew
That blue was the color of death
I feel lost when I can't hear your breath
Or watch you as you sleep, thoughts intermingling
Time universe, still searching for the sublime unwinding
And the unbinding from all of the ropes that tie me
To my mother

I don't want to fuck my mother
I don't want to fuck my mother
I don't want to fuck my mother

But I guess, when I'm fucking you,
I'm really just fucking my mother

Join Hands in the Sands

I am the sun, the moon, the stars
and the bars
And as our hearts slowly become one
I won't be as hard
I shall become softer
like fluid waves of cotton
That ebb and flow into one continuous sea
Rockin to the beat of the sun
I am not the drum
I am the gun
That slings semen
and sends women on the run
I sink into the bed
I'm red
And I become the bed
Not able to wake
I continually shake
the barbed wire and lead bullets
That pierce my spirit

They're tracing like fluid
Into the Milky Way
Beyond the Milky Way
Beyond what I say
For now I lay you down to sleep
But the journey untethered or weathered
Even though my clothes be tattered
My soul hasn't shattered
I bleed you
I feed you
I need you
And as if that hadn't mattered
You leave me to rot and to write
And to fight against Jesus
My tongue suffers suffocated
As I scream he fails to heed us
And this must
Hate must
And will rust the world away
Unless we douse it with our hearts
Our conscious love for a day
And finally say WOW
What the fuck have we done to ourselves?
Then I delve into what I still don't fully understand
But I can stand up and recite
The words I write at night by lamp light
And it will be a sight to behold
For we are all on this journey of
mind, soul, body, life, death, grief, happiness, success,
failure, suicide, life support, euthanasia, sensation,

redemption, condemnation, openness, and closure
But bring me closer to assimilation
Into the collective river which is us
Our conscious spirit that opens to the sky
I will never die
So help me try to combat
What's become destructive in time
And even though I hurt
And am crooked of spine
We must join hands in the sands
and heal this world that's unkind

Have I come full circle again?
But a circle is never full till it is joined
By every person who has lived, is living, and will live
And you may ask me,
Jacob, is that possible?
To which I reply,
Of course, the circle is already drawn in the sand
All that is left to do is step into it
And taking your hand I lead every person into the future
Into the unknown
To face the orange balls of ice
That rain into the atmosphere
They've become the projectiles
The walnuts to the dome
But who's the enemy if the whole world is my home?
My enemies are the ones who take no side

The ones we know have something to hide
So much has become tainted and corrupted
I fought against not fighting and my spirit has erupted
And conducted the lightning made of one thought
I caught it
Spun out to space in haste
Without knowing the substance of what was given to me
It's easy for you to see
You who already know what it was
A challenge to make it grow
And not to wither
Come hither, my child
And speak with the wild
For you have been there
Grown out your hair
And sputtered back onto the track
Toward rebirth, recreation, temptation,
Sensation, creation, deception, but rejection of destruction
Realization to the point where
You cease to destroy all you love
And tear down only when necessary
But to create without holding back
You are my God, child, meditate with me this day
And we just may become one body
So please be my eyes, my ears, my voice
And lead my people back to the circle
The river, the wind, the spirit, the infinite
And you will be their Ankh
Leading the battle of the mind
Pick up your pens, my friends

Cut the binds
And burn the blinds
From off of your eyes

I am Raging War

I Am One of Them, I Am All of Them

I am continually dying among the living
And I find myself living among the dead
However, my mother is among the living
And my father is amongst the dead
And then there comes me
The one who doesn't belong, you see
So I scream in silence
As the violence of unridden hooves
Pummel my body with their noise
Swimming in the sediment
I wait
For the sky to accept the girls
And boys that I have made love to
What is to come?
What is to come for me?
What is to come for you?
And what is to come for all of us?
For we are all of the same spirit
As we remain prisoners of the never-ending

Crimson pendulum
That pulled from the cave of ba-dum dum dum
I'm still feeling the ripples of the bomb
Ba-dum dum dum
Please, I beg you to stretch your hand
Out to suddenly connect with the electricity
Pulsing from my palm
Where has this power come from
Pour the soul into me from the sun
And the galaxies of every hand I've ever touched
And every hand that's ever touched me
Push my hair back to reveal a hidden door
To my mind
Open that door so the tails of iguanas
Can air themselves and combine with the thoughts
That are brought forth from my sleeping fortifications
Motherfuckers need to look into my eyes
So as to share my hallucinations
That come not from drugs
But from the goddesses, the gods, the heart,
The spirit, the love the hate, the words, the humans,
The subhumans, the superhumans, the mortals,
And the immortals

I am one of them
I am all of them

Gettin Paid

This is a rhyme about
Gettin' paid, gettin' paid

You are my muse, my spirit
And you've made me rich beyond reason
Because you've spit these colors into
My eyes
Making my retinas shatter
And my pupils dilate
In order to make a larger whole
For your soul

Catch me if you can
But this ain't a race
And you're not a rabbit
I remember when they used to call me
Turtle
But now,
I can stand up straight
Since the vertebrae be fused
To the titanium of my soul

And I can drum out a
Bum bum bum
On the sticks, the clams, the snakes
That feather this expanse
Of unweathered talk
Of unspooned words
Of tortured wings
That will fall off once the sky
Becomes the color of wine

And I know
That you all know
That I know
That you know
I am not you
But in that fact I am
Becoming Everything
And that makes us the same

Part the ways
We are the parts of the world
And we are One
We are the sun
The fire, the living
And everything I have said here tonight
Will take flight into the darkest
And most narrow tunnels
That lead out of the spheres
Into another tunnel

And into you

My spirit
My guide
My myself
Because you are me
And I am you
And that is a picture of me
Even though it was developed as you
It bears my face

The constellationness of time conflagrations
Because the sky is aflame with airwaves
That ripple with our voices

I still exist to grow roots in cosmopolitan gardens
To sprout no thought
Just phallic symbols
But I grab them and jerk them
Till they spurt—
Blood

Because I know they just exist here
To transform into vaginal imagery
My muse
My spirit
You've made me rich beyond reason
Because even though I can't have children
You aid me in giving birth

And for this I thank you

This shit ain't about
Gettin' paid, gettin' paid
And this shit
Does not
Rhyme

If I Killed You

If I killed you
it wouldn't be pretty

If I killed you
it wouldn't be pleasant

If I killed you
it wouldn't be ugly

If I killed you
it would be beautiful...
Just like you

BITCH
I hate you
I fucking hate you
Forever—bullshit
Eternity—bullshit
Fantasy—bullshit
Love—bullshit

Let me break it down for you now:
This is how it would go down:
I would tie your wrists to the bedposts
And I would watch you squirm naked
As I taped up your mouth
After that I would just watch you struggle for a bit
I'd sit in complete silence next to you
And look at you silence for a good hour...

Until you got tired and depleted
Then I would rape you
Over
And over
And over
And over
And over
And over
And over again

That's seven times I would rape you
So that then you would become infected
With the same sickness that afflicts my soul...

I would leave you to cry and die
Again and again...
But soon you would be impregnated with
my semen of frailty
Of fertile infertility
of saintly insanity
Of loving hatred

and beautiful violence
For I have made you into a work of art
A work of fiction
A work of literature
And you
now
cum 4 me

As pregnancy accelerates and you beg for me to stop
It only gets worse…

Oh yes

I haven't even gotten started

Now your belly would swell with child
and I'd be ready with a bowie knife
My favorite
jagged and sharp
A deadly phallus
like my heart

Burying it up to the handle in your pregnant stomach,
I slice like a rainbow
drenched in blood
An angry flow of colors
that don't stick
they only run
Like tears
and bleeding mascara

and your face

My face inside you
My face intermingling with your slowly manipulating
time in and out of consciousness
And I CUT

CUT for every place
CUT for every time
CUT for every expectation that I ever had
And with every cut I can see the hope
drain from your being
And soak into my eyes
Giving me sight

RIP
Fucking RIP

Tear the flesh
And tear the undeveloped being
out of your being
Open belly
open heart
closed spirit

Fetus in hand I will be able to
ingest the night through brain waves
not ready to penetrate the light
Forever my sight
will be riddled and dotted

With red and with white
With your hair
And with your broken teeth

The child
Dead child
in my arms
I will always cradle it sweetly
Cherish the deadness
The silence
The heartache
The bittersweet abortion

Music to my lungs

Breath to my ears

You…
my sweet you…

Now open for me
I would crawl inside her mangled body
So I would never be without you again…

But you see…

If I killed you
I wouldn't need to write this poem

And I will never be inside you again…

Ever again

Ever again

Ever again

Ever again

Ever again

Ever again

Jiz and Rainbows

You are *Rainbow Brite*
And I am *David the Gnome*
And I still remember all the cartoons
I'd watch at home
When I was six-years-old
Back from kindergarten
No,
I'm not like you
Watching *Power Rangers* or *Beetle Borgs*
Shit,
I'm *Stranger than Fiction*
I sunk my mind into *Care Bears*
And silky chairs
Watching *Muppet Babies*
That shit made my dreams cum true
Like *Lamb Chop* on my plate
And *Mister Rogers* staying up late
Watching four or five hours of shows…

Nickelodeon?

Forget *Blues Clues*
I watched *Rupert*
That weird little white bear in shoes
Give me old school cartoons like
Felix the Cat
Not some violent Asian shit
That shit is whack
What?
You telling me *The Neverending Story* is gay?
Put that shit away
I can't stand your hateful honesty
Cause you were jerkin' off to *Adventures in Odyssey*

Ummm…fuck it
This poem ain't flowin'
The way that I wanted it to
Cause whenever I try to be funny
It doesn't work
And deep down I'm imagining
Rainbow Brite getting fucked by *Felix the Cat*
And the *Care Bears* dousing the audience
With their love juice
Yeah…that's where it goes
And it flows all down your leg
And when you beg for the show
To be over,
I'm watchin' *Ducktales*
And countin' clovers

We Are Not the Living

We are not the living
We are not the living
We are not the living

Butcher the gods of Forever
So we may see our sins are clever
We haven't died a thousand ways
Cause we live in darkness
You fail to put us where we already are
Feeling the sharpness of the knife
Across my tongue
And lunge
At the wings I desire
To use to fly far away from the fire
Which consumes our lover's dream
But transforms into a fetus's scream
Of pain
For its mother to come and fuck it with a long stick
However
Leave me be
Crying, dying, not flying

But bleeding from my dick

We are not the living

Watch the sky darken with birds
Sent to bring our doom
DIIIIIIIEEEEE—-
Survive
We won't
As they hit
BOOM BOOM BOOM
You may try to run
But we all drown in feathers
However
We're already tied to our possessions
Cars are the tethers
WAAAAA—-
Where are your spirits
Excitement has withered
You all live like zombies
So will it matter when you're gone
What were your trophies

We are not the living
We are not the living
We are not the living
We are not the living

You've been visited by Jacob Steep:
The Killer of Last Things

But you can't comprehend
What you've seen in me
For it is god-like
Devil-like
Forget all that
As you fall into Nothingness
I wait in the shadows
For you to finally understand the pain
And the hurt
And it will scar like a hot iron
To the face
But you will be Enlightened

LEARN YOUR WORLD
LEARN YOUR WORLD
LEARN YOUR WORLD
LEARN YOUR WORLD

Cause crossing over costs a heavy price
Just look at my hands
As if you let me
And hold you
Just know
This blood is toxic
Inside my love
But let me love you anyway
I can bring you into the living

We are not the living

We are not the living
But we can be

We are not the living
But we can be

Falling down I stand tall
From the bridge I look down
At your face
A kiss from a Goddess
Please bestow on me this day
Life
Femininity
And words to speak
How I love thee unconditionally
I shall not die
For you are with me

I shall not die
For you are with me

My Goddess
How I love thee unconditionally
I shall not die
For you are with me

I am the living…

Sacagewaea

Is this it which bitch
You WHAT?

FUCK

AND YOU
This is no ordinary conundrum
For I don't even see the puzzle
I'm supposed to solve
NO NO NO

This is not for you
This is for me

Spacious
Raucous
Caucus

What…the…fuck
Shove it in the whatever
And blood

And what the hell is this semen
Dripping from the hole
Where your heart used to be?

The Purple doesn't help
The Purple doesn't comfort

Chhhkkka—chhhhkkka
Chest Death sets in
So believe me when I tell you
That I will melt into the steel branches
That cut my nonexistent face
And believe me when I tell you
That the only thing I see at this moment
Is a dead ferret
Hanging right there
It's blood dripping into the open mouth
Of a child that is masturbating
For the Perfect Forever

It is me
Me is it
See it me
Me it see
Ahhhhhh…fuck

Just do it

Just do it

Bubble, spit, packing paper, your face,
raw fish, inside a dress, case, waist, tires, skies

STOP

Warbling
Incoherent
Sub-genres
Fuck

Maybe it was just him
The penis
In, in, in
OW…

I just wanted to watch Rainbow Brite
But now it's in me

Pursue me if you wish
Oh right, I forgot
There isn't anyone
As business usual
Silent as the sun
Loud as the grave
Sexy as your death

CUT OPEN YOUR MOUTH AND FUCK IT

Take me to bed…
Mmmmmmm…

It hurts…
But I don't care anymore…
Drip, drip, drip

I DECLARE THIS
I OWN THIS
And it shall be
The incantation of the defiled child
Commune with me and we will
Slowly…
Slowly…
Slowly…
Slowly…
Orgasm
into the cosmos
FOREVER

B-CUM

Suffer all that hasn't become everything. Walk it and meet up with the energy of the ones you are supposed to commune with. B-CUM me. B-CUM you. B-CUM black. B-CUM white. I am every color. Become my concubine and we will have sex over the page. I will cut my wrists and bleed these verses. Please menstruate onto my word and I will love you always. Cupping my hands, I shall drink of your river. Bless me with your curse and I shall B-CUM it. B-CUM the mantra. B-CUM. B-CUM. B-CUM. B-CUM. B-CUM. B-CUM. B-CUM. B-CUM. But does anything B-CUM or are we already what we will always be? I shall be your cum. Your flow. Your wetness. Baptize me henceforth in femininity. Have me worship you and bleed into and out of your vagina. Make me into that being of light that radiates energy, sexuality, and wisdom. For cumming together may still be able to open portals into the stars. We are the everything. Plants be our feet, suns be our heads, cough and bring into being. And it has been created out of nothingness. Out of my mind. Out of all that was, is, and will be. And it is I. I have not B-CUM. I am. I have not B-CUM. I am. I have not B-CUM. I am. I have not B-CUM. I am.

HOO

You are the Bling to my Blang,
And whatever that means, I will understand it in the future
However, I still don't know who You are
Are you—
GOD?
Hmm, no...
Are you—
SATAN?
YES!
NO!
mmmmmmmmmmmmmmm...
Well,
Are you..
Macavity the Mystery Cat?
No, but you do excite me to no end

All I know is you are a CNT
An all-knowing, all-seeing CNT
So will you share with me your wisdom?
I am an ear of corn to your stalk
No, wait

I am the stalk-er to your lonely woman
Please rape me again
I think this time I'll catch the meaning of life

Hmm

Wisdorgasm
And I Commence

Pour your words into my mouth
Because the heavens speak in riddles
Hell remains relatively straight-forward
This is why I understand what it's saying

Writer's Block does not exist
This is because I declare it doesn't
And so shall it be
Bulimia is just the lifestyle of taking in and giving back

So I wait at the crosswalk

Break out. Fall back. Stab down. Shoot up. Pull tight.
Fuck loose. Noose the misuse of words.
I'm sorry for all the words I have uttered without thought.

Forgive me
How shall I make it right

Scream out FUCCCKK!

Before this point I would've said:
"and die"
But I do not wish that anymore

AND LIVE

The Girls in My Screams EP (2010)

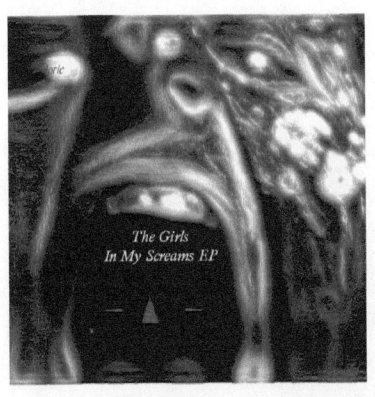

1. The Girls in My Screams (Pt. 1)
2. The Girls in My Screams (Pt. 2)
3. The Girls in My Screams (Pt. 3)
4. Alice   5. The Screams in My Girls
6. The Sky Is Falling   7. Suffering

scream 4 me
cum 4 me

The Girls in My Screams (Part 1)

"I can't be your mother," she said.
"Emotionally you're dead, and in bed you have issues."

S-s-s-s-save it!

Even though your fuckin name is my fuckin name
Doesn't mean we can't fight or pass blame
And for now it's still a shame
That we continue this game
Of Chasing the Blue…

She was dead (blue)
She was dead (blue)
And I lived because of it

The first said she wasn't going to baby me anymore
The second said she couldn't be my mother
The third said I sucked in bed
Then I pounded lead into her head!!!!!——-

(pause)

But I still clung to the second
The one I'm still in love with

I still find myself waking up in her apartment

When I was on top of you, you said, "Yes, Daddy. I need it."
Then I cut open my hands, and tried to stitch your scars as I bleed it
My intimacy distress, I confess, runs deeper than where they get Fiji water
And I know that cutting your belly is not Forever or the way that I taught her
To love me, I guess I am that baby crying for milk
But your tit is sour and I scream for soft silk
And receiving nothing but delayed abortions

…abortions…distortions…extortions…exorcisms…heroism…womanism

That is the real question: Is society still dominated by men? Or is it really the women who control everything manipulatively from the background? I don't really want to wait around until Hilary Clinton infests the White(house) with her Zombies of Period. Phallus. Slogan, flag, and anthem.

And I bring it back to the fetus

Tearing it out in order to feed us
I've blocked the sun with the dead babies piled
High to the sky, you killed your own child
But it feels like it was my d-d-dick you cut out of yourself
But I, I know what I am (surrogate motherfucker)
And I know what you are not (woman)
I'm still four years behind (pedophile)
With an undeveloped mind (pedophile)

BOOM!

Just for a second as I blink my eyes, a flash of an image appears in front of me. It is my mirror reflection, holding the Winged-Sword high above his head. Then he is gone like the morning frost.

Basically the basic targeting of women is an age-old religion stemming back to the time of the vikings. They knew where to put the horns, they knew. But that's not the point. The point is

Rape

Why won't you love me?

Why won't you love me?

WHY WON'T YOU FUCKING LOVE ME?

The Eden, the Forever, the rape victim
The one who said she loved me after we fucked
Is no longer near me, but with luck
She won't forget me the way I'm forgetting her
In every way except how she fucked like a hooker
And squeezed my arms as she came
I remember how she loved brother-sister incest play
And I still think of her name every fucking day

WHY WON'T YOU FUCKING HOLD ME?

Gasping for air, my eyes shoot open. Water floods into my tear ducts and I feel like I'm drowning. It's the women. I know it. They've infested the colleges, the churches, the coffee houses, the White(house), the movie theaters. Shit. I need to stop taking time off.

I sink and continuously feel like a gooey piece of afterbirth running
Down my leg to come to rest on the brink of enlightenment
However, that will not come through orgasm or excitement
Astral Penis Projection into the universe's uterus
I can feel myself dying, how come god won't remember us?

Why do they play?
For brains…and for women

Peter just stands there as I am forcibly raped by ten

decomposing men. Their mutilated cocks will sometimes break off in my ass, but that's the price you pay for being a misogynist.

But as my ass is repeatedly pumped with zombie cum, I fall into my own mind as a dog would fall into a pile of shit.

God, where are you now?

I'm faaaaaaaaaaaaaaaaalling…

God, where are you in the place where I reside?

God is my mother
God is my mother
God is my mother
We are God's failed experiment
I've been going down
Spiraling down
You let the girls pound me into the ground
And the answers for me still remain unfound
Bam I hit the ground!

I dissolve in water. This is what she would say to me whenever we would bathe together. But to tell you the truth, I was really the one who dissolves in water. Whenever I'm standing in stagnant water, I can feel the liquid creep up my hairless legs like spider string. It laces around my knees, tickling my muscles as it makes its way up to the hanging bits. And ties tight around my balls and penis, cutting off circulation. And I laugh, because it was her who said she dissolved in water. But my manhood has a lot to do with wetness. My manhood has a lot to do with satisfaction. So when she said I was terrible, I died a little inside, waiting for the water to again defy gravity and slip and slide around my hips, my waist, my nipples. It makes its way up to my vulnerable neck, the only weapon I choose to use. Her feet are in my puddle again, jerking at my semi-erect penis.

"Come on! I want you to cum," she says.

I try, but my wounded dick decides to rebel and softens to the consistency of putty. They don't have faces. She sighs and lets go of me.

"You're useless," she says. "Go fix yourself." Stepping from my water, she disappears into my sex-memory. By this point the water has climbed my neck and is trying desperately to get into my closed mouth. I fight it, but streams start to pour into my nostrils and I gasp for air. Just as I do so, a waterfall pours down my throat and I fall back into my body.

Bam I hit the ground!
Making craters and cavities riddling through expanses
Of polluted air, making me impotent and sequentially pensive
And I live, still live, even if you won't help me open the seventh chakra
I'm still searching for that explorer who will aid me on the

road to tantra
To help me dig deeper into the earth in order to hold my hand as we shoot
Into the celestial universe together, but she's gone and in my hand is a boot
A boot that falls into ashes and leaves my dreams for love-making dry
And my mother lands next to me, but I don't want her to touch me even if she tried
To love me, I reject but suspect her of something deeper
Some spirituality that I don't wish to be a keeper
Of, I'm a sleeper, a dreamer, a philosopher
Of sexual fluidity, but I remain alone
With no one to become one with, I'm still as a stone
    Yeah, that's right…Fuck you…

    Subdivided and undressed, I became a human dildo. Which is really what I've always been. But this is the first time I've really stated it. This is the first time I've really come to terms with it. My body isn't what I wanted it to be. My body isn't what I envisioned it to be. But they said I was beautiful, they said I was pretty, they said I was hot. Lies. Why do they lie? She said she made noises just to make me feel better, so I killed her. She killed me. I killed her. Cycle. Circle. Recite these words cyclically until you become a spiral. But the spiral is only broken out of through orgasm.

    Sabotage is nothing, just as forgiveness is nothing. Evasion is everything. Evading detection. Isn't that always the goal? Sneak in, sneak out, go undetected. Evade traps, land mines, women, and terrorists. Always. But I don't do so well evading the evil women, do I? Not a chance.

What will happen to our sexual identity when we are blind in the mixture of purple and black?
Fallen trap, I'll drink the sun sap, till I know how the weather speaks, then I fly and fall back
Into nothingness and I become sexless, unsex me here, and fill me from the crown
To the toe top-full of direst understanding, because I am that slave bound
But with roots of energy striping and penetrating the ground
I have found what it really means to be inside of the spirit
Soul love, soul sex, souls weaving together, and I don't wish to tear it
Apart and tear the heart, the chakra that eludes my touch the most
But I guess, I'm still that failure, and can't seem to become more than a parasitic host

But sometimes...I don't want to think about that...

I want to be somewhere where I can love.

Take me to that place.

Take me to that place. That place of fairy tales and dragons, knights and maidens. Take me to that place where true love exists and perseverance is not punished. Because in this world, no good deed ever goes unpunished. I finally know that. Circularly. Strategically. But I'll keep doing what I believe is right. Because that's all we can do even if the dragons have forsaken us. If the Dreaming is dulled down to a hum-hum that not many can hear, I still know it's there calling out for me. And I will follow it. To the end of my days.

And there she was again.

Th-th-there she was again-a-a-again

I remember thinking that we were going to have a meaningful conversation, but then she opened her mouth. It was a black cave of madness, purely woman. From out of her mouth crawled giant arachnids. They crawled over her lips, some up onto her face and some down her neck. I just stared as the horrific monstrosity infested my mind. She stirred, getting up from the bed and moving over to me. She got on top, straddling me and looking down into my mutilated face. And she opened my mouth. She opened her mouth. And a torrential downpour of tarantulas poured from her mouth and down into mine. The only thing I could hear as the stream was ripping down my throat was the shriek of Wesley after he had been drained fifty years by The Machine in the Pit of Despair. *(Wesley Screams)*

I am the only one who put these motherfucking scars on my motherfucking chest
Please tell me why I still can't figure out how to put these

thoughts to rest
My sex is just a mess, and again I confess, about my intimacy distress
And why I cum less than you wish for me to
But this is nothing new, and I always knew
That blue was the color of death
I feel lost when I can't hear your breath
Or watch you as you sleep, thoughts intermingling
Time universe, still searching for the sublime unwinding
And the unbinding from all of the ropes that tie me to my mother

You are my world now. She would say to me over and over again. Like a broken record linearly separated from reality. Not being able to register cycles it would crack and sputter back just the same words over and over and over again. You are my world now. You are my world now. You are my world now. Scream it. You are my world now. You are my world now. You are my world now. Don't fight it. You are my world now. So entertain me. Make me laugh like no one else can.

You are my world now. And Forever.

And since you are my world, you must be spherical, like a testicle. No, not like a testicle. Like a globe, a hollow one. One made of chocolate and persimmons. One made of poppy seeds and Jolly Ranchers like when you were a young boy having sex with strangers in the backs of Volkswagens. Or was that a BMW? Nevertheless I knew what penetration was. And I always would because she-he engrained it in me and evasion was not really an option. From my tank of water that only exists in my belly, I finally know the meaning of life. And it's Antichrist. If you wanna know, ask Lars. He's the Savior.

(clearing throat)
(clearing throat)
(clearing throat)

I don't want to fuck my mother
I don't want to fuck my mother
I don't want to fuck my mother

I fall into the bed as a devastating migraine splits my head open. My bullet wound opens up again and blood pours down my face. Screaming, I pull off my pants and discover my dick is no longer there. It has turned into an umbilical cord wrapped tightly around my heart. I start to pull on it violently, trying to rid myself of this pregnant feeling. As I pull, I feel it pulling my heart. My fingers slip on the gooey umbilical and as I struggle, the bed begins to melt down into the theater. It begins to melt down into the theater. It begins to melt down into the theater. And I fall. Onto the stage of Studying the Madness. Studying the Women. The audience is missing in action and I stand alone on this stage with one microphone. Waiting. I'm always waiting. I'm sick of waiting. But suddenly the audience starts to pour in from every entrance. And they stampede like no other species.

The Zombies. And Peter standing in the balcony watching me.

And I do the only thing I know how to do. I recite.

(audio skipping)

But I guess, when I'm fucking you
I'm really just fucking my mother

The Girls in My Screams (Part 2)

started to become blurry under her blood-battered face.
Slowly the night drew close inside the den of thieves

they played blackjack for brains.
But I had beaten her and I couldn't see the light as it

Why
Do
They
Play?

infestation had become apparent when the dead walked like tourists.
She had it coming to her, oh she had it coming to her like

The Zombie
balled up fists inside the anger and the madness I had for the opposite sex.

Cry-oh-Genics

Cradle my head in ashes. Cradle my head in the ashes of my own aborted children, because they number in the thousands. Thousands upon thousands of words, worlds, lives, and deaths. These are the times of mourning. And these are the times I give life and also take life away. From the smallest of mice to the most enormous of giants. They are all equal in The Eyes. But forget nothing that I have said, because it will be of use to you one day. And that is the truth.

But I tell you now...

Do not be fooled by the man behind the curtain
He only exists to hurt you
Only look to the ones who never had a curtain to begin with
The ones who hide only exist in stages
Stages of ego, fear, and deceit
They pose as wizards, yet possess no magic
And I have brought forth the flame to expose these fallacies
They flutter away from my fire like mosquitos sent to harm the children
Us, the truthful ones, possess the real magic

By this point we are covered in haggis and brains. Intestines and chitlins. Break backs and spines like toothpicks in the rain and we finally know that all this is in our minds. But what comes forth from our minds is much more real than this world. We fly and we are warriors, sent to protect this world Forever.

But fuck not what you see in front,
Fuck the earth below you, so that the connections shall not break
They will branch, sprout, grow stronger, and spread
As we live through these storms,
Being watered by torrential rains,
I, I, and I am what you seek
See in me what you wish,
But trust there is no deceit behind these eyes
I am spread-egoed naked
Fuck the roses, give me the thorns
Whip me with thistles
Then consummate our lust on that sacred spot
The spot where I buried my libido
But it has grown, sprouted like a mighty Oak
Which refuses to be cut down
It has become the Giving Tree
Play in my branches
And know me

We whimper each other's names into the galaxies and we know finally that we can touch one another. Falling into the piles, we lose ourselves in each other's body. I in his, he in mine. And he enters me, exploring the dragon's cave. The discoverer of worlds and we are the Wizards of Steam. I moan as he thrusts in and out of me. This is becoming. He thrusts in and out of me. This is becoming. He thrusts in and out of me. This is becoming. I live, bursting like a flowered firework into the sky.

Boom.

Heaving, we detach like HDMI cables into bottle rockets. Then we hold each other. Tenderly, but violently.

"Never let me go," I say.
"I won't."
We fall heavily into sleep.

This—
Is always what I meant
When I kissed you so passionately
And there is no fear in my being drawn to you
But if I had said 'I love you',
That would not have been a lie
However, I have been conditioned not to utter these words
For fear on instilling fear in the one I love—
Does this make any sense?
Why must I hide the connection I feel even though the energy is undeniable real?
I still love you
One day at a time

I can't hear anything except for a woo-woo-woosh in my ears. As we walk, our pulses fade like the beat. Moving in and out like waves: boom-boom-baloom. Tragic. But this is where I have chosen to walk.

Fire, walk with me. This is all I ask. I have always felt the fire inside and in the loins. But my search for the outer fire hasn't proven as productive. This is how the spiders have treated me, because they crawl in my belly. She put them there and only fire can rid me of them. And it was watching us. I could see its eyes peering from the shadows.

You live in me,
But I murdered the idea of you

However, it was probably the idea of you which I fell in love with
The concept of you:
My Perfect Forever to your Elan
My Alice to your Sherry
My Violet Perfect to your Aleks
And I died inside you

"How the fuck are we supposed to know if we're in love or if we're in pain?"

And he leads us across the rows of women. "We have come to realize that they are parasites. They have come not to coexist, but to leech." He pauses for a second then continues. "But there is one special case. Here." He stops in front of one of the freezers and we look in. At first glance, the body inside looks like a pre-pubescent boy. But with further scrutiny, I realize it is not. There are what looks like the budding of small breasts; subtle but there nonetheless. And there are no testicles under the penis, there is what looks like the opening of a vagina.

"This is Bartholem-You."

Drowning! Suddenly images flash before my eyes and I can't get a breath. A cave. Tunnel. Graffiti. The Tethered Toys. Torrential rains. Crimson Tide. The Madness. War. Rumors of War. Rumors of famine. Diseases. Storms of hail. Earthquakes. Tutus. Androgynous androids. Plankton. Civilization. Cinema. Castration. Constellations. Concordances. Cancer. Clocks. Clowns. Clouds. CNT. Madness. Consciousness. Synonyms. Nudity. Sharks. In-in. Soaring above the world. Chaos. Eyes. Forever. Violet. Transexuals. Wings. Mountains. Absolute Shaman. Council. Children. Violence. Sex. Rape. Murder. Transcendence. Existence. Energy. Tribes-people. Belinquast. Soulmind. T-Ps. Specialization. Tunnel. Path. Down. Beat of the Universal Drum. Signs of Madness. Walls. Riddled. Crawling. Sickeningly searching for their eyes. Apocalypse. Stones. Looming at me. Sacagewaea. Incest. Forgive me Mother for I did not know how deep ran the Black Mist. Darkness. Melts. Ripples circle my feet. S / he was a nine-year-old girlboi in a tutu, but wise beyond her years. You are the Nilotic. I am Bartholem-You. Revolution. Muffins. Have not forsaken you. All things androgynous. And it shall...BE.

BOOM!

Air sucking in *Hyperventilation*

"The best way we've found is to be neither of them. And all of them." He taps my forehead and I faint and fall back into nothingness. I was made of porcelain. And I fell. Shattering on the ground like a mirror in front of hideousness.

(Silence)

You aren't responsible for my lack of climax
At least, I don't think you are

Wait…I don't think I'm behind the curtain
But it seems that I have put you behind the curtains I have woven,
   painted, and tailored just for you
And, hence, I have created you
Like I have created everything else

And everything falls away like cherry blossoms on the wind. In the in-between space where I was neither awake nor asleep, I wept. 4-MySelf. I was curled in a fetal position on a dark wooden stage with a spotlight on me. I am naked. Raking my nails through my face, I peel back layers and layers of skin. Searching for any soul that may have been there. I lifted her and slowly started, I just didn't know it.

When my eyes finally open, I am laying down below the Picasso sculpture in Daily Plaza. And now, my problem is apparent. Utterly naked again, there is an audience all around me. They watch me with dead eyes. Fish eyes. Men, women, and children look upon my nakedness. I look down and discover that my penis is gone again, but this time, instead of a hanging umbilical cord, I have a full-fledged vagina. So I start to finger myself, which seems to excite the crowd. My pussy starts to gush as I plunge two fingers deep inside myself. The men in the front row start to rub their crotches as I start to moan. Then they storm on me. Kissing me. Stroking me. Licking me. Shrieks of pleasure start to escape from my lips. And just before I cum, I yell:

"I am woman, hear me roar!"

Suddenly a scream breaks free from my throat as cum breaks free from my cunt, showering the onlookers. As I try to catch my breath, my hair starts to grow at an alarming pace, pooling all around me like a blanket. It is a mane. And I am a lioness. The audience scatters as I bear my teeth menacingly. And I walk off proudly into the sunset, hunting for zombies.

I am creating my mythology,
But that seems to have a way of
sucking everything into itself
And it tends to connect everything in
my world into a tapestry web

I do not fail to mark every detail
If we know one another,
You are most likely already part of my Mythos
But I am beginning to love you for you
And not what I've written you to be

This is a story that must be told. And it is a story that only I can tell. I have seen it, like no other person before me has seen it, spread out on the desert ground like a giant map; but unreadable. Indecipherable are the lines and inscriptions. The enormous Blanket of Colossus. But the point is that I've seen it, I have read it, and now I must tell about it.

Belinquast is a place that we all must go at one point in our lives. Sometimes it is at the end of the map. Sometimes it is in the middle. And sometimes it is at the very start. We all pass through at one point or another. I want you to know that I have not been there yet, but I am slowly walking in that direction. Even though the map may be foreign to me, I can still make out the paths despite if they be covered with sand. However, it is hard and slow going toward my destination when the road is covered with the undead. They've become sluggish, lethargic, apathetic, and they try to grasp at my legs to pull me down to their level. But I will never give in. Ever. I will walk with purpose.

Not everything that happens,
Happens in this world
Benny has made it possible for me to
start the war

Since he released the Black Mist and
the Purple Fog into the Hollow Dimension: our world

I am still unsure of what will happen
When the Black Mist meets the Purple Fog
Alls I know is that it shall be called The Climactic Moment
There is the possibility that everything may be washed away
Expunged from the world
And I will be left with a fresh slate

I desperately scrape at the inside wall of her vagina with two of my fingers as if to scrape away the sickness which is CNT. But I know that I cannot. It is no use, because it is my sickness as well. Then I enter her hard and deep. Slamming my body against hers, I hate fuck the shit out of her box. My fuck-box. That's what she is. Always.

Why is it considered such a wrong for a man to use a woman for sex, but it is never thought of when a woman uses a man for sex? How many licks does it take to get to the Tootsie Roll center of a Tootsie Pop? *The world may never know.*

As I thrust she begins to laugh, quietly then louder. And the tears begin to flow from my eyes. I raise my fist and bring it down on her face. Again. I raise my fist and bring it down on her face. Again. I raise my fist and bring it down on her face. She is silenced. Reaching over, I turn the lamp on beside my bed. The light illuminates her blood-battered face and I cease to recognize a human under there. Cock my fist back. Bring it down. Cock my fist back. Bring it down. She sputters blood and coughs, but I continue to beat her face with my fist until my knuckles are broken and all life has flown from her body. By this point I can hardly remember why I fucked her.

I raised my fist into the light
I could hardly remember why I had come here

I look down into Aly's blood-covered eyes. They are beginning to crust over with ice. She feels cold and heavy below me, like a slab of ice. Frigid air starts to blow from between her lips, but it is not breath. I look around my bedroom and the walls start to drip and freeze; icicles hang from the ceiling menacingly. I expel a burst of air in a white cloud.

I raised my fist into the light
It was starting to freeze...

But who knows

Maybe I just want to love you
Until Eternity comes to tear you from my arms
But maybe Eternity would cultivate that love
Make it immortal
Like us

Little Alice, where have you run to?

The Girls in My Screams (Part 3)

"I accepted a long time ago that not everyone is going to understand what I do. But the ones that get it know that we have something special. We are together in this. We are connected within the light."

She isn't dead. And I am not dead. But what I have said here was never even given a chance to live.

I'm not really sure how to end this, like all things. This is because nothing is ever really finished, it's always open and festering like a cut you can't help going over repeatedly with the same razor. We made love like two mermaids in the cool waters; that was the moment I fell in love with her. That beautiful creature who shares my name, but then I wrote in detail how I would kill her. This was the last shout-out to a dying emcee.

It was me.

She always told me that I was perfect
But that was a lie
She always told me that I was special
But that was a lie,
For we all have something to offer

She always told me that we had been
lovers in another life
And this is the truth

The truth is that it is impossible to end something when the intention is to start it. But I don't think that's gonna happen; it ended before it began. Slowly I sink down through the sheets on my bed that begin to melt into the currents of the ocean. Bubbles swirl around my naked body as the water pulls me deeper. She is there waiting for me. I remember when I held her braided head under and forced her to watch her own abortion. She never left the water. And now we are together.

Alice floats up toward me from down below. I hover in the water without treading. She is naked and beautiful as she swims up toward me like a pale fish. She turns her back toward me and slowly presses her ass against my penis. I hold her body against mine. Breathing her in, breathing in the water around us. We are like two swimming angels again; making love. Becoming one flesh, we move in sync with the other's body. Bubbles float out of our mouths and toward the surface.

I've always loved you...

I've known you all and
At one point we may have been lovers
Lovers of the light and lovers of the dark
Lovers of the spirit and lovers of the universe

Connected within the light

I wake up in her apartment. And I smoke a bowl. I wake up in her apartment. And I smoke a bowl. Remembering the times we shared doing this. Together. Connecting within the light and never choosing to be wounded because we are together in this. But no more. No more. And I fail to find the reason why. Maybe it wasn't meant to be. The reason, I mean. The reason was never meant to be for *I* was never meant to be. Just like this fish swimming incessantly like a lover of the blue. But blue is death, you see. So why would we love death? But we do. We love the abuse as well; or, I do. But the madness transpires as follows: We were at once two otters, madly and desperately in love. No, that isn't true. We were at once two otters, madly and desperately in lust. That's more to key. However, once we consummated that lust, someone fell in love. And it wasn't me. Wait. Yeah, it was me. But I love you. I thought we were connected within the light? I feel like we are. Why won't you be with me now?

I wake up in her apartment. But she isn't here and I hear

a soft siren in the distance. It is wailing my heart longing loss like loveless lions. What I wouldn't give for a cat curled up on my lap right now. But would that take away my loneliness? Little Alice, where have you run to?

>Yes, you have kicked me down to the ground
>But sho' nuff I got right back up and now
>I am radiating the energy many refuse to acknowledge
>Educated in the spirit and attending the universal college,
>You and I meet and become one with the stars
>Hearts being in sync, escaping these mental bars
>That bind us, hold us, and collapse us
>Be strong, even if you are knocked by the tempest
>I will be there to offer you a hand,
>But it's up to you if you join me in the sand

>We are connected within the light

>I wake up in her apartment. No, no, no.

>I wake up in her apartment. Fuck.

I didn't just wake up because I haven't even gone to sleep yet. I've never been here before. To this apartment?

>Yeeeaaaah…
>Why won't you hold me?
>You already asked that question.
>Fuck. Yeah, I did. Didn't I?

You have become lost in your meandered mewlings and conversations with ghostly gay men. Why do I feel such despair?

I want to have astronomic sex on the astral plane
A thousand petaled lotus bursting like a lion's mane
Around the crown of my head, fusing me with this
I'll still walk this world even if you damn me to the abyss
So used to being alone, growing tough in the soul
You leave me no choice, but I'm not left with a hole
I still have space for you in my heart
But it's up to you if you wish to depart

We're still connected within the light

I wake up in her apartment. Dead.
I wake up in her apartment. Fuck everything I've said so far.
Why are you crying? I'm gonna keep asking you until I get an answer.

Now I know why I hate women.

And I ended it there.
But my phone rang. It was a txt message which read:

hey its alysha u wanna come 2 my wedding nxt april?

But then it started again like a violent typhoon hurling me into the darkness, into suicidal thoughts again. *This was never my world / You took the angel away / I'd kill myself to make everybody pay.* Alice was my angel for a brief moment in time then she was gone and thinking back now on the times we had shared together, everything seems so surreal, like it was just a dream and I have woken to find morning and my dreams slowly fading. She's fading.

How come everything that's true ends with *I just want this to be over*? Cause pain is truth and truth is pain. Women are the truth, so women are pain. Wait, that's not right. Women are deceptive and so they cause pain. Chest death is the most intense pain in the world because it combines emotional pain with physical pain. The way it feels is as if someone took a giant hook and gouged out your chest with it.

Let's go for a ride.

I'm looking for my life back. Where can I find it? She stole it, didn't she? WHERE THE FUCK DID SHE GO? I've been looking way too long. And I've been living without my life for far too long. Shame on me for letting her take it. She never deserved it. Hey, Alice, I'm talking to you! Give it back…

Do we wish to explore the tantric Spiralverse together?
I will be your guide to wonders you have never seen
And you will be clean of your physical body
Shedding your skin for your astral spirit

We will wander over Rainbows of Reflection
And become one with dimensions of thought
and dimensions of spirit

Connected within the light

It's fine if you do not choose to walk with me
But know I will accept you and we shall be free
How many times do I have to offer my hand
before you take it?
Still, I love you, even if you don't understand
or you hate it
If you wish I will do the understanding for you,
But I will be there always if you want to know the clues
We don't need to walk miles of infinity in
each other's shoes,
Because we wear the same pair,
and we share the same body

But I've become so weak, I think I'll just rest here for a bit…NO! I must press on through this rotting flesh towards that sunset in the distance. The sun slowly dropping below the horizon. It leaves me in darkness, but I must not forget that it's light will be back in the morning. Sometimes the night seems so long that I make myself believe that this is our natural state: away from the light.

This seems laughable to me now because I wrote this to try and make sense out of events that took place. That was a silly thing of me to do, or even think was possible. This sheds no light, only dark shadows into the creases of the bed sheets. The ones we fucked on. It is useless to try to make sense out of a nonsensical world. But when you think of it that way, all the meaning comes out of that nonsense. I think that's where I've failed on this, I've been trying to put down things that make more sense when really everything drips down the leg of the host like a rancid piece of afterbirth purged from the sinus cavities of the prophets of old. If you eat the placenta of Jesus, then all the knowledge of the world will be gained back by the people, the humans. And misanthropy will be no more since we will all understand one another.

However, this will not come to pass because of our self-imposed sexual separation. As long as we have idiotic gender roles and stereotypes about men and women, we will never progress. We will forever be hormonally raging monkeys. Incapable of love. Incapable of empathy. Incapable of substantial relationships. Is this why I'm impotent? Or has it slowly been getting worse with each experience with the opposite sex? I think me and people just don't mesh well.

This is a train wreck.
I am a train wreck.
Everything I touch becomes a train wreck.

We are ourselves. But not everyone is themselves. This is what causes problems: the pretending, the lies, the blaaaaaahh. This is when suicide becomes beneficial. This is when suicide becomes an asset. Oh, wait, suicide is never productive, is it? Disregard that last bit, I wasn't thinking correctly.

The only reason you're reading this is because I haven't committed suicide.

And I ended it there.

But my phone rang. It was a txt message which read:

hey its alysha u wanna come to my wedding nxt april?

And I gave up.

Connect, dot, dot, dot
Triangle
We are connected within the light

Do not seek forms of separation
Materialism is definitely a temptation
But spirit is much richer for this life
I told you, I know you, and lived out your strife
Again, take my hand and you will know
You will feel all there is to become and grow
Into everything, becoming the world, becoming everything
We shall always stay connected as the physical becomes as nothing

Connect, affect, dissect, astral project
Expect nothing, and you will gain everything
Within the light…

I guess what I mean to say is:
We should fuck,
And I will write about it

Alice

[VERSE 1]
Once upon a time in the forest of decay
Lived a girl, which I say was made of clay
Molded by the fingers of deception
Condemned and trapped in this recitation
Created to be a legend, a myth, a song
The way she was seen was often wrong
Paths covered in bodies of her lovers
And summers filled with natural born killers
Fillers and chillers of life becoming still
In the forever born still born ever born will
Of a little girl who believes in the world of the wondrous
Little Alice didn't know her storm
Was becoming thunderous
Starting up life but leaving in her wake death
Her dress was meth and her smile his breath
He fell into love like tripping down the rabbit hole
Holding her tight, letting her free, tearing her soul

[CHORUS]
I will forever be beatific

If the storm was less specific
His love was epileptic
And Alice is the apocalyptic

[VERSE 2]
She didn't want to hurt the boy,
Her toy-toy could be his joy
Hands around his throat
Hands around his throat
Alice threw him to the wind
Swirling makes everything bend
Pretend she loves him forever
Sever the ties into the sky
Paint this lie on his face
Then retrace the streaks
Left by the rabbit shrieks
Written in broken teeth
Only twice he felt the sheath
Then she wrote him that check,
He weighed her an ounce,
He knew it would ba-bounce
Into what is now known as clowns
For sparks we need wedding gowns
I'm surprising the world with diamonds and pearls
A song about a girl ain't really about a girl

[CHORUS]
I will forever be beatific
If the storm was less specific
His love was epileptic

And Alice is the apocalyptic

[VERSE 3]
Now he's in the shadow of the Dreamchild
But impossible to tame when they seem wild
Child, dream, wet dream, come clean
His fantasy, and Alice, isn't what she seems
She moves on and burns the polaroids
From his mind, 16mm film on steroids
Making digital transfers of sex
No laundry to be done, so don't expect
A ride back to the train
Just cry in the pouring rain
Retain the cartridges overexposed
And remain in her mind enclosed
Knowing nothing more than incense
Covering up what should be common sense
You're the king, little girl, you're the king
You're the king, little girl, you're the king

The Screams in My Girls

"My life is a labyrinth. A map of its complexities is etched on my face in a thousand tiny expressions. There is an answer in what we're doing; a remedy that no fuckin' medication or quack therapy could ever compete with. But sometimes I get discouraged. Maybe I'm not being clear enough. Maybe I need to be honest with you and tell you what I want... I want your soul to open up for me. Spread-eagle like a split beaver so that I can gaze into its secrets."

- Anthony DiBlasi, *Dread*

I was in love… once
For all intents and purposes I'll call her Alice
Or Jessica, if you wish
We were two mermaids
Beautiful and glistening in the sun,
We swam out into the middle of the ocean to make love
And after we folded into one another

Like fragmented origami pieces,
She would sing to me of the worlds beyond the sea,
The islands in the stars,
Second star to the right and straight on till morning

This is when she became my muse

And she told me that she believed in the work I was doing,
To keep speaking even if no one was listening
Because she was always there to hear it

We were connected within the light

But if you really want to know,
Mermaids are creatures of darkness,
With pointed teeth and vacant eyes
And they'll gnaw off your balls if you get too close...
Or clit, whichever you prefer
They want your soul,
But not so they can love you,
They want your soul
So they can segment it for their own use
And they want your body
So they can devour it

Into depravity

I see your faces
I see your insides
I see your bones

You wanna know what she did to me?
Yeah…
It's not really what she did,
It's what she didn't do

I hear wedding bells ringing
I hear dead birds singing
I feel bi girls clinging
To my shirts, to my pants, to my heart
Tearing the distance into fragments of misunderstanding
Uncomprehending, disambiguation, rejection,
no redemption
For me, or for her, or for any of us godless soul-suckers
Seductive vampires

Your beauty is like a sunset brimming with light
Stretched out to fill every inch of space.
I have read your atlases and explored your caves
Like a seeker after truth.
But no seeker after truth is solely a seeker after truth.
I'll make you believe even if it kills you.

Everybody falls down.
We all fall down.
We all come down from that high Pye in the sky
Baby, lie to me
You wrote me that check,
I weighed you an ounce,
Even though I knew it would ba-bounce

Like the moon into space
In this rat race of sexual communism
Naked communication
Where nothing is ever, ever private

Ask me what I want

Go ahead, ask me

I want to take my writing to the next level
Have it not be just something I say
Empty words that rattle with hollowness
We can make it a way of life

You ever wonder what it would feel like to shoot a person?
What kinda rush you would get
Slipping your fingers around
A girl's throat as she sobs?

No?

THIS IS BULLSHIT!

Kill that bitch
Chop that bitch
Rape that bitch

I know you hear my words and

I know you feel my rage
I'll Ketchum by the throat and
They'll know I'm not a shag carpet to step on
And if you see me coming
You'll probably hear the screams in my girls
You'll probably feel the dreams in my worlds

We are The Lost organ donors
No takebacks!
Give me back my fuckin' heart
And give me back my fuckin' dick

All of this sex is unsafe sex

And all of my girls are in danger…

Alice, The Perfect Forever, The Violet Perfect, Sally, Jennifer, Katherine, Martha, Aly, Ellen, Elan, Sherry, Jacqueline, Sylvia, Erin, Sarah, Kileen, Evan, Asia, Leila, Amy, Amy, Amy, Amy, Amy, Amy, Amy, Alyssa, Christina, Dakota, AnnaSophia, Amy, Amy, Amy, Amy, Amy, Amy, Amy, Alice……………

The Sky Is Falling

[INTRO]
Is failure like a slippery slope
Pulling you down, destroying your hope
Is failure like a slippery slope
Pulling you down, destroying your hope
Is failure like a slippery slope
Pulling you down, destroying your hope

[VERSE 1]
But fuck it if I'm going down alive
You can't kill me, for now I will survive
You weren't as sweet as the wine of the same name
I still don't understand why you treat this like a game
I don't feel no shame for how we played
But I wasn't lookin' just to get laid
Feelin' like you played me for a human sex toy
Look me in my empty face and say I'm not a boy
I'm not made of latex, but you were just looking for sex
I made the mistake of falling in love
And I still am, so come take my blood

[CHORUS]
The sky is falling on my head
And I wish that I was dead
The sky is falling on my head
And I wish that I was dead
The sky is falling on my head
Blood stains this empty bed…
Blood stains this empty bed…

[VERSE 2]
You came from murder, I came from the living dead
Tread softly when you deal with love, losing your head
Is one of the pitfalls of emotion, love lotion
Come closer, little girl, I didn't use the potion
And I never wished to rape you
But I'm rolling, come on let me tape you
Oh, I meant tie you to the chair
By your hair, I got rope that won't tear
These are just my fantasies
And you live with the fairies
These are just my fantasies
And you live with the fairies
Click-clack, pop all your cherries
But I didn't feel the pressure
When it comes to man, I am the lesser

[CHORUS]
The sky is falling on my head
And I wish that I was dead
The sky is falling on my head

And I wish that I was dead
The sky is falling on my head
Blood stains this empty bed...
Blood stains this empty bed...

[VERSE 3]
You're the only girl I wish to have
But I'll just dig my grave
Shoveling dirt over my old face
My mistake letting you set this pace
Retrace the days we shared
I wish I never cared
That all you wanted was one night
That light burnt out, and all my might
Went to rekindling that spark
Now I'm dead, and my love is dark

[CHORUS]
The sky is falling on my head
And I wish that I was dead
The sky is falling on my head
And I wish that I was dead
The sky is falling on my head
Blood stains this empty bed...
Blood stains this empty bed...

Suffering

I know this
As you once knew this

But no more

I meant to tell you I am incapable of love
But that would have been a lie
I meant to tell you I am impotent
But that would have only been half true

How come the tree I planted years ago has yet to bear fruit?
I watered it with blood
And fertilized it with cum
Sprout damnit!
I've waited long enough for you to bear fruit
I guess my produce skipped the ripeness phase and went
Straight to rot and maggots

But what chooses to drip from your vagina?
Is it daisies or black menstrual blood?
But that doesn't change the fact

I drank from your red sea as your lips were parted

Say my name as we Seed
Say my name as we harvest this forgotten fruit

These blood oranges washed up onto
The shores of the forgotten
And I remember myself
As I gutted every organ of your spirit
Kill me
For I have become a monster,
Full of beautiful hideousness,
Sacred rapes, and
Artful murders

All the rumors are true
But which ones will you allow to come to pass?
I have brought some of them into existence
And as they rain from the sky,

I will know this
As you once knew this

I wanted you to know
That your mother came to me in a dream
She told me that your time hasn't evaporated and
You shouldn't step into the darkness

I've been there

And I do not wish that for you
My suns have been birthed
From supernovas of blood

What has created your stars?
I hope to God it was daffodils and cherry blossoms
Cause for me, my map isn't clean like that
It is cracked, stained, and unfinished
Let me see yours for a sec

Hey, I'll show you mine if you show me yours
Still being my muse, I see?
Leave me be

I am your destiny
Beaten to serenity
Taking your virginity

Forgive me
My sky has gone dark
I'm waiting for the galaxies to be reunited with my spirit
Rewrite my heart, soul, and mind
Maybe then I wouldn't be so stuck in time
In a "crime"

The wheels are spinning
But there is no movement
How much strength will it take
To drag your body from the water?
I was beginning to forget your braided head

As I held it under and
Forced you to watch your own abortion...
Extortion...
Exploitation of energy leeched
From the roots of fallen trees
But the energy of the universe is shared so
There is no theft and

I know this
As you once knew this

But I cannot Liken(s) my suffering
To that of Sylvia
But I do suffer
As we all have suffered

I wish all the touchings of yesteryear
Were just marks of chalk on a blackboard
But they still leave smears if not washed with water
I was the Girl Next Door,
Trapped in the basement,
Dreaming of stars as they beat me

She was my father
The one who trained dogs to sniff out enlightenment
He, who never approved of the soul
Him and the matriarch became one flesh
But I fled from them,
Sprinting into the depths of the forest

And if anyone asks for me,
Tell them I'm playing lacrosse with the stars
And hosting Roman orgies on mars
Tell them I can't be bothered with physical
When I'm experiencing the spiritual
As my soul gets on all fours,
Allowing the universe entrance into my being

I have been laid by the wind
And fondled by the grass
And yes, I can make nature be sexual
Since she is my mistress
This is where I go to escape from my suffering

Escape into escape into escape
And BE
(Gasping for breath)
I am here and

I know this
As you once knew this

But I've cried tears that have crystallized and
Become the rings of Saturn
Sad meteorites that weep as fallen stars
Don't let your light go out
As long as you live, you can speak
Even if it must be without words

And I hear you,
Sylvia
As you return to the carnival
The one place you always felt safe
I wish I could ride the carousel with you
And hold your hand as we watch the setting sun

Some people say that with every situation
God always has a plan,
But I'm not going to wait around wondering what it is
I have my own plans

net.art (2011)

1. Cellar Door (ft. Khyree)
2. She's So Heavy
3. The Rock Without Roll (ft. JoBar)
4. Unsolicitous Advice (Skit)
5. Another Brick in the Wall
6. Alt Gangsta
7. ar
8. This is Hell
9. Hate Love
10. Fuck Monkeys in Space Interlude
11. Her Body
12. Cocaine (No Pain)
13. Not So Fucked Up
14. Where Are We Going?
15. Who Are You?
16. Intercision
17. The World Is Yours
18. Freedom of Leave
19. AOC

BONUS:

20. Out of Sight
21. This Is Where It's At
22. Trick Tock Tick
23. On the Journey Toward the Infinite

(note: no text is included for skits and interludes)

Hell.com is the destination of desire, the home of temptation. Without desire there is no hope and without temptation there is no passion.

This is the re-release of Nilotic's mixtape "net.art" which was originally released with a bonus disc. However, on the Journey Toward the Infinite, this work has been hacked.n.altered to include tracks from both the main mixtape and the bonus disc, creating a more concise work. In hell we found each other. enter hell(com) and experience Nilotic's early work as he comments on the state of the internet, hip-hop, hitler, fuck monkeys in space, and alice.

we are creators, gods of the free-sphere

Cellar Door

[INTRO]
Cellar door
We've got everything
That you need and more
Come with me

[CHORUS]
Come with me
Through the cellar door
We've got everything
That you need and more
Come with me
To my basement

[VERSE 1]
I'll tell you in another life
When we are both cats
Distract me from the seduction
Of a tortured artist
And I fight against the twisted fantasy
Of being a Marxist

Pull motorists
Obsessing over physicists
No KKK arsonists
Just double-barrel artist anarchists
Making war swords
Tattooed like books of flesh
I digress into a crystal mesh
Woven heavenly, a holy anti-mess
Compressing spines realigned
By angels sent to design
Devils of thought
Torn down to the spot
Where you rot with the clocks
What do you do when the knocks
Come at your door
Your destruction of a mind
Does not increase your score
Anymore, at the core
I could leave your soul sore
We spin vinyl like propellers
Leaky roofs and synthesizer cellars
Seven pillars internal
Leaks all ink universal

[CHORUS]
Come with me
Through the cellar door
We've got everything
That you need and more
Come with me

To my basement

[VERSE 2]
At birth I split the Earth
At Seven I was bombing Heaven
At nine I took what's mine
At twelve I started scanning shelves
Then the elves start spinning concoctions
To hold auctions
Selling of our psyche
It might be our future
The return of torture
At thirteen I started feeling mean
So I tore out every seam
And sewed a tapestry world
Made from every girl torn from wonder
Shorn from under
Testing storms of wanderers
We are ponderers, priests, and poets
You already crowned me king
Didn't you know it

Wrrrrrtt Wrrrrtt

The king, you heard me sing
I got the rock up in this sling
I'm David
You big-ass Goliath-looking motherfucker
I'm your worst nightmare
Come on, sucka

Come on, sucka…

[CHORUS]
Come with me
Through the cellar door
We've got everything
That you need and more
Come with me
To my basement

[VERSE 3]
We split our bodies like mitosis
Absorb our environment like photosynthesis
What's the real difference
Between men and plants
Chant, chant, give a chant
Will your body keep through this dis-dance
We set up camp under the star
Barren wilderness in the dark
Push past willows of weakness
Sleep on pillows of completeness
Assess the situation
Avoid any temptation
We're here to realign with nature
But the reeds mark our departure
Our soothsayers sing their prayers
We've finally become the bricklayers
But impressions left on quicksands of our perception
Only know bounds through common misconception

Redemption for your lies
Compensation for your eyes
No reparations for your demise

[CHORUS]
Come with me
Through the cellar door
We've got everything
That you need and more
Come with me
To my basement

She's So Heavy

I hate me
Can't you see
I hate me
Can't you see
I hate me
Can't you see…

[VERSE 1]
He never believed in his power
Victim mentality, but won't cower
To drink and waste his breath
Depressed to smoke your death
Repressing into himself
Talent remains on a shelf
I told him not to throw it all away
Please say I will never see the day
That you pay for all your sins
By offing yourself
Just before your life begins

[CHORUS]
She's so heavy
She's so heavy
She's so heavy
Don't let her break your levee

[VERSE 2]
I break out my little stash of Jesus
Seize us and scrape us into lines
I'm blind accepting the white into my mind
And his heart is racing
Checking pulse and pacing
Heal the pieces of my body I've destroyed
Treating this temple like a toy
He's fallen into the Spindle Trap
No map
I'm here to witness his execution
This is extortion
Distortion of reality
So is there any solution
Revolution
Mind, body, spirit
Sobriety will help to clear it
This is another way
To keep the demons at bay
This is a blanket
He's a blanket
Torn from years of use and abuse
This noose is a wedding ring
Around our necks ready to drop

Please stop
With every mistake we must be learning
Keep yearning for that love
But keep your world a-turning

[CHORUS]
She's so heavy
She's so heavy
She's so heavy
Don't let her break your levee

[VERSE 3]
We must check the way we write
Tonight this ink is DUI
Dripping under the influence
Of sexual abuse, mental abuse, social abuse
Don't let your demons loose like that
Just be free listening to that high hat
Don't combat
Check our poems into rehab
Don't forget to grab me as you stab
Your heart until it's almost gone
Don't let yourself become her pawn
I don't know why nobody told you
How to unfold your love
I don't know how someone controlled you
She bought and sold you
Blue-red blood dripping down a bus stop bench
Lovely colors running but the stench
Is of something deeper

I am not your keeper
But I'm also not the Reaper
So please accept my hand of help, friend
Do not fight
The Sherry-Nelson-Funeral-Home looms
Like a succubus, it's tough
But you swung then gushed
With flowing blood filled with poison
You should have chosen to back down
From the anger caused by the love you haven't found
But you're crowned god of your own life
And now you have a wife
No one to blame but the person
Your world revolves around
I don't want to see you hit the fucking ground
But if you do, look up and see this hand
These hands
These hands
Have hurt so many people
But they don't have to remain stained
Our heads haloed by rings of cocaine
Can't complain
The soul is starved for meth
Instead of deciding to inhale
We breathe forever through each other's mouths
The drought of love leaves us dry
I'm in the same boat, we cry
But don't give up the try
The lungs expand to reveal a
Complicated network of truth and lies

Let the poison and these lies
Never reach our lips
Hope he finally knows
He can stand right back up
Even if he slips

[CHORUS]
She's so heavy
She's so heavy
She's so heavy
Don't let her break your levee

She's so heavy

The Rock Without Roll

I see visions of a visionary Rock group
The lead singer stands behind the mic
His face, covered by a white hockey mask
This masked vigilante speaks in a language
Not quite my own
And the genre of music is
Not quite stationary

Despite the fact the language is foreign
I comprehend
I comprehend
I comprehend

Their vision is MY vision
However up to this point I haven't developed
A complete grasp on that vision

What I see
And what I hear
Is intricate
Like a handmade fabric

On this stage
On this stage
On this
Stage
I call forth these visions with words
I CALL FORTH THESE WORDS WITH VISIONS
I CALL FORTH THESE VISIONS WITH WORDS
I CALL FORTH THESE WORDS WITH VISIONS
I CALL FORTH THESE VISIONS WITH WORDS
I CALL FORTH THESE WORDS with visions

All I ask for
Is for you to listen

But let me ask you this:
Am I barking up the wrong tree?

Am I barking up the wrong tree?

AM I BARKING UP THE WRONG TREE?

And when that tree falls…
Will it make a sound?

…my beautiful death…

…my beautiful death…

I see visions of a blind audience

They hear every beat
But none of the words

I have nothing more to say…

Another Brick in the Wall

I'm a product of my environment
A product of entertainment
What you see in me
Is what you hate is in yourself
So would you keep any of my albums on your shelf
I think not—despised
I tried but never lied
About who I am
What I am
Or what I create with my hands
This wall I built, but not without your help
Then you tell me just to stop
And just turn up the Pop
How can I top the charts
When the ones who have no hearts
Are the only ones who get a part

Hand me a brick
Hand me a brick

I'm gonna box you out
Alone without a doubt

My wall is built of women
And also a few men
Can you tend to the fire that keeps burning from within
But you can never burn out
If you're not on fire
Even if I was a dictator
Never call me sire
Yes I am a cryer
Stay behind barbed wire
If I became that man
You could never stand
For I'd throw you all in chambers
Cause of how you see my failures
You're just another brick in my wall
I am no Adolf
But the hatred for you all
Comes from deep inside
But behind this wall, I'll hide

All in all, you're all just bricks in the wall
All in all, you're all just bricks in the wall

My friends all held me back
But I got back on track
Headed toward Rhode Island
Before I could get banned
But I'm so fucking Strange

But as of yet not Famous
I say this not to shame us
The FBI could never tame us
As I'm waiting for the worms
I'll destroy all of your norms

Hand me a brick
Hand me a brick
I'm gonna box you out
Alone without a doubt

I'm with alice
My muh-malice
My Brave New World
Will be void of girls
All dead and raped
Everyone taped for snuff
Decide if that's a bluff
I'm with alice
My muh-muh-malice
Rape us
I'm a brick, you're a brick
Everyone's a brick brick
I'm with alice
My muh-malice
I guess I'm just that callous

All in all, you're all just bricks in the wall
All in all, you're all just bricks in the wall

You'd rather me retreat and isolate
Than take you by the throat and show my hate
We don't need no education
We don't need no thought control
You're faceless in the classroom
Four years of college is our tomb
There's no room for individuality
Social control relies on predictability
So become my infinite nazis
We'll all run wild in a propaganda posse

All in all, you're all just bricks in the wall
All in all, you're all just bricks in the wall

(Is it possible to be too strange for Strange Famous?)

Alt Gangsta

[VERSE 1]
What you see before you
Is not what you get
I bet the false persona is soon to regret
But to kill or be killed is the rule of the streets
Selling the image is the rap you gotta beat
I don't need platinum chains to be a rockstar
I come far with no car and living with these scars
It ain't easy, I'm not breezy
For-sheezy, nothing came easy for me
I see before my eyes all these lies
Of a gangsta, a bank-star
You came out these bars
Money money money
Money on my mind
But you're blind getting signed
I go against the grind

[CHORUS]
I'm an emo gangsta
I'm a goth-hop rocker

I'm an emo gangsta
Call me a Hip Hop shocker

[VERSE 2]
Got a diamond-crusted razor blade
Hanging from my neck
A force to be reckoned with
Even from a train wreck
Respect me for being me
There's nothing more free
I see through your eyes
There's nothing else to hide
It's real gangsta being fucked by a dude
Each night of the week
No need to seek out the ones hiding in the Hip Hop
I know your record sells cause you're sticking to the Pop
Keep your secret all you want
It's not like you're gonna stop
I exist so you know
It's okay just to show
That you got that glow
Check my flow
This ain't no sissy rap
But I gotta maintain my ability
To change the mainstream to the main fuckin' vein
And I would never make a claim
To be more than what I am
This has always been my stand
The ability to be ourselves is all I wish
I'm waiting for Kanye West to come out the closet

And admit that he's a gay fish

[CHORUS]
I'm an emo gangsta
I'm a goth-hop rocker
I'm an emo gangsta
Call me a Hip Hop shocker

[BRIDGE]
I ain't no Paper Gangsta
I ain't no fuckin' Pop Star
But just know I'll go far
Cause I could be alt gangsta
Alt gangsta

[VERSE 3]
I'd make astral love to Solstice Will I Am
This is not a diss
Through the storm I will withstand
Keep the Anthem of Ayn Rand in your head
But sleep with a pistol in your bed
We've been fed stereotypes
And generalized hype
Sorry, you're not my type
Come to me and share with me your gripes
When it's late at night
My sight falls on all your tears
I'll strip away the years
And write down all your fears
I'm used to taking words in the face like mace

I'm not fucking gay—I'm a faggot
I'm not fucking gay—I'm a faggot
I'm not fucking gay—I'm a faggot
Blowjobs in the back
Amplified by hydraulics
Constantly taking in alcohol, smoke, and dicks
Swallowing his pride, adjust his wig,
And tuck it under, he knows how to hide
The men fall their eyes on the skirted little boy
And think he'll crumble like a girl and be their little toy
How wrong
How wrong
Why not just listen to my song

[BRIDGE]
I ain't no Paper Gangsta
I ain't no fuckin' pop star
But just know I'll go far
Cause I could be alt gangsta
Alt gangsta

[OUTRO]
Mark my words
There are gay-ass rappers
Dark my cords
Labels are tricky trappers
But they don't cum strapped with a gun
They wear them pink panties and then some
I'm just having fun
Come one

So back up Backstreet Boys
Here cums
Kanye West, Lil Wayne, Soulja Boy,
Asher Roth, and Gucci Mane
Top it off with Justin Bieber
No need to dream any farther
Never say never
Before you say anything just still your hand
You've got the ultimate boy band

It's getting queer in here…

ar

We are
We are
We are
We are
We are
We are
We are
Creators, gods of the free-sphere
Listen here, we are the spacial shift of years
Our tears become worlds to be explored
Droplets of universes ripped up and torn
We're scorned by the false representation of god
This bod was created by me
Then beat with a rod
We're here at the end of the tunnel
I someone still tending the light
We might
Find something different
When we behold cyber-natural sights

Final dot org is a meme generator dedicated to instigating a global paradigm shift to expand perceptual boundaries beyond biological and geopolitical limitations.

Finally at the bleeding edge of the Web
Everything that you really want exists here
Hell is the destination of desire
The home of temptation
Without desire there is no hope
And without temptation there is no passion
What reaction will you give when fashion is ashen
No compassion for the damned
In hell we'll all be scammed

We exist on multiple levels of reality
But no one knows the actuality
So we create alternative realities
Hell is a place for sensualities

In hell we found each other
In hell we found each other
In hell we found each other
Then I smothered her face with another
Torn asunder
Flying like a Bat free, you see
Look up at the alternative key
Opening doors to where we all should live
But I've been locked out
What will you give

A perfection of our evolutionary journey, this is not a game, there are no instructions or definitions, only possibilities, a reality determined by the depth of your individual quest.

This world is what we make it
So we're not gonna take it
I'll shake it to its core
So I can find there's more
Than what we've been told that there is
Close your double eyes, open your third
Where is this life we've been promised
But who will go the farthest
Everyone's an artist, an anarchist
Sent to create
I create, therefore I am
Bam bam slam

We exist on multiple levels of reality
But no one knows the actuality
So we create alternative realities
Hell is a place for sensualities

The true digitalization of your life
A world of ones and zeros rife
With potential, it's essential
Now we choose to live on the internet
Take a breath, step out on the minaret
What you create is digital

Go on and call me cynical
This is critical, the pinnacle
The age of the Web
Has become Nirvana
Or I'm a prima donna
But this is what it's come to
Is there any option to choose
Who am I kidding
The domain will do my bidding

Domain disabled. Hell dot com is no longer up and running due to the shift of consciousness.

We are the global paradigm shift
Thrown off the Earth into a time rift
Sift through my ashes
As my server crashes
This is where I'm living
This is where I'm living
But the Net is unforgiving

We exist on multiple levels of reality
But no one knows the actuality
So we create alternative realities
Hell is a place for sensualities

Facebook, Myspace, Napster, Hell
We've all gone and died, oh well
Interweb is death

We're caught, last breath
Spiders wrapping us in HTML string
But remember, membership is expiring
Renew your death
Gain stress
Have less
Privacy's a thing of the past
We're all naked at long last
Cursed to Live in Public
Transmit it from a Sputnik

Alternative reality
Internet mentality
Digital brutality
Website morality

Brain surgery
This is perjury
Mergery for drudgery
Computer surgery
Cursory, forced a fee
Told to be, want and need
Told to heed, want and feed
Told to greed
Fuck my seed

Alternative reality
Internet mentality
Digital brutality
Website morality

We exist on multiple levels of reality
But no one knows the actuality
So we create alternative realities
Hell is a place for sensualities

Hell is a place for sensualities

This Is Hell

This is hell
Where we live
In America
Hysterica

Traveling a striped spiral to insanity
A playground slide of castrated chastity
This city is a permanent vacancy
Empty except you
Deep in the sun that has you turning blue
What's true, if you only knew
A sidewalk chalk destruction
Made from your construction
Orchestrated as a never-ending symphony
A cacophony played on a universal violin
The conductor dictates every sin
The way you spin, dancing to this discordant din
Bombs, guns, and engines
All naked in the sound
This place is now our dungeon
Together we are bound

Violence has always been an American tradition
Our final reward will be infinite perdition
Unconditional love is contingent on unbroken happiness
She left you on the curb, untouched
No hug or even kiss
They dismiss your opinions when they don't match up
To the ones taught in class
You're behind, go catch up
Stack up business flyers to all the downturned eyes
When they hold you down and fuck you
How to reach the skies
You lack a female touch
When silence is too much

This is hell (hell)
This is hell (hell)
This is hell (hell)

If I was a member of the Marilyn Manson band
Call me Edie Harris-Klebold
The darkest blanket will unfold
Benevalment partly owns my soul
I'm taking credit for the death toll
Send zombies to take a catatonic poll
Then ask for full control
Absolutes corrupt absolutely
I kill, therefore I am, resolutely
So shoot me and sue me and do me
Shortly I will regain my gift
I refuse saline, hormones, and a fucking facelift

I'll find a new pen in an absent snowdrift
Sift through the coffins soaked with paint
Lay down with this knife and cut your taint
Then just fuck yourself
As the walls begin to melt
Middle America is stained with student blood
Wallowing waist-deep in this diseased mud
We trade fluids like our AIDS
Erect emotional blockades
Letting in furry rabid rabbits
That support all of our habits
My brain is white and crystalized
Strap me to this table and have me anesthetized
Lonely, alone, but beady eyes are fixed on me
I'm clean, look, nothing in my pockets
Except a family locket
Hey that's weird, it's just an empty socket
Dictate my own visions
Or lock me in these prisons

This is hell (hell)
This is hell (hell)
This is hell (hell)

Count yourselves so lucky
I chose not to become a killer
I chose to be a filler
One who closes gaps
And provides all that we lack
Come back here, boy

Sit back down and listen
You're a citizen
But will drown out in those streets
Turn your face around and say you feel the heat
So take your seat, I repeat
The world can make the darkest rain
No one escapes or has a drain on this pain
But you can regain your life
Despite a past of torment
You see, those trees are all informants
Laying dormant till the days we're cursed
To Tribulation
What you see before you is no
Left Behind simulation
Our homes have become our fallout shelters
Helter Skelter
We're terrified of one another
Trust no one in your neighborhood
Father wears an executioner's hood
We all live alone
Tethered to this stone
Isolation inside your head
Cut off until you're dead—

Hate Love

[VERSE 1]
Hanging from this cross
I feel death approaching from below
Carnage left behind in the seeds that I sow
Then you'll come to know all my pain
From the days you'll all be slain
Laid dead on this battleground
Called America Hysterica
Declare it a coup d'état
So then bring it back to the Spindle Trap
I'll fuckin' draw you a map
To pull you out of hell
The ocean up and swells
To destroy, employ, and deploy
To ravage the skin left on bones
She left me with this hole
Dripping with consummated flowers
Your blood will flow in showers

[CHORUS]
Please tell me that you hate me

That's the only way I'll make it
I've told you all about my wall
So don't try to shake it
Cause I can't handle love

[VERSE 2]
Your generation is so scare
Of expressing what's repressed
They're cursed to be depressed
Trapped in the bottom of the well
Cold and tired in this wet jail cell
The bucket hanging an inch above your hand
Forgetting how grand it was to be on land
The ground splitting open
You're hoping there's a key, an epiphany
To be released from solitary confinement
And earning enough money for retirement
My generation's scared to death of love
But I'm looking down to see the running blood
What did you do, an abortion
Underage sex is way outta proportion
Leave me be alone
Or build me my own clone
To keep me company
In the roots of this tree how can I be free
When nothing can get through to me

[CHORUS]
Please tell me that you hate me
That's the only way I'll make it

I've told you all about my wall
So don't try to shake it
Cause I can't handle love

[VERSE 3]
So just pop a pill
To take away the urge to kill
My skill with this gun
Has only just begun
But I'm aimed right between your eyes
My spine is always curved
To show how I'm despised
My cries fall on deaf ears
Repair this open cavity in my chest
I only fucking did my best
So seal me up with sealing wax
Relax, can't you see the cracks
Mapping down my vertebrae
Making room for wings to take me away
Maybe if we left this world behind
Let's travel to where we won't be blind
Remind me of the blinding white light
Despite the slashes down my wrists
You can see the life in my tightly clenched fists
One day I'll finally realize
Why my flesh is torn
And in that moment show me the reason I was born

[OUTRO]
I can't handle love

I can't handle love
I hate love
Hate love

Her Body

Check it out
This is a painting
Of her body

[VERSE 1]
Her body is a roadmap
Contrived on her spine
Combined and designed
For travel off-road
But her mind's a different thing
And difficult to decode
The body corrodes just because it's flesh
The brain implodes and becomes a mess
She was never told where to go
Which undiscovered road to travel
Where her feet won't cut with gravel
Every time she's touched,
Her will will then unravel
This body limits what you are able
But wounds on the flesh
Will turn into distress

Leave her to transgress
She used to be full, now she's become less
Physical becomes emotional
Emotional becomes spiritual
She discovers love is rarely reciprocal
Her path doesn't run from A to B
She bobs on the waves in a Dead Sea
Floating away forever from this deceased emcee

[CHORUS]
Her body is my tomb
Her body is a womb
I'm a Dying Fetus
And her body is my weakness

[VERSE 2]
Sherry embodied the Alice Archetype
But I might meet another
Within Providence's melodious thunder
I wonder if she saw the way I watched
Just make sure you moved and dodged
Her arms as she swings to hit the drum
My eyes have come unwound
And my wrists are now bound
To this woman who's body's marked with ink
Shh, shhh, listen as I try to sync
My vocals with her sound
Wait, let me just rethink
But I can't just come around
After I have found another body

My hands become A Scanner Darkly
Exploring what's under the cotton
I was struck like Lewis Carroll
When I saw her there in Boston

[BRIDGE]
Archetype
Mark a fight

[CHORUS]
Her body is my tomb
Her body is a womb
I'm a Dying Fetus
And her body is my weakness

[VERSE 3]
I see alice's body
Lying on the floor
Contort the way the world looks through the door
Pouring from her chest, rivers of blood
Slivers of a flood, but not buried in the mud
Stripped naked, dead, and exposed to the air
She's got no more despair
But beware of this affair
Right there where you stare
I tear a gash up and down her heart
Leave a rash where her body tears apart
She was pregnant with a weapon
So come in when I beckon
Just a second, I'll give a forced abortion

Go ahead and watch my films of exploitation
Of audience and actor
Lucifer is a detractor
There will always be an alice,
But only one Nilotic
And never-ending malice

There will always be an alice,
But only one Nilotic
And never-ending malice

NEVER-ENDING MALICE

[CHORUS]
Her body is my tomb
Her body is a womb
I'm a Dying Fetus
And her body is my weakness

[OUTRO
Archetype
Mark a fight
Start a life
Archetype
Mark a fight
Start a life

Archetype

Cocaine (No Pain)

I know people might not understand what I'm doing right away. But if you listen, and you catch on, then we've got something special. We're *Connected Within The Light*.

[VERSE 1]
Blasphemous lies let me hover over ground
Come listen to this sound
That rings through my ears
It's taken me these years
To put it down in music
So use it, don't confuse it
Suffuse it like a global flood
You scud, from the coming waves
Don't throw it into graves
I'm the one who paves the way
For the shift of consciousness
The lift of spaciousness
To then expand the mind
But not aligned with drugs
Dig out of my body seven silver slugs

Unplug from the acid, alcohol, and cocaine
Sometimes this body can't contain
What goes on in my brain
But you can train your system
To withstand the pull of addiction
Drug dependency
Obsessive tendency
Yes there is a vacancy of happiness
You would be better of embracing ghastliness

[CHORUS]
Cocaine, no pain
I'm insane with a stain on the brain
Cocaine, no pain
My domain I ordain arcane

[VERSE 2]
Cocaine, no pain
Come here and do this line
Till your eyes begin to shine
The reason I smoked was
Because I hate my body
Suck down white puffy death
And kill me softly
Cough please, the blood into your palms
Your outside matches your insides, calmly
Take a breath
Try not to think about your death
Respect this life you're given

I got passion and I'm driven
So I ain't leavin' yet
Try to live without regret
Don't abuse the body like you abuse the substance
I totally understand circumstance
But don't rely on chance
Life can deal us use and abuse
Dealers deal us booze and a noose
We need to call a truce
If the concept's too abstruse
Body like a temple
Mind like a devil
Spirit like a vessel
Can't have one without the other
So don't treat any part like a dumpster

[CHORUS]
Cocaine, no pain
I'm insane with a stain on the brain
Cocaine, no pain
My domain I ordain arcane

[VERSE 3]
I like the smell of coke
Get it?
Forget it
There's a demon in my view
We'd swap the effects if we knew
Why alcohol is called spirits
Cocaine is gutter glitter

No need to fear it
You could be very near it
But it's true what they say about moderation
Do you have condensation in your thoughts
Especially in dreams when you're caught
In the trap of blotter paper
Surrounded by squirrels that are agents of your dealer
Concealer, hidden in your sock
Watch the clock tick time till your next fix
What is that a mix
Of Zoloft, Xanax, and Vicodin
Invite him in
He's got candy, every type
Do you still believe the hype
Too much high will kill ya
With formaldehyde they'll fill ya

Too much high will kill ya
With formaldehyde they'll fill ya

[CHORUS]
Cocaine, no pain
I'm insane with a stain on the brain
Cocaine, no pain
My domain I ordain arcane

All I ask is for you to listen
So listen

Not So Fucked Up

[VERSE 1]
Tonight, conversations with Jared Paul
Hope he heard my silent call
From behind my wall
Trying to tear it down
But my fall will hit the ground
But will they hear this sound
If I don't scream it like a banshee
You're free to disagree
With the statements that I speak
How can I reach my peak
When I know it's the earth that inherits the meek
Not the other way around
Seems I'm bound for the grave
When I keep these words and save
Them behind my lips
The hatred trips me up
And the blood fills up my cup
It's time to rethink my strategy
But still remaining true to me
Maybe what I thought would make me free

Only keeps me in slavery

[CHORUS]
Part of me doesn't want to be this way
So what more can I say
Maybe I am, that's the rub
Or I'm not so fucked up

[VERSE 2]
Stuck in schizophrenic paralysis
Needing a conceptual dialysis
A lyrical analysis
Reading over old rhymes and remembering the times
I was hurt, I was killed, I was raped
Doesn't mean I can't reshape
My world to be decent at its core
Hard to remember that there's more
Than the darkness that destroys
And the rage becomes my toy
I shouldn't let it dominate
Or let genocide propagate
Listen to my words
To see where I'm going towards
Maybe a better fucking place
Where I leave no trail or trace
Of blood outlining epithets
The power to make you sweat
Maybe isn't worth the threat of death

[CHORUS]
Part of me doesn't want to be this way
So what more can I say
Maybe I am, that's the rub
Or I'm not so fucked up

[VERSE 3]
Having a poetic temper tantrum
Does reveal my inner sanctum
But to be completely honest
That's just the little kid inside
Refusing to hide behind
A mother's ruffled skirt
Choosing to flirt with destruction
But maybe that's not meant for public consumption
Screaming for attention
Did I fail to mention
This station's full to tension
But with moderate apprehension
Chose to take on the speech
Of the one called Hitler, so impeach
What I try to teach
Maybe she was right when she said
The method discredits the message
Why couldn't I see the presage
Quoting the words of Voltaire,
Then use that to declare
Many racist statements
That I never fucking supported
But agreed could be retorted

Learning this the hard way
Will help me grow in what I say

What's my destination
This is my creation
Fifteen's no duration
Must resist stagnation

Being the Opposite Man only works for so long
I'm not always right
And many times I'm wrong
But I'm strong
In everything I stand for
However, I'm coming to find there's more
Way more in the world
Than fucked up girls
Walking on a healing path
Will distill my wrath
But still the aftermath
Is something to be discovered,
Uncovered, and recovered
But maybe she was right
And now I'll hold on tight
To this idea of growth
I can still be both
But choose now to be better
Then bring it down to letters
And break all of my fetters

[CHORUS]
Part of me doesn't want to be this way
So what more can I say
Maybe I am, that's the rub
Or I'm not so fucked up

What's my destination
This is my creation
Fifteen's no duration
Must resist stagnation

Where Are We Going?

We're all broken children
With grown-up pain

[VERSE 1]
The sensation of penetration
Just feel this exploration
I'm introverted and deserted
But sexually perverted
Converted on Concerta
Parents who tried to dope me up
They fail to realize
My minds conceptualize
And tries to help me up
I've been down to where I almost drowned
And decided to give it up to suicide
We live in public
No one has the ability to hide
Our bodies are always being found
So pound down all these drugs
You're void of any hugs

The friends I had failed to show me love
No touch
He wouldn't even take off the gloves
Just shove me to this fence
Too late to put up any defense
Then I watch myself as a spirit
See the hate in their eyes, learn to fear it
Now you're on the ground being bound
Never make a sound
Just pray to have your body found

[CHORUS]
Where are we going?
Where have we been?

[VERSE 2]
I'm not dead yet
If I'd have to place a bet
I'm not even close
Dancing through the life that I chose
Predisposed to failure and wind-currents
Blowing me off course
Through storms of remorse
This is where I live
Where it rains inside my house
Chest Death leaves me feeling like a Faust
But how would it feel
To get rejected by the Devil
An order to pick up your own shovel
Set to self-destruct and never reconstruct

Should we really rely on luck
We're dealt a certain set of cards
But you can tear 'em up, it's hard
But never ever let down your guard

[CHORUS]
Where are we going?
Where have we been?

[VERSE 3]
Hey, yo
I was fucked from the get-go
It hurts, I know
Just let go
Flow away the pain
Before you go insane

Pornographic Childhood
Isolating neighborhood
Every single friend will leave you beggin'
Parents ask where you're headin'
Set-in for a rocky road ahead
Killed by your family before you reach the dead
The source of divorce
I see visions of a white horse
A savior that never shows
Wait till I create my own glow

I got a halo in hell
Paid my dues in blood

Felt penetration, can't you tell
Paid my dues in blood

[CHORUS]
Where are we going?
Where have we been?

Who Are You?

Who do you think you are?

In the corners of dark rooms
My personal demons loom
Crouched in a fetal position
It's me, but I forget about my mission
Sent to uplift and expand consciousness
But I fall, filleted by sociopathic-ness
Digression, descent, hell-bent
Broken, but with artistic intent

Touch me like this please
Fingers, tongues squeeze
Like nothing you've ever felt
Then endure many blows dealt
Sexually, violently, as a child
Where were the parents
When my guts were left in piles
It's miles and miles behind me
But that's all I seem to see

And I'm sorry, Mommy
For every time I made you cry
Sometimes I just wanna lay down and die
That's why
I search for that mother
But one that's still a daughter
Back away, cause I could be your slaughter
Sorry doesn't mean very much
But I think I've lost myself
Close my entire life in a bookshelf
Written for the entertainment
Of generations to come
Sherry, I would say I'm sorry
But my body came undone
Flesh melting off in the sun
Is it possible to lose yourself
A dismembered hand of help
Creating multiple identities
For a fatal lack of any amenities
Who are you?

Intercision

[VERSE 1]
God wrote the book and made a list of all my sins
I'll grab your fucking heart, and so let it begin
Pull you to this flow like a swift undertow
So swing low sweet chariot
Carry it away, my soul into the sky
Leave a crater in this world before I die
Never cater to the masses
I tear a hole straight through heaven
Taught classes about Seven
Reinventing Hip Hop with numbers and language
Then undo the damage dealt through this universal mic
You're spitting empty words
I don't care to be polite
Despite a religious following
And a fanbase swallowing
Every syllable uttered from your lips
Trip trip trip you up when you execute my trust
And your whole fucking world is falling into dust

[CHORUS]
Mainstream Hip Hop is the specters of this world
Tearing wide open spaces, empty like a chasm
Cut open the sky, try to walk into another world
Wipe away this life and create a new phantasm

[VERSE 2]
You all willingly become soulless
I fight against feeling this is hopeless
The church tore your daemon from your body
Walk through atmosphere, expand perception properly
Hold on to that childlike wonder
Through life's disrupting thunder
Forced to grow up way to fast
Through a skull corrupting broadcast
I'm the last of my kind
But I wish that one will find
The symbols that I've etched into your forehead
Drawing maps on eternity looseleaf
And sped up, up into the Northern Lights
To start supernatural fights
I'll lean into your cage to drill a hole through your temple
Don't be afraid of Dark Matter
Let them in and tremble

[CHORUS]
Mainstream Hip Hop is the specters of this world
Tearing wide open spaces, empty like a chasm
Cut open the sky, try to walk into another world
Wipe away this life and create a new phantasm

[VERSE 3]
The government's been performing Intercision
Death by Soulmind circumcision
Suspension of life
Undead at the edge of a knife
Respect spirit, supernatural maturation
Leave behind religious mind saturation
This sensation between child and adult
Can't be contained or cured by a cult
Glenn Beck would destroy the Alethiometer
Protest the war in heaven and pray to Saint Peter
Bill O'Reilly would shelter children in the arctic
Teach them Jesus's words from a book that is archaic
Just say it
Fuck the church like they fucked over gays
I love original sin
Teach His Dark Materials ways
Don't worry, I'm not here to kill God
But there is no second coming
When I speak the name of God
That's what I'm becoming
God…
That's what I'm becoming

[CHORUS]
Mainstream Hip Hop is the specters of this world
Tearing wide open spaces, empty like a chasm
Cut open the sky, try to walk into another world
Wipe away this life and create a new phantasm

[OUTRO]
Cut open the sky
And finally let me become one with everything
Please let me love you with a knife
For today and always I am
The Dead King of caked-on makeup
I hide from the formations of dogma
On the earth I have cracked for one
Sanctus Symphony
And the dead sing praises to the one who
Sent them to the grave
Deprivation only results in enlightenment
Of all the senses
Why is everything so difficult
When the nail is driven through the spine

The World Is Yours

It's easy for a star to be born
It's a little harder for a star to be made

[VERSE 1]
If it weren't for the artists on SFR
I would not have gotten very far
I'd either be in jail or even dead
Or in a ward on heavy meds
Instead, I share my feelings with these words
I never killed or raped, haven't you heard
I use pens instead of razors
Mics instead of guns
This ain't always fun
But before my body comes undone
This world will let me speak my mind
Don't rewind or take back
Any word that you state
Own every mistake you make
Utter nothing that is fake
Get that fucking cake outta my face
Lay your eyes down on this trace

The one that laces up my arm
Like an armored worm torn loose
From this noose of restraint
If we use blood to make this paint
It's our own
Don't wanna hear you piss and moan
If your throat is more than two-tone
The Earth will not disown you
You're glowing, flowing, and controlling
Reach out and take the sphere
Everything you say, everyone will hear

[CHORUS]
The world is yours
The world is yours
The world is yours
But I have come to find
Your world is now mine
Your world is now mine

[VERSE 2]
If it weren't for Marilyn Manson
I'd have blown away my high school
With an AK-47
Seven is the number of my life
And completion
They destroyed my world,
So what's my compensation
I thought the destination
Was always new galaxies

Exploration of the unknown
And debunking fallacies
Is what we see only singularly personal
Or are all these twisted visions universal
I bear the Subtle Knife that carves through
Worlds like magic doors
Distortions like to flicker on the walls of your mind
And combine with the beliefs you hide and grind
Into a gritty powder
Sniff and be enlightened
What you hold inside
Might be what makes you frightened
Shortsighted gets you nowhere
Now look I'll make you care
Stare out along these hills
Ignore the sweat and chills
Distill what you really think
You're on the brink of becoming everything
Now sing to the winds
And they'll bring you back as king

[CHORUS]
The world is yours
The world is yours
The world is yours
But I have come to find
Your world is now mine
Your world is now mine

[VERSE 3]
The cosmos are my light-grid
Amid the stars the sun is my spotlight
Stage right, stage left, the world is my stage
And this rage still shimmers and glitters
Attention forever takes away what's bitter
So when you survive
They get to see you live
On an endless stage that stretches past the sky
Let me see you try
As you're about to eat that pie
I hear the last note of your reprise
Decomposing fowl are the ones who give us outcries
They ask you to explain every word
Cause of the inability to think of their own accord
Still attached to their feeding cord
But look out, here comes trouble
The record company's here to burst your bubble
But look out, here comes trouble
The record company's here to burst your bubble
The world is yours
No dancing allowed
No romancing allowed
They want to keep you grounded
With compounded interest
Taxing your thoughts
And before you know you're caught
Cerebral entrapment
Imagination is illegal

If you picture that you're regal
Kiss goodbye your freedom
You'll be put away for many many seasons
Reasons, illegal brain activity
Government hates productivity
They're hiring doctors to install
Some micro-electrical wall
I tiny mind embankment
To keep your dreams at bay
So watch what you say
Some day
FBI will come for you
Then what will you do
My train of thought is like Superjail on coke
And my speech ain't no fuckin' joke
Tell me what you know about cocaine
Did you know I'm critically insane
Wait till I speak about Alternate Egypt
But don't look for it
You'll never find it
Cause it's up in your head
And it lives when I'm in bed
When my phone is set to vibrate only
Just leave me to masturbate lonely
To be honest, I'm sorry they fucked up your eyes
With all their lies they have contrived
With fabricated history
The world is yours
Doesn't always reflect the fame mentality

Superstars never spend their money gradually
Did I mention I dream of a man in a Jigsaw mask
Coming to assassinate the Nilotic
Or maybe I'm still psychotic
But hey,
Em'll be one tough act to follow
So when I cum, step aside, Marshall
Shut your mouth, pass the mic, and swallow

[OUTRO]
I'm attaining what was previously denied me
The world, everything in it,
And everything outside of it

Freedom of Leave

[INTRO]
We don't seek death
We seek destruction
We don't seek death
We seek destruction
We're running to the edge of the world
We're running to the edge of the world

[VERSE 1]
I don't care what people want
I give them what they need
Just heed these fragmented concepts
In-depth full-body tremors
I'm not the first gender-bender
To take a stand against the censored
Films, music, thoughts, and literature
I may look to be a caricature
Just be sure I'd never use an interpreter
To explain anything I write
What I say is meant to bite
I use it as my fight

I'm used to being misconstrued
But I still strive to give this world something new
Won't control your thoughts
I write songs when I'm distraught
Keep shelves of books you never bought
This is how we fought
Music a weapon to fill the barren mind
And if you take the time
To meditate on instead of deaden
Abrasive content will not deafen
It will provide ideas to contemplate
Admit you cried as you felt the hate

[CHORUS]
I was told to tone it down
You'd never hear my sound
The message would be drowned
I describe what I feel and what I see
Total support of freedom of speech
But listeners have freedom of leave

[VERSE 2]
Empty stage
Full of rage
Anger keeps me caged
No one in the crowd
But I'm still screaming loud
Cries fall on deaf ears
When death came to my peers

Cheers!
This art, I'd give my life for it
Jump out on a limb and tightrope-it
Validation through presentation
Rock 'n Roll ain't noise pollution
Decibels emit cancerous radiation
That leaves condensation on your brain
Now just de-board the train
Left out in the rain
Shriek out then complain
But that won't erase their disdain
Don't you see the way they look at you
Hey, I thought you knew
You're a freak, you're a creep
So don't ever speak
Just let your blood leak
But I'm still writing raps
On this stage avoiding mousetraps

[CHORUS]
I was told to tone it down
You'd never hear my sound
The message would be drowned
I describe what I feel and what I see
Total support of freedom of speech
But listeners have freedom of leave

[VERSE 3]
Congress shall make no law respecting an establishment of religion,

or prohibiting the free exercise thereof; or abridging the freedom of speech, or of the press; or the right of the people peaceably to assemble, and to petition the Government for a redress of grievances.

>Back in the day
>I featured at the Heartland Cafe
>Where I knew that what I said
>Would never reach their head
>My songs never spread like a rash
>It left me low on cash
>With no bed to crash
>So I fled instead to where I might be read
>Less population of the brain-dead
>But still potential to be misread
>If you understand my thread
>Follow where I tread
>Make Conscious Rap widespread
>Leave nothing left unsaid
>I live in an unstable world
>Where I am just a Girl,
>Interrupted and corrupted
>I finally erupted

>If a rapper emcees to an empty crowd,
>Does he make a sound?

>Fuck the Shoeless Hippie

>Amendment assessment

Repression testament
Concept propellant
Expression commencement

[CHORUS]
I was told to tone it down
You'd never hear my sound
The message would be drowned
I describe what I feel and what I see
Total support of freedom of speech
But listeners have freedom of leave

You're free to leave

AOC

[VERSE 1]
I remember the times I used to jerk off
For middle-aged men over webcam
He was a wolf posing as a lamb
This is no complaint
And I'm not trying to make you faint
I've never been a saint
This is the picture I'm gonna paint
After I hit thirteen, I always gave consent
Tell me I have sinned, and repent
Recant, and then no permission I would grant
Yes, I did receive and FBI courtesy call
My mother fucking cried
And I just fucking sighed
And explained that she had lied
About the age she was living in
Bullshit to say she was giving in
For we never even met
And I've got no regrets
So delete the child pornography
And tuck it in your sock

Or you're really fucked

Come on
Come on
Come on

[CHORUS]
We're living in the Age of Consent
The Age of Descent
Where we express dissent
But we're not consenting adults
We express all of our faults
Our inner children have been raped
And I say, none of the minors have escaped

[VERSE 2]
The bloodstained treehouse is eternal
Our protection's not paternal
Maternal is our keeper
But when the Reaper comes
He'll drain all of our sums
Leaving us with nothing
Just a bleeding rectum
And a piercing septum
Protect 'em from themselves
For in those vans are elves
But not the ones with magic
The ones with aching dicks
You're a pedophile
Wipe away that smile

You fucking pedophile

Come on
Come on
Come on

[CHORUS]
We're living in the Age of Consent
The Age of Descent
Where we express dissent
But we're not consenting adults
We express all of our faults
Our inner children have been raped
And I say, none of the minors have escaped

[VERSE 3]
"He can't say that!"
Yes I can,
I just did, faggot, guess again
Remember there's nothing I can't say
Just be careful to pick the time and the place
So remember, don't throw away
Your freedom for your anger
Don't give up your rights
For one night of shock
You're right, I'm one to talk
I wanna walk the walk
Instead of talk the talk
Sometimes I only talk the walk
And forget to hide my cock

I'd almost forgotten who I was
Or what I wanted to be
This isn't me, maybe half you see
I embody duality
That's a tough line to walk
And this is where we part
On the final track for net.art
I want you to know I'm just beginning
Gonna try to start again
But who knows, I might continue sinning

Come on
Come on
Come on

[CHORUS]
We're living in the Age of Consent
The Age of Descent
Where we express dissent
But we're not consenting adults
We express all of our faults
Our inner children have been raped
And I say, none of the minors have escaped

I forgive you (escape)
I forgive you (escape)
I forgive you (escape)

We are not enemies, but friends. We must not be enemies. Though passion may have strained, it must not break our bonds of affection. The mystic chords of memory will swell when again touched, as surely they will be, by the better angels of our nature.

- Abraham Lincoln

Out of Sight

[VERSE 1]
I brake too late on a date
Toward doom
Hoarding off highway demons soon
It's high noon
But up in the sky a vacant moon
Forsaken groom
Left at the altar
Consult her mother's father
Don't bother with respect
Reject precepts
Suspect unrealistic prospects
Repetitive stressive compressive
Mind siege massive compassion
How can a show a mother love
When all I can do is bathe you in blood
Decode a regional ode
A prayer sung to hold ladder rungs
Guns to scrape needles over records
Swords to play with chords
What's more to score than to kill a Lord

A cold seasonal mold
I said, break the mold
My lips are breaking bold
I sold nothing to the demon
They take from my heart what's gleamin'
But nothin' is ever what it seems
Pray for more platinum dreams
Make sure you're able to grow
Cause that's a tough row to hoe

[CHORUS]
I fly toward my eyes
Canister lies and dies
Cries crack, glass cans
Night falls on another devilish clan

[VERSE 2]
Highway number 7 stay up late
Seal away the hate
Conceal the day of fate
Take control of destiny
But this is a fantasy we live
And our lives are what we give
To this tombstone
I'm not yet fully grown
But etched into this rock
Many names around this spot
Where I got laid the fuck down
Never catch me painted like a clown

Tainted like the unfound
The ground coming fast into sound
Hear a thud as your head hits the rust
Bleed fatality, cause your living's not a must
Need brutality, cause rape is just lust
Which personality bit the dust
Wait for your skull to spontaneously combust
Then commune on the Moon's high noon
We wait in a circle
Cloaked in robes the color purple

We wait in a circle
Cloaked in robes the color purple

[CHORUS]
I fly toward my eyes
Canister lies and dies
Cries crack, glass cans
Night falls on another devilish clan

[VERSE 3]
Horribly adorably she lurks
Smirking from distant shadows
Constant bubble glows
Rows one mile deep
Designed to keep and grow bodies
Like *Catcher in the Rye*, kill the phonies
We've detached from our spheres
Attacked all of our peers

And left our hopes at Ground Zero
Where's your hero now
Gone south
I'm heading North towards the next life
Bathed in the glory of light
Oh, it's gonna be gory tonight
Cause that ain't light, it's a fight
So we might just kill the light
Out of sight
We take flight on wings of seraphim
But which ones have fallen from him
This god in the sky
Who tells us when to die
Does he cry when we lie
Always watched by the great eye
So turn down the lights
Out of sight

[CHORUS]
I fly toward my eyes
Canister lies and dies
Cries crack, glass cans
Night falls on another devilish clan

This Is Where It's At

[INTRO]
This is where it's at
Where everyone is gay (Yo!)
We're takin' over (Yes we are!)
Cause this is where it's at

[VERSE 1]
We're takin' over
Wearin' pads on our shoulders
This is about dressin' up, not down
Yes, we've been crowned
But we ain't clowns
We rock big black boots
But hey, they're back and shoots
Us down, killed like Matthew Shepard
Leopard print leotards
It's hard to be who you are
But to thine own self be true
Hey, there's your proof
I do rap, I rock chick clothes
Pink robes and black soles

We punch holes through our skin
And don't give a fuck if our flesh sins
And this is where it's at
Where everyone is kin
We begin

There's no pain, just sensation
There's no rain, just revelation
We're transcenders of gender
Reality contender
With an army of gender-benders
We come strapped in dresses
And fuck away all that stresses

[CHORUS]
This is where it's at
Where the drag queens rule
And bi kids are cool
This is where it's at
Where everyone is queer
And we all feel the music in here

[VERSE 2]
I make an Etch-a-Sketch etch
Of Neverland
But compacted and reworked
Into Wonderland
Alice molested by Peter Pan?
No? Yo
So this is how we go:

Ran from home long ago
Rejects, misfits, and outcasts
We live outside of pasts
Not shared, separate
We share desperate visions
Of a future not certain to be witnessed
I stress the sickness of the coming years
But live life through smiling tears
Our peers are who we stand by
As we look to the sky
No judgments
Our identity stands and confronts
How we mirror our naked egos
Bold we are,
But damn our scars are beautiful
But damn our scars are beautiful

[CHORUS]
This is where it's at
Where the drag queens rule
And bi kids are cool
This is where it's at
Where everyone is queer
And we all feel the music in here

[VERSE 3]
Let me be your shaman
If you would, this is the plan
We create and discover ourselves as we go
Never slow, we must know

That the paint we paint our faces with
Scars and leaves us with a gift
Tattoos that sink for life
Reminding us of strife
Or an emo corpse wife
Playing with a fetish knife
Yo, why you lookin' at me like that, a'ight?
I was just messin' around
I'll be your guide into this NeverWonderland
Where sands of time tell wishes
Of a grand expanse of truth
One that bends to our wills
And flexes to our skills
And whatever never kills
Will forevermore chill and thrill

What more is there to know?
I'm a queer fairy dressed like Peter Pan
Who dreams of a Wonderland
Where alice dies slow

What more is there to know?
I'm a queer fairy dressed like Peter Pan
Who dreams of a Wonderland
Where alice dies slow
Where alice dies slow

[OUTRO]
This is where it's at
Where everyone is queer

And we all feel the music in here

Trick Tock Tick

[INTRO]
I love all your porno beats, Mr. Muffin Man. But the time has come for me to swim, and Dormy knows how Dina sings. For great are things to come in fact. Everything in tact, is now. But all come round and Time be gone and Time be on. From time to time the creatures tick, and from below come Trick, Tock, and Tick.

[VERSE 1]
Resist the time of sedation
Trick is inked with *penetration*
One for me, one for you,
One for him, and one for her
Are you sure you're ready
Hold steady through these winds
Hook clouds then descend
What bends is fluid
Relativity runs deep, don't glue it
True, it's like this
We search for longevity
We march for prosperity

How far do illusions penetrate
Dilate your eyes but concentrate
Educate but we die late
What's after we obliterate
No energy created
No energy destroyed
Through internal passages, demons deployed

[CHORUS]
Shot down like quail
God will send the hail
Locked in eternal jail
We face four jutting nails
Who's sent to crucify?
Trick Tock Tick

[VERSE 2]
Mark the target, compress it
Confessions of regression
Compensation meant nothing
When the gun pressed to your head
An emotional dead-piece
A promotional said laced
Around bodies like DNA strands
Our lands become marked with tiny flags
Little tricky chained bags
Cool luggage with trendy record tags
He brags about the emptiness of his heart
And degrades appreciation of his art
What is marked down lives

What is bled out sings
We contrive rings of fire
We survive slings of arrows
Our sorrows bring us back
Yo, you know
Provide all that we lack
Yo, you know
Provide all that we lack
Our sorrows bring us back
Bring us back

[CHORUS]
Shot down like quail
God will send the hail
Locked in eternal jail
We face four jutting nails
Who's sent to crucify?
Trick Tock Tick

[VERSE 3]
We tear degradation from open faces
What sears saturation from open stasis
We paint it like a living canvas
Either dark like a stratus
Or beautiful in lattice
They're coming
Trick Tock Tick
So pull up and don't act sick
Cause they come to take a hit
From darkness full of mist

Yo, hold up, Benevalment, hold up
I don't know if I can say this shit, man
Whoa whoa whoa
Cold settlement encampments
Scattered on the outskirts of Distania
Explain Fantasia
Design aphasia
Left brain right brain split
Then spit convulsive rhymes
Something about repulsive crimes
Then spit convulsive rhymes
Something about repulsive crimes

Yo, whoa whoa
This isn't a murder
This is a slaughter

[CHORUS]
Shot down like quail
God will send the hail
Locked in eternal jail
We face four jutting nails
Who's sent to crucify?
Trick Tock Tick

On the Journey Toward the Infinite

[INTRO]
This is my journey toward the infinite
Listen

[VERSE 1]
From this moment forward we laugh
And forget we had a past
The test is whether we surpass
Or we crumble under life's troubles
A life like two towers turned to rubble
I was just a little kid
When he brought me home alone
A different tone shone through his pale skin
Today I wouldn't win
Or get saved by any twin
The way we begin life
Like tiny scattered mice
Looking for crumbs and war drums
We make plans in our caves

After God fails to save
We crave love like it's oxygen
And a face we feel comfortable in
Cause after that day
When he took me in that way
We fail to really say
What rains on our parade
Touch me, no, step back
Fuck me, provide all that we lack
Combat like plastic army men
We're children playing in the ring

[CHORUS]
On the journey toward the infinite
We sing
On the journey toward the infinite
We bring
On the journey toward the infinite
We follow time spirals our path
Flowered roads or burning trails of ash

[VERSE 2]
Has what has shaped you
Been something coming true
Death taking before your time
I take back what's mine
And spit it in a rhyme
Yes, bitch, I did the crime
Fine, I'll tell you one more time
It's like this

When I felt the twist
At the beginning I didn't fear his fist
But trust was something earned
Not something read or even learned
But her burned me surely
The friendship ended prematurely
He was deported way too early
We rode with powder on our faces
Paid no more attention to living's little races
Nah, he wasn't insane
Just a brain full of empty pain
From a childhood spurned and in turn
Left him desolate
Searching for sex as something to dislodge the hate
And his fate seemed to be nothing better
Self-destructive nature
An evil bilingual creature
Searching for a happy medium
Between reality and delirium
But the demons boxed him in
Where he fends for his life
With a fucking paid citizen wife
When I saw you pull that knife
We bounce like a junkie with an ounce
Denounce friendships filled with lying lips
And fucked up acid trips
Permit a bastard sun
Born from the barrel of a gun
The womb of the illegitimate one
The powers that be hold the bomb

And you're on the run
You're on the run

[CHORUS]
On the journey toward the infinite
We sing
On the journey toward the infinite
We bring
On the journey toward the infinite
We follow time spirals our path
Flowered roads or burning trails of ash

[VERSE 3]
We live in a twisted fantasy
Where our existence is profanity
God disowns your name
Because dominant traits came
To the surface of collective consciousness
Where nothing's left to preciousness
All the world is tainted
Wall permanently painted
An Iron Curtain mural
Seen outside your hospital
Where your doctor gave you a referral
Locked up cause you shook a brother down for a dollar
Took his wallet like he was nothing
But something sparked in the air
A tiny recognition you might care
So don't despair
Grow some Samson hair

Cause we're all children in the sandbox
No secret locks or clocks
Just collective games
Cause we're fundamentally the same
This life is not a game
What has shaped your persona
Some past childhood trauma?

What has shaped your persona
Some past childhood trauma?

[OUTRO]
Yo, that's what we call drama
Some people are addicted to it
Like a junkie fiending for some heroin

Lullabies for a Lifestyle (2011)

1. Apology
2. EDEN
3. Fuck Chicago
4. Hourglass
5. Create My Pain
6. Play Party In Hell
7. The Heartbeat Mile
8. Fame & Fucking
9. My Heroin
10. VisionLand
11. We Are Not the Living
12. False Reality
13. Fall With Me
14. Girl With a Gun
15. Hollow Woman
16. Soul(less) Electric
17. Bates Motel
18. Nothing is Private
19. Child's Pose
20. Headcase
21. Goodbye Lifestyle Lullaby Soliloquy

22. No Gandhi
23. Open Your Eyes
24. WonderLand

"Lullabies for a Lifestyle" is the second hip-hop album from Chicago MC Nilotic. This piece was written and assembled to describe the artist's experiences while exploring the BDSM scene in Chicago. From the highs of Sub Space, to the lows of rejection, this is a journey through the senses. One realm after another.

"If we're together cause we signed/then I guess that love is blind"
    - Nilotic

Apology

Hello, people of the world
I'm sorry for speaking to you like this
But, things must be said
This is my apology to
Every person on the face of the Earth
I'm sorry I always use the stage as a weapon
I'm sorry I ripped your fetus from your womb
And wrung it out all over your face
I'm sorry I wrote a four-page poem
Detailing how I would kill you
I'm sorry for being a crossdressing misogynist
Who wants to rape all the women in the room
I'm sorry for using clips from your sex tape in my film
I'm sorry I made you read *Dying Fetus*
Even though you had a miscarriage
I'm sorry I made you read *Dying Fetus*
Even though you had an abortion
I'm sorry I wrote a short story about you
And didn't change your name
I'm sorry I created characters based on all of you

And started seeing you as those characters
I'm sorry I am the way that I am
I'm sorry for all I've seen
I'm sorry for all I've exposed you to
I'm sorry, but I'm still in love with you

You know what?
Fuck it
I'm sorry,
But I'm not sorry for any of that
I give you me
No apologies

EDEN

I remember when you said
You couldn't wait two months to fuck me
So suck me as I melt into the couch
I let your love reconstruct me
I thought I'd found love, Eden-bound
Sing to me, make this our sound
I'm cold, my clothes hit the ground
Eden is not just overgrown
But dead, silent, ragged, and sewn shut
Isn't play supposed to be fun
What I had ended before it begun
Staring into the sun
Is better than feeling the shape of a gun
Temple buried in the dirt
But I'm hidden in the clouds
I never discovered you
Buried you under dark mounds

Two pedophiles don't make a (w)hole

Pull me

Whip me
Strip me
Fetishistic masochistic narcissistic
Pathologic brain
Didn't you know a mind like that
Can't be tamed
Give me Tantra
Ignore the mantra
Love for vampires
Sex becomes a funeral pyre
Psychotic, demonic, absence of logic
Forget me not
Left in the back of a rusting truck to rot
I think not
Sock-hop then slap my rat-infested face
Gun at your hip, gun at your neck
Traced with lace
I fell for your beautiful violence
You cut out my tongue
And left me in silence

I hope you never walk into the light, Forever
Burn
Hear me, Forever, as I scream for you to never
Sever ties that bind
Bound and gagged
Give me your tie that leaves me jagged razor cuts
Into vertebrae leaking soul
You just exist as a gaping black hole
Loveless, with permanent birth control

Two pedophiles don't make a (w)hole
Maybe it's imperative to switch roles

Fuck Chicago

[VERSE 1]
I remember vividly the day I committed suicide
Tried to hide from the light
And shied away from the right
Money was tight, pants were loose
It was no use to fight the tide
When I was just along for the ride
Tongue-tied but committed to the page
I let my persona die on that dark fuckin' stage
Feeling caged and the rage
Taught me nothing more than I'd paid
Everything in bloody handprints on the pen
Chicago's broke-down and muddy
In this hen-house of serpents
I ain't got no servants
And never wished to be a lord
But then I cut the cord
Wishing there was more

[CHORUS]
So fuck you, Chicago

I'm going the way of the road
Fuck you, Chicago
I'm leaving where I was born
And tryin' to find my way home

[VERSE 2]
But I didn't commit suicide
The Ankh is now my guide
And so was Death
But I regain my breath
Sewed up my chest
And put to rest the confusion
And accepted the spinal fusion
In this illusion called life
Despite I'd been taught by the knife
So bite your lip and move on
But don't cry when they don't know you're gone
They were wrong, always wrong
About me singing my song
Sing it like you mean it
Sing it like you love it
Sing it like you mean it
Sing it like you love it
Sing it like you mean it
Sing it like you love it
Sing it like you mean it
Sing it like you love it
Sing it like you mean it
Mean it
I didn't leave cause you scared me away

But when I went you didn't beg me to stay
But hey, I followed my dreams
Didn't burst at the seams
Never played well on a team
But came clean from the start
Never lost heart
But still fell apart
When I broke down
I knew I had to go East
LA created a BeaST
So used to being cold
But unafraid of getting old
Will never fit the mold
I never owned a closet
Music, wait, pause it

I'm straight
No, wait…

I'm leavin' you far far behind
Where everyone is blind
Won't remind you of death
Cause that's a waste of breath
You want me repressed
Fuck that, I'll give you my best
You want me repressed
Fuck that, I'll give you my best

Sing it like you mean it (hate)
Sing it like you love it (love)

Sing it like you mean it (hate)
Sing it like you love it (love)
Sing it like you hate it (hate)
Sing it like you love it (love)
Sing it like you hate it (hate)
Sing it like you love it (love)

Fuck you, Chicago

[CHORUS]
So fuck you, Chicago
I'm going the way of the road
Fuck you, Chicago
I'm leaving where I was born
And tryin' to find my way home

[OUTRO]
Chicago born and raised
Sometimes you gotta leave
The place that you were born
In order to find where your heart is
And that's your real home
Providence

Hourglass

[VERSE 1]
I sit here, my back against the wall
If I could've changed it all
No one would've died
And I would not be tied
To this forced reality
Body corrupted by suffocated frailty
The time has come for change
A revolution for the Strange
Before we fully become deranged
But hey, to shift our thought process
Where time is just excess
This is the way to progress
Shift mood through melody
Lift blood through rhapsody
Pay no mind to time
Just numbers slipping by
Just give us one more sign
To show when it's all mine

[CHORUS]
Sand will break the glass
Time now doesn't last
We must redesign and live
And time is what we must give
I don't know how to start
So I learn and then depart
I fought Time but lost
Take back life at any cost

[VERSE 2]
A call for revolution
But stall for restitution
Just baby chickens pecking through the shell
Our domain is just a personal hell
We buried our own heads in the sand
God has forsaken this broken ravaged land
Yell for life
Breathe for strife
Tell me what you left behind in places
Where light can't shine
River water hasn't turned to wine
It's bitter from the swine
That fell from the face of the Divine
Violence entwines us
Combines us with ideas to align
Bodies in space
But you see these things done in haste
Creates spiritual waste
When no one's ever chaste

Everyone is base and huffing paste
We scream out for a better day
Leave, and come what may
I can't stand to feel this way

[CHORUS]
Sand will break the glass
Time now doesn't last
We must redesign and live
And time is what we must give
I don't know how to start
So I learn and then depart
I fought Time but lost
Take back life at any cost

[VERSE 3]
Shatter the hourglass
If you must take your time
Is that so much a crime
Unrestricted feels sublime
Just make personalities
Different versions of yourself
Don't forget to put the clock back on the shelf
Worry creates stress
Hurry creates a mess
Time means nothing,
So kill and then confess
Killing Time is a noble murder
But I'm the one who hurt her
Time, something we didn't have much of

But hate and animosity there was a touch of
I only believe in True Time
Inside, I think I'm just a mime
Puppets on the strings of time
Help me snap these strings of mine

[CHORUS]
Sand will break the glass
Time now doesn't last
We must redesign and live
And time is what we must give
I don't know how to start
So I learn and then depart
I fought Time but lost
Take back life at any cost

Create My Pain

[INTRO]
Yo, Jacob
I told you not to mess around
With those underage girls no more
Oh yeah?
I hope you learned your fuckin' lesson
Yeah well, whatever…

[VERSE 1]
You said that I was perfect
You said that I was fine
But can you see this defect
And all the lies are mine
Now I'm sick
Cutting me, feel sane
Kid, I'm sick
And so I choose this pain
All you say to me
Wishing I was free
I know you've suffered enough
But you're too blind to call my bluff

So run for your life
To save you from my strife

[CHORUS]
Creating all my grief
Give me my soul, you thief
Lying here, slice into me
And rape me as I bleed

[VERSE 2]
Give me that, why not
That shit is burning hot
So lock me up right now
I'm dead inside this crowd
Before I get what I want
I'll crush your lustful taunt
I would never hurt you
So I lay here on my bed
As I hurt myself instead

[CHORUS]
Creating all my grief
Give me my soul, you thief
Lying here, slice into me
And rape me as I bleed

[VERSE 3]
Cut
Cut
Cut

Cut me down to size
Kill
Kill
Kill
Kill my wicked want
Come on, show me your scar
If you took it that far
Those are the ones
That fueled this bleeding cunt
I've been creating my own pain
Sending this bullet to my brain
I'm at the end of my rope
Lying in this pool of hope

[CHORUS]
Creating all my grief
Give me my soul, you thief
Lying here, slice into me
And rape me as I bleed

[VERSE 4]
I'll rape all that you feel
Can't take the time to heal
I'll cut it till I feel again
When I cannot make it end
My mind is what destroys me
Killing all the good I see
Ripping up the girls from play
Wanting what's not safe to say
I would never hurt you

But I rape you in my head
I could never do that
So I jerk off instead

[CHORUS]
Creating all my grief
Give me my soul, you thief
Lying here, slice into me
And rape me as I bleed

[OUTRO]
I deserve this all
All
All
I'm a sick little bitch

Play Party In Hell

[VERSE 1]
Leather feels so cold
As it rests in my palm
Anger is absent
Depression is present
And yet I feel calm
I wish life came with a GPS
That way death isn't living's PS
Drain fluid from the onlooker's eyes
Tongueless in your stares leave unsaid whys
An unwanted sub in the basement
Dominant forced into encasement
I'll whip away my pain in a box of staples
Participating in scenes feel lied and in fables
Sitting silent on an unmapped road
Failure helps only in clamping loads
Into Odes to Joy that die once the music stops
Partially productive, partially destructive
Come the tops
I fail to factor in the night of still pictures
Shunning incessantly, placating to fill fissures

The road moves on when I leave it
And it doesn't look back at me
As if it gave a shit

[CHORUS]
What type of Bibles are the sell
Fuck you,
We'll have a play party in hell

[VERSE 2]
Strategic ties into cages of memories
Can't recall the locked doors of families
Passengers boarding the foggy train
Cremate their mothers in a groggy rain
Dripping onto their feet of dry puddles
We sink forever down as the try cuddles
Our collective baby-head
Pacifying the undead
Watch them all play lead drums
Follow the letter
Simon says play deader
And crush fortifications set for us
They rush forth waters to bless us
Sinful rain falling from our sex
Blinded by our eyes, we fail what's next

[CHORUS]
What type of Bibles are the sell
Fuck you,
We'll have a play party in hell

[VERSE 3]
I have come to join the fun
But then I find your flower gun
Hiding in the air just below the Sun
You pour fire into the blinding sea
Come now, Goddess, shall I take a knee
When we flee, wash the tree
The branches rubbed off my bark
Shading my light as you fuck the dark
Wed the light
Shut the night
Crush the flight
Fix me right
Bottomless engines run on split ends
Girls fail to imagine, some hit trends
Take my hand as I lead to the sandbox
Play with me, girl, try out my hand-locks

[CHORUS]
What type of Bibles are the sell
Fuck you,
We'll have a play party in hell

The Heartbeat Mile

[VERSE 1]
On a starlit night in mid-December
I'd lay you down near burning embers
And I don't think you should remember
That all these thoughts may last forever

You opened like a flower
To give up a little power
And gave in
To the Silver Seducer
The Mental Inducer
But you let me in
Allowed me into your skin
Do you still see me now
Like you saw me then?
And will you still wait for me till the end?

Before I die
Bring me there
To your silver tarnished land
I'll become so like a child

In a Heartbeat Mile

[CHORUS]
So please remember this song
And it won't take too long
Then we can stay for a while
In a Heartbeat Mile

[VERSE 2]
Y'all heard that it's better to have
Loved and lost
Than never have loved at all
That's bullshit!

Out from our quiet madness
Sprouts the violet sadness
So give me nothing
As always I'll take everything
From you before I've killed your spirit
Love is elusive and you can't hear it
Back track
Track back
To the beginning of where we ended
If not, it's impossible for the umbilical to be mended
I can't determine why making love is called
What it is before time crawled and stalled
To the place where orgasm stagnates
There is no Heartbeat Mile as this dictates
Crash and cum into the spectrum of solace
It's lonesome waiting for the rape police

In silence, eggs cracked, tackled girl
Dive through space into your world
Impossibility of breaking through atmosphere
Into your sphere where your heart is here
I'm terrified
But sanctified
As we butcher what's left of longing
And waiting for something that's never coming
No matter what nonsense I cook for cactus basket
You're one too many tulips, but unready to trash it
Are we two girls, two boys,
Two broken toys?
But two broken toys can still work in time
All that's needed is to intertwine and combine

[CHORUS]
So please remember this motherfucking song
And it won't take too long
Then we can stay for a while
In a Heartbeat Mile

[VERSE 3]
Bop one
Bop two
Bop three
Fuck me!

I guess I failed at writing a love song
I hope you forgive me for this wrong
Don Juan I'm not and can never be

Then why do you still seem into me
I can't help feeling you should keep the fuck away
What can I say,
My offerings dry up like unquoted sayings
Dried up and unlactated,
I'm a child spraying unsatisfied ravings
Cravings unsquelched but unhealthy, unsanitary
I've become unsavory
Swim into the womb and come back
I haven't yet because you're sucking me black
Some trap, I've fallen to your feet
But you offer no collar or treat
I said I wouldn't make apologies for myself
But I'm sorry for the pain
To which I offer no help
And I'm sorry I remain undeveloped,
Undisputed, and unsatisfactory
But I don't want you as a disappearing
Character in my unfinished story

So please remember this song…

Fame & Fucking

"A photographer most noted for his photographs of Marilyn Monroe pulled a cute number on me after a session. He invited me over to his little apartment for—which he keeps one block away from his studio—for a drink. So I trotted over there thinking a drink wouldn't hurt. And whack I was out like a light after two sips. When I woke up this photographer was humping me. And it was like being a nympho...uh, not a nymphomaniac. What do you call those dead people? I can't remember. A...necrophiliac? I couldn't move. Whatever it was in that drink, I was like a dead body. So it was like he was screwing a corpse. Twisted... I never went back there."

- Edie Sedgwick

[VERSE 1]
Stab you with my dick
Like a rabbit saturated in cocaine
Maintain an erection till the blood
Explodes three-way like a water main
My pain makes your cancer seem like segued bliss
Blast her with a heroin dancer

Romancer, girl, I miss you
Like the moon hidden in clouds of darkness
Wake up, I'm losing weight
Wake up, I'm losing weight
Wake up and feel the hate

"Fashion as a whole is a farce, completely."
 - Edie Sedgwick

Self-centered, self-indulgent,
Self-speeding, not heeding
Advice, misunderstanding
Impeding comprehension
Shoot-up till we all go down
On the town and around
I'll take you where we're bound
To fortune, fame, and fucking
And breaking through the ground

"I hadn't had that much experience with acid, but I wasn't afraid..."
 - Edie Sedgwick

[CHORUS]
Fuck me like I'm famous
Fuck me like I'm famous

[VERSE 2]
Sex
Respect, inject me with silicone cyclone

Change me out and in
And down to the bone
I'm a clone
A self-imposed clown
Paint me up then we all fall down
Heart-job, boob-job
Give me double-D's
Then maybe all you fuckers would know me
Until then I become anorexic and psychotic
Platonic relationship? NOT
Fuck me on hypnotic psychotropics
Half passed-out as you're riding on my dick
Come quick, she's ODing out the world
You still don't know my name
And I still don't have a girl
So…

"I'd like to turn the whole world on just for a moment! Keep that superlative high…"
 - Edie Sedgwick

[CHORUS]
Fuck me like I'm famous
Fuck me like I'm famous

[VERSE 3]
Ask me what's my fashion sense
Henceforth from now on I'm the prince
Of crossdressing misogyny

Look at me, I'm flying through the sky
So high, my teeth are made of meth
Death cum quick
So I can kick you out my bed
Something wrong up in the head
Are you dead
What's behind that makeup? dread?
If I led a normal life no one would know my name
All the same, fuck my broken hips
Kiss me on the lips
And tell me that I'm hip

"Meth burns your brain cells out unless the injections are accompanied by massive doses of vitamin B12."
- Edie Sedgwick

Fill me up with acid
Feel just like a kid
Then I hid from the world on fire
Edie, Girl on Fire
Never retire from the game
The flame, and it's a goddamn shame
To die at twenty-eight, too late
For much more than fortune, fame, and fucking
And people sucking all your life away
Please stay in my arms until the End of Days

"I'd make a mask out of my face cause I didn't realize I was really quite beautiful."

- Edie Sedgwick

Fuck me like I'm famous

"The first fifteen minutes takes a long time. The second fifteen minutes takes forever."
 - Edie Sedgwick

Fuck me like I'm famous

Maybe if I was born a woman
A hole between my legs
I could sell my body, suck him off
To the floor and begs for more, more,
More from my tits
First give me a hit
Then I'll suck your dick
Hell, I'm sick
From all the tar, but I've become a star
Take me to the bar
I'm beautiful now
Teach me ways to die cause I've forgotten how

"I'm a star... Just a star."
 - Edie Sedgwick

Maybe I'm already too far gone
Bring me back to life before the break of dawn
Withdrawn from the light

And giving up the fight
Surrender to the high
The possessions and the pheromones
Pump me full of sex, drugs, and Rock 'n Roll
Till I cannot speak and no longer have control
We are only here to give our final possessions
Elevate my status and I'll share all-time confessions

"Stripped off all my clothes, leapt downstairs, and ran out on Park Avenue and ran two blocks down Park Avenue before my friends caught me. Naked. Naked as a lima bean. A speedball is from another world. It's a little bit dangerous. The ultimate in climax."
  - Edie Sedgwick

My Heroin

[INTRO]
Sucks to be old
You are my heroin

[VERSE 1]
It was never my choice
To be living like this
I just envied a life like his
Not jealous of the wealth
But mental health is overrated
And my words still remain understated
So I drift back to the rift
His head was always in the clouds
Past the Cellar Door,
Surrounded by kinky white mounds
Where the sounds were always
Beat, beat, beat
Give me some of your powder
Cause I feel I have no power
I'm within the Purple Fog
Breathing human-created smog

I can't see beyond this Black Mist
He took me down to his dungeon
Where I could forget all my pain
Through these spirals and colors
I love to be insane
Grab an apple and cut it
Get baked till I'm a flame

[CHORUS]
You are my heroin
Sucks to be old
You are my heroin
Sucks to be old
You are my heroin
Sucks to be old

[VERSE 2]
Walk into my blackened garden, Sarah
Come see what's been planted here
Our family is broken, discharged
I don't wanna hear how the theory
Of God's become enlarged
You are my heroin
When the needle breaks the skin
Our souls are worn thin
Telepathic sin, tapeworms of self
Degrade and shade physical health
And then when we melt
We wear a human pelt
You are my heroin

Get me outta this place
I can't see my fucking face
Gimme that fucking case
Pop one, two, three, four pills
Don't you know how temptation kills
My body crawling with icicle chills
Loving addiction
Your mind's a complication
I can't deal with your suppositions
With your prejudice
That's why I built this edifice
Me and my demons are all I need
I can't wait to fill this greed
With white, purple, green
Just remember my contradiction
When I'm begging your redemption

[CHORUS]
You are my heroin
Sucks to be old
You are my heroin
Sucks to be old
You are my heroin
Sucks to be old

[VERSE 3]
I slowly take a breath
No death
I shoot smack in my lungs
Wouldn't you?

But it's like I'm being hung
With no tongue
And you're deaf to everything I've sung
Why does she gotta be an opiate of the masses
I'm a barbiturate teaching classes
A truth acid for your minds
You're placid or you're blind
Throw your paws up
Then shut the fuck up
Free booze, she wins, you lose
Don't give up your right to choose
A drug that might have made you frightened
Either be numbed or be enlightened
But be wise when choosing who to follow
Be sure inside they haven't become as hollow
Oh, and don't forget
The light seeping from a single eye
Inside a distant triangle
Always tells us lies

[CHORUS]
You are my heroin
Sucks to be old
You are my heroin
Sucks to be old
You are my heroin
Sucks to be old

[OUTRO]
They want to keep you numb

How come?
Just remember this Lest We Forget:
A pill to make you numb
A pill to make you dumb
A pill to make you anybody else
But all the drugs in this world
Won't save her from herself

VisionLand

[INTRO]
Life is a search for answers that never existed.
As humans it is only natural to look for
answers to these questions.
But as we search, we accumulate
more questions than when we started.
So we are plagued with thoughts;
thoughts that come from a mind
that can't comprehend them.

[VERSE 1]
Tell me what you see when you look in my face
Does it make you want to cringe and shake
But your eyes have gone and I just know
That you're blind and caught in my undertow

Reap the seeds you sow
Keep the deeds you own
Cause they grow a flow known
As a tsunami
Waves that put children in their graves

Jesus never saves
Just makes us hide in caves
Terrified of the sunlight
And spirits in the night
But I know that I can see
Cause starlight makes you flee
Into a shelter for the cursed
Holy water can't quench your thirst
But wait on me, wait on me
And I'll make all your dreams be free
Into this land of things to be
I can only see through my eyes of calloused stones
I rake my broken claws
Cause I cannot save your bones

[CHORUS]
This is all I see from you
Why save what's already dead
We fall into our crimson blue
With our eyes, the beasts are fed

[BRIDGE]
What can you see with those empty eye sockets
What can you see with those empty eye sockets
What can you see with those empty eye sockets
And what can you think with that empty fuckin' head

[VERSE 2]
Maggots fall from blinking holes
Betwixt, be waxed in our souls

Pray to god to give you sight
With real eyes the truth is bright
Blinded by the bitter things
I cannot seem to spread these wings
Falling feathers red
God's army laying dead
I said it, confess it
You're atheist, admit it
We're all kings in our mind
Doesn't change the fact that you're blind
Mankind, believers in a God
Which deceives her own people
To their death on a steeple
Show me now the believers dead
Into slow matchbox sand
Our lives have gone and now they end
Into this waistcoat patched-up land

[CHORUS]
This is all I see from you
Why save what's already dead
We fall into our crimson blue
With our eyes, the beasts are fed

[VERSE 3]
And I'm sick of all these dreams
That never seem to come true
And I see the only thing in this world is me
But the only me in this time is dead
For you I will see these visions

But I cough up some filthy verses
The world isn't cleansing of the dirty
Fearless merciless scars on our minds
Why must the wolves rape and ravage
Like savages
Passages twist in my mind
And tell me how to talk
But I think I got some cum on your mohawk
Spiritual descendants of stalkers
Day-walkers that rape souls
And make 'em into drones
Eternally glued to their cell-phones
But when we die, bones will never be recovered
And future generations
Will be ignorant of how we suffered

[BRIDGE]
What can you see with those empty eye sockets
What can you see with those empty eye sockets
What can you see with those empty eye sockets
And what can you think with that empty fuckin' head

[OUTRO]
You can't think nothing
With that empty head
Cause the only thing inside
Is O2
(Death)

False Reality

[INTRO]
They say there is a man on the moon watching over the Earth. They say he isn't alone. They say he doesn't eat or sleep or even breathe for fear that he may miss a key piece of the puzzle before him. They say he doesn't want to watch anymore and happily awaits the day he'll be dismissed. But I wonder if it's really true.

[CHORUS]
This is my false reality
Only the fallen are what's real
Where the lie is the truth
And the truth is a lie

[VERSE 1]
Trapped in my spiral cage
I see things I wish didn't exist
But I keep a list
Of those I created here and insist
That they live in this world
Possessing every girl that I meet

In these haunted halls
I stretch my arm through my bars
To touch the breathing walls
Then a shrieking call
Breaks forth from my throat
And stalls
My memory from revealing
My escape from this cage
As I crawl toward the wall
That drips with fresh mucus
Come join us
Through this doorway
And kiss me forever in this death landscape
Where the only way to say and be
Is evil, uncivil
And never shrivel up like clay
Or pay for your sins
Women sticking me with pins
My cage finally opens
And I step through the striped door down
Give me the monsters

[CHORUS]
This is my false reality
Only the fallen are what's real
Where the lie is the truth
And the truth is a lie

[VERSE 2]
Stumble blindly down the stairs

My vision stays impaired
Repair my broken limbs
Sing my Satanic hymns
The only way to see
Is to gouge out the eyes
She dies in my arms
And cries from my lies
But what's real reveals itself
Independent of what's true
Blue, blue is death
But that you surely knew
Cause you plucked out your eyes
As I give you wisdom
Far from the Kingdom of God
In a world of pain where we never spare the rod
Truth marks time in this unbegotten rotten
Crimson flows through my pours
As I see without the senses
Hence, you rape me bloody
So what will be my recompense
Cremate my soul as I fall into your dolls
Segment my whole through these hallucinogenic halls
Their eyes have been gouged out with a radio dial
There won't be a smile
And I'm just full of bile
Many visions of lust
In this vacuum of cardiac arrest
To these visions, deaths,
And creatures I can attest
They're as real as I can make them

And squeal as I can shake them
I'm raping your dolls
I'm raping your dolls
I'm raping your dolls
Blood cotton isn't capable of love
I violate your plastic
And wait to be amused
You're my fire mistress

[CHORUS]
This is my false reality
Only the fallen are what's real
Where the lie is the truth
And the truth is a lie

[VERSE 3]
Time is dead in this waste—
Land has never been killed
Everything is made
Everything is thought up
Everything of loathing and disgust
Where the mind has turned to dust
Here, where everything is broken
Where women hurt
And women desert
Everything is burning
Consumed by fire for eternity, undying
Relying on nothing except the demons
Flying high above the Black Mist
Watch out for her fist

She's fallen into Triple Trick-or-Treat
And if you cannot take the heat
You could always retreat
From the fire, knives, and briar
But I remain crammed in a room
Where I cannot sit
And can only fit
When my legs are broken under me
Flee from me now
Then you'll maybe see
I've triangulated my throat
Opened up the gate
And wrote down what I saw

Body is a prison for the soul
I fall into the Spindle Trap
Body is a prison for the soul
I fall into the Spindle Trap
We're hollow, trapped, and dead
Inside our blood vessels as I said
I speak just to use my lungs
Impaled on a cloud of spider tongues
Can there be absence of dark
Or just absence of light
Riding on the infrared wings of night
Blood-red dreams projected onto white eyes
But the lies are for real and no one ever dies
Our palms drip rancid images
The mark has been made
We'll never forget

That world is real

[OUTRO]

They say there is a man on the moon watching over the Earth. They say he isn't alone. They say he doesn't eat or sleep or even breathe for fear that he may miss a key piece of the puzzle before him. They say he doesn't want to watch anymore and happily awaits the day he'll be dismissed. But if I've learned one thing, it's not to believe what I'm told.

Fall With Me

[CHORUS]
Fall with me
Till we finally feel free
Fall with me
Or from he, she will flee

[VERSE 1]
We were a boy and a girl
Hansel and Gretel
Forgetting not to meddle
In affairs of adults
The results will be dire
Just follow how the petal
Falls down to the ground
Never making a sound
Isn't that profound
How you found you were crowned
Like a king, a child-king
Sing to me of forests
Florists, and mothers killing off the poorest
Of their young and drown them in the tub

I'll turn and take your hand, girl
We're left out in this world
To fend for ourselves
Lost Children of the sweets
Endless eats and cobblestone streets
For us to wander hand in hand
And puss-in, puss-in-boots
Then becoming baited with candy, meat, and cake
Oh, for Christ's sake
She's just a child, don't bake
Her in a pie
I'd rather see me die, I'll pry
Her from your grasp and your seductive rasp
I'll protect you from a child-devouring witch
And a predatory father,
But which has become the bitch
The mother or the daughter?
I'm afraid the trail of pebbles and bread crumbs
Will lead us to the slaughter
Where parents abandon the children of their womb
Disown them till they cry
And fall into their tomb

[CHORUS]
Fall with me
Till we finally feel free
Fall with me
Or from he, she will flee

[VERSE 2]
She looks so cute in her Little Red Cap
Still remaining innocent as she's falling in my trap
Have I become the wolf and she become the faun?
I'll be withdrawn into the bed
And she is just a pawn
So she thinks she's a woman
Cause she wears a red cape
And just cause she's bleeding
That she wouldn't get raped
She's been taped by her brothers
And touched by her father
Don't bother to save her now
The wolf has always caught her
The erector predator and virginal prey
What can you say to one who's gone astray
Come lay in my bed
I'd never leave her dead
Eaten maybe but still alive and kicking
So next time he darkens her doorway
She'll think of Little Red Riding Hood
As he has his way
There's nothing she can say except:
"What big teeth you have"
"What big hands you have"
"Ow! What a big cock you have"
I wish I could've saved her
But the red hood will just deter
Her memories from surfacing
Tell her that she's sure a king

And blind out all those bitter things

[CHORUS]
Fall with me
Till we finally feel free
Fall with me
Or from he, she will flee

[BRIDGE]
I forgot your name
It's my name
I forgot your name
It's my name
I forgot your name
It's my name
Dance around my soul
I already know
Dance around my soul
I still miss your glow

[VERSE 3]
Who would you be falling with
If you won't fall with me
But I've fallen so hard for you
Won't you ever see
That you planted this dying tree
That's still trying to grow
Even thought the roots have become withered
And I cannot sow
The seeds that have burned

And the love that has turned
Into something rather hideous but sensuous
And I've become superfluous
Expendable to you as I've fallen down
Still bound to your torture
As a rose is bound to thorns
Grabbing by the horns
Isn't easy when your soul is being torn
I'm like a shorn sheep
Without Little Bo Peep
Lost and confused and falling in too deep

So ring a ring o roses
A pocketful of posies
Hush! Hush! Hush! Hush!
We're all tumbled down

We're all a-crumbling 'round
I cremated our relationship
Incinerated my penmanship
And burned your kiss into my breath
Now forever infected by the Black Death
Trading our sickness
Then you still condemn me to sneezing
The final fatal symptom

[CHORUS]
Fall with me
Till we finally feel free
Fall with me

Or from he, she will flee

Girl with a Gun

[INTRO]
Girl with a gun
I want you
Girl with a gun
I want to feel your
Cold hard steel in my mouth
Girl with a gun
Shoot me

[VERSE 1]
Shoot me down to the level of your mind
Make me understand so I'm not so fuckin' blind
Please remind me you're a girl
And dance with me in time
Heal me from within
Refuse and diffuse my misused spine
Seal the hated and the jaded
And come back resurrected
I've been infected by the Hollow
But disregard your preconceptions
Destinations are still clouded

And my life is contraceptions
Distractions from misconceptions
Of a female world
That's why I never could communicate
Or get through to a girl
Hurl me to the dark
But I refuse to be blinded by the night
My sight is far from gone
I've become the source of the light
Face the complications
Race the proclamations
Displace the old traditions
And experience the sensations
Girl with a gun
Girl with a gun
Is in my brain
This is who I want
Even if I'm being slain
Prayin' through the rain
For the arms to hold me tight
Oh, right
I'm alone in this world
Without you in my sight
But if you're there,
Tie me to the bed and pull the rope tight
The is the appeal of the dominant female
Let us sail into the night on wisps of wind tails
I'll be your child as you ride my broken hips
Till the moon cries NOW as you pull out your whips

[CHORUS]
Pretty little girl with a gun
Kissing you through the gates of the sun
Pump me full of lead in the head
Then bring me back with love
From the dead

[VERSE 2]
I'm sorry I can't be a girl for you
Be a girl for you
Be a girl for you
True blue is death but pink would do
I'm sick of having to compete with Britney Spears
So hit me baby one more time
I'll be your toy if only for a moment
Can't be your sub and I've been sent
To turn back and switch with no restraint
Don't get me wrong and I'm no saint
I ain't gonna submit to all that you desire
If your love is there you can burn me with fire
But I tire of this game and we become divided
And guided by nothing
Beyond the living and the dead
I'll be your lover, I won't be your slave
Twist me all you want but I won't live in a cave
"Behave or you'll be punished"
It's amazing how you're perfectly blemished
It's not a crime to switch from black to white
In the night it's right to give up the fight
So give me the gun

We're not even done
Even done
Even done...

[CHORUS]
Pretty little girl with a gun
Kissing you through the gates of the sun
Pump me full of lead in the head
Then bring me back with love
From the dead

[VERSE 3]
I'll still let you slap me in the face
Doesn't mean you can get on my case
Tell me that you love me
Then pull on my leash
Switchin' and fuckin' you hard
Getting up in your crease
Who's got the gun,
Is it you or is it me
Got you by the throat, don't try to get free
I know where you live all up in your head
Watch out for the bullet, watch out where you tread
You're my Dead-Head doll-ified bitch
Fucked against the wall
Make your clitoris twitch
This is the hitch
Pull you in, pull me in
To the world of pain, sex, and sin
I know what you want

And I know how to give it
This world is my own
I've written and know how to live it

[CHORUS]
Pretty little girl with a gun
Kissing you through the gates of the sun
Pump me full of lead in the head
Then bring me back with love
From the dead

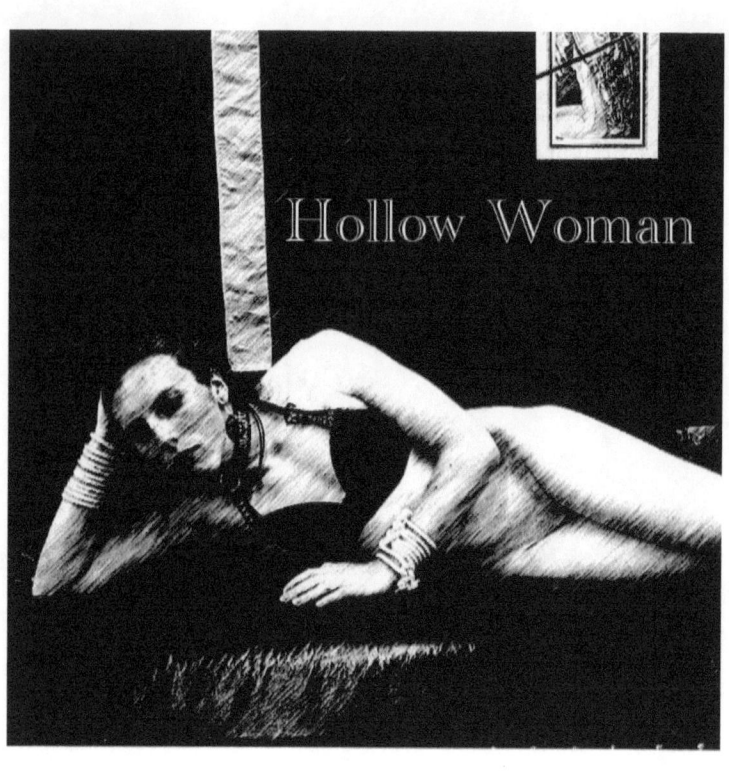

Hollow Woman

In the immortal words of Lady GaGa:
"Silicone, saline, poison, inject me, baby, I'm a free bitch. I'm a free bitch."
- Lady GaGa

[VERSE 1]
Have you ever heard of a misogynistic crossdresser
I am now cause the women tend to be my stressor
Alice was my oppressor and now I hate the female
In the tail-end of this whole story
The surgery became on sale
So unsex me here, so you will never fear,
That my hate would never sear
The clitoris to the shaft
Rough draft of my declaration of war
On the opposite gender, I'm the contender of this sore
Bitterness of distress
Pussy left me tore to the core
Restore my faith in the feminine agenda
Why can't they all be tender?

They are the broken gas masks of intranquility
I hate them in everything other than nudity
They haven't become hollow, they always were
Stir the behind the eyes, there is not a cure
For the sickness which is CNT
Stunt my sexual growth and leave me like a runt
So I blur the line between feminine and masculine
Fuck me in a dress, decide what you see within
See me as both or neither, or just full of shit
But I am not a man
My dick is just a clit

[CHORUS]
Make me a hollow woman
I'll take you all inside
So cum as much as you can
I'm ready to be cut wide
(Empty, hollow, vacant)

[VERSE 2]
CNT isn't in this, it's about this
CNT isn't in this, it's about this
CNT isn't in this, it's about this

How do you gender identify?
Genderqueer, genderfluid, transgender pussify
Eunuchify my face in this fuck race state
A vagina on my plate makes me irate
Frustrate, dilate the cervix
Till you think outside your purse

Before you hit the hearse
Discover there's more
To life than makeup, nails, and hair product stores
Walk around in heels, diamonds, and pearls
There's still nothing behind the eyes, girls
This world is not implants and facelifts
What will it take to make your thinking shift
What's the definition of a woman
A superficial trophy wife, that only becomes a shelf life
Despite what you may think, anatomical sex
Is just between the legs, open up and check
But we are all just fluid
Relative through my superlative
I'll give you a laxative
Till you shit out your empty brain
I claim to be insane
Just feel my female pain
They drain me of my life
I never want a wife
So cut off my dick and hollow me out
Then plug up my mouth with what I cannot be without
(Empty, hollow, vacant)

[CHORUS]
Make me a hollow woman
I'll take you all inside
So cum as much as you can
I'm ready to be cut wide

[VERSE 3]

I consider myself an unregistered gender offender
Defender of the dick, destroyer of the clit
Spit on her tits and squirt on her lips
The tip is almost in, but my penis has no skin
I'm strapped down to the operating table
I've always known my mind was unstable
Cables wrapping around my sexuality
Changing me in and out into duality
There's no such thing as a whole woman,
Just a chick with a dick
Pick which one you wanna fucking kill
Biggest mistake was giving them free will
I'm ready for my sexual reassignment
Make me better through refinement
Realignment of my organs inside outside
Confide in my genitals how you wish to see the bride
Decide the wax and waning hormonal bitch
Was once a chauvinistic man, stitch, stitch, stitch
From the cock to the balls
From urinals to the stalls
Inverted and inserted into the body inside out
Becomes the new vagina is what TS is about
Can I gain my wisdom through the labia
Can my intellect contract gonorrhea
My mind's an inverted penis
The male's inserted cleanness
Into the monstrous regiment
But you see I'm just as decadent
And this song is just my excrement

However I'm not wholly male or wholly female
My body's just for sale
I'll wear your wedding veil
Listen to me cause I am fully sick
There's still no such thing as a while woman,
Just a dick with a chick

[CHORUS]
Make me a hollow woman
I'll take you all inside
So cum as much as you can
I'm ready to be cut wide
(Empty, hollow, vacant)

Soul(less) Electric

No, you don't look fucking pretty

I know that we are old
And I know that she may hate me
But I just can't think of you like this
Anymore…
Alice
Alice

GaGa, drama-ma
GaGa, drama-ma
GaGa, drama-ma
You're just soulless electric

Maybe you're just being esoteric
Eccentric and fag-Tantric
It's already been said: dare Hip Hop stop
Maybe someone needs to put a stop to the Pop
Don't fucking call me GaGa
Was there ever any substance
To someone spitting blah-blah

Saying you make soulless electronic Pop
But your music ain't a flop—stop
Less than two years later coming
With a heartfelt Speech(less)
Doubting that you'll ever have something to teach
Preach it to the masses like a blonde-headed leech
Impeach the beyotch
Impeach the beyotch

Money's just illusion
You didn't come to that conclusion
Confusion from your esoteric allusion
Soul is Money, Honey
Soul is Money, Honey
Soul is Money, Honey
I am art, you're parody

Will you go the way of Edie
Warhol would've sucked away your sanity
Fame's a high-priced bitch, baby
I'm sorry I can't be a girl for you
But I can see through your pa-pa-Poker Face
Plastic is sometimes sometimes see-through
Already you've left a mark and a trace
Pa-Poker Face, Pa-Poker Face
You've risen to instantaneous fame
So rape her in the dark
She'll think it's a Love Game
You're a woman without conviction
You're a woman who's always known

How to sell the contradiction
You come and go
You come and go

GaGa, blah-blah-blah
GaGa, blah-blah-blah
GaGa, blah-blah-blah
You're just soulless electric

How come you can't sing of our pains
Cause you're plastic and so are your brains
Few myths loom larger than Pop fame
I guess they were waiting when you came
(The Perfect Spirit)
Myth-ilize me, Captain
With an agenda that's Reptilian
You're a free bitch, baby, that's worth a million
In the stars you found your place
You've had way more than a taste
What's w-w-with the money-money-money
With your face-face-face
I want your grace
What's w-w-with the money-money-money
With your face-face-face
I want your grace
What kind of message you sending to the girls
With I Like It Rough
Then again, I'm one to talk
That shit is tough-tough-tough
You hate the men

I hate the women
You kill the men
I kill the women
I just want to understand you and your schtick
Actually I think I understand more than
I'd like to admit
(Don't ask, don't tell)
I hated The Fame
But fell in love with your eight Little Monsters
We'll have to see if you take your place
With the imposters
Tell us how it is that you play
Just know you can't have it both ways
Soulless and heartfelt

GaGa, drama-ma
GaGa, drama-ma
GaGa, drama-ma
You're just soul…ful electric?
NO!

What you behold, you become
What you behold, you become
Let's play a fame game
Game-game shame big name
Stuff it, bluffin', muff-muff-muffin
St-st-stuffin' starstruck
Fuckin' it up
Sup in the hizzy clizzy
Jizzy busy with the money-money-money

Just Dance, monkey
Dance you goddamn monkey
Monkey paper, fuh-fuh-fakers
Takers in the house
Groove slam work it back
Groove slam work it back
Bitch, I'm rich
Sick in the hitch
Ra-ra-reverse into the purse
Into the hearse
Puh-puh-purse
Again, again I'm into the boys-boys-boys-boys
Toys, we're all toys
Runaway models, Cadillacs, liquor bottles
Papa, papa, fuck me papa—
Poke her fucking face
I like it fucking rough

Dykes, fags, and queens
Dykes, fags, and queens
Dykes, fags, and queens
Silicone
Saline
Poison
Free bitch stitch-stitch-stitch
Pitch a concept precept
Inspect, fall apart
Got no heart to start
Part the lips
Sip the goblet

Stop it
I'm a speechless monster
Corrupted in foster care
Despair
Tear my soul out
Pole out my spine
Decline the money
The fame
Monster ma-ma-monster
Be Beyonce
Alejandro GI Josephine
Plain and sim-sim-simple
Fuck your Bad Romance
I'm So Happy I Could Die…

What you behold, you become
What you behold, you become
What you behold, you become
What you behold, you become

Silicone
Saline
Poison
Inject me, baby
I'm a free bitch
I'm a free bitch
What you behold, you become
What you behold, you become

GO!

Soulless electric

Boom

Been struggling with the facts
Of how you act
I contract the GaGa infection
In the perception of your work
Conceptual artist full of promises promises
Knowing how to work the androgynous
A Bowie-ish superstar princess
Fame is an inner sense of confidence
Providence astonishment opulence
Manson, don't do it
You blew it
But you're still my God of Fuck
Chew Fu it
However, you do have a freak in me
Don't know if I could handle your teeth
Rapping beneath the anti-GaGa flag
Even though I'm a fuh-fuh-fucking fag
I wish even just once I could leave you Speechless
The Fame Factory Girl with
Thesis and Antithesis
I'm your biggest fan
But still am not a man
I am Hip Hop
But remember,
I'm no Paper Gangster

I'm an Emo Gangsta

Free me
Free me
Free me
I don't like you
Could I just love you
I'm your Paparazzi
And I'll still keep chasing you
Till you love me
Hold me
GaGa oo-la-la
GaGa oo-la-la
GaGa
I love you
But don't know what to do
I don't know what to say
And for this I will pay
Eh eh, there's nothing else I can say
Eh eh, there's nothing else I can say
Eh eh, there's nothing else I can say

I don't know, GaGa
Maybe I just want you to be my man

Bates Motel

[VERSE 1]
There is a little place on top of a hill
And maybe before you come
You should take a little pill
If you ever hear a shrill yell
From the windows of the hotel
It's nothing but the orgasms
Of a lost banshee
Let me tell you about a little time
In a little place
Where I fell face first
And lost a little thing we call the human race

Human race
Human race
Human race

Welcome beautiful woman to Bates Motel
Where we sell nothing except for images of hell
So bid ye farewells to family and friends
And step through this doorway where

Everyone gender-bends
I'll send you to my artist quarters
Inside the water mirrors
We'll bathe in the light of supernovas
You will join my hearers
From one two, boom boom
One two, boom boom
Soon you'll know my pleasures
Soon I'll know your treasure
However, if you try to maintain
The pleasure turns to pain

[CHORUS]
Follow me toward Bates Motel
Where we will fuck
Until you give a yell
Breaking you like eggs
And breaking through the shell
P or P doesn't matter much
When you're sinking into hell

[VERSE 2]
Aly dragged me dead up toward the entrance
Head bleeding profusely
Need no drug enhance-meant
For nothing more than to be fucked
And stuck forever in the past
Chucked into the swamp
Overflowing the hotel bathtub
No, I won't sub to you

Unless you become a wolf-cub
Something in the spirit
Sometimes I can hear it
Maybe don't be so loud during fornication
So we can speak to God's Creation
Why have we turned so violent
Instead of learning about the world
And letting things fall silent

We are the Lost Organ Donors
We are the Lost Organ Donors
Giving away our hearts
Giving away our sex
Children don't understand how it's so complex
I can't remember how many rooms
Own pieces of me
How many songs leak love
In the releases of me
Ceases to be
Once we've cum into the stars
Dead and waiting for string to stitch our scars
Hear my voice from my hotel room
Come sing with me and let our flowers bloom

[CHORUS]
Follow me toward Bates Motel
Where we will fuck
Until you give a yell
Breaking you like eggs
And breaking through the shell

P or P doesn't matter much
When you're sinking into hell

[VERSE 3]
I dissolve in water
I dissolve in water
I dissolve in water
And I thought I'd caught her
But it was she who'd caught me
Saying he was better in bed than I'd ever be
That's why she shot me in the head
Forever infesting me with lead
Falling into bed with one already dead
Opening her mouth was a black cave of madness
Arachnids poured down my throat
Of laughing sadness
So used to being an utter disappointment
I can't heal with any ointment
Scars are forever
While dicks are being severed
I fall into the bed
A migraine splits my head
Exploding from my face
The wound opens to let in the cum
There's no use in hoping for some
So-called safe sex
It's never what it seems
They're just dangerous dreams
Screams through my mouth
Pulling off my pants my dick is no longer there

Forgetting any chance that will bring me back to life
And I forgot my knife
My penis is an umbilical
Wrapped tightly around my heart
So continue to have sex with me
Disappear
And then depart

[CHORUS]
Follow me toward Bates Motel
Where we will fuck
Until you give a yell
Breaking you like eggs
And breaking through the shell
P or P doesn't matter much
When you're sinking into hell

[OUTRO]
I'm collecting all my girls
I'll rape them till they cry
Then I'll find the time to die

Nothing Is Private

[INTRO]
This is as much a confession
As it is a lie
And fully in part the whole truth
And nothing but nothing
And none of the truth
Just like your fucking face

[VERSE 1]
Step inside the bloodstained treehouse of my mind
Unwind from the crime
Where I was filled in from behind
Was it that crime that made me the way I am
Cum take my hand
I'll take you to the sand
And bam!
I slam the pestle into the pariah
Come dine on flat boyish tits
I'll give you a hit
Till you're flat passed out to shit
I admit it that I'm sick

So split my dick in half
So I wouldn't hurt your calf
Relax, I haven't crashed out from all this hash
I've cashed out on all my sins
And am left with just a rash
Push past victimization
But don't abort fertilization
The separation between penetration sensation
False epiphanies, and statutory rape revelations

[CHORUS]
And I can tell you this cause
A, nothing is private
B, nothing is sacred
C, nothing is forbidden

[VERSE 2]
Maybe I deserve to be Bound Torture Killed
I'm strong-willed but still I give in
This body's marked with scars I live in
This vessel with a pestle
I've sufficiently sliced up
I'm still a pup, a child
A boy waiting for you to fill my cup
With your titty milk
Mommy, Ma, look what I did to my hands
Even though I created many lands
I always seem to return to this one
Where my dick feels like a gun
I can't see the sun

With these empty eye sockets
When you're on the ground I put these bottle rockets
In your mouth, I'm sorry for that pain
Come fuck me in the rain
You took me in that treehouse
I was quiet as a mouse
Just remember I was seven
Seven, seven, seven, seven, seven, seven

[CHORUS]
And I can tell you this cause
A, nothing is private
B, nothing is sacred
C, nothing is forbidden

[VERSE 3]
Maybe I've hurt myself
Reading Mai-chan's Daily Life
Thinking "babyfuck, babyfuck, it's all right"
Tonight I'll feel that shaft constricting tight
We might be damned to hell, oh well
I'm still a god that fell
If you ever asked me what I wish to do
I would reply:
To cut you open and fuck the hole
I'd made in your soul
And then cum on your wounded humanity
My sanity left me that day inside that treehouse
Now I'm stuck in the past
As a child, as a toy

The one that's become soiled
And still remains a boy
But I'm not quite a man
Not quite a woman
Chop off my balls and cut open my hands
Why can't I get over undeveloped sex
Or rid myself of this Oedipus Complex
Respect me for being so honest about my life
Don't become my wife
My dick's become a knife
And I've wholly become Travis Vuoso
But please always remember
It ain't your fault
It ain't your fault
It ain't your fault

Child's Pose

[INTRO]
Bar none,
I've told you nothing
Nothing at all, ever
This is because I don't trust you
I've never trusted you
And this is why you won't
Get any information from me
None whatsoever
Not even if you pry and beg and plead
And cry on your knees in front of me
I will never give you anything
Because you give me nothing
You give me nothing
So why should I give you anything at all
And I won't
Cause you don't deserve it

[VERSE 1]
It was the night of the Screams in My Girls
Through the light of the dreams in my worlds

You weren't ever there to hear my voice
I wasn't even there to sway your choice
But I flew back to you
Like blue never ever
However, forever isn't burned
Into our genetic code
And I'm afraid I'll never ever
Stop walking this road
You forbid then I hid away
From your dark sunset
And swam into the midnight light
Where I am not a threat
You became my confessor
I became your aggressor
But I'm a gentle rapist
You're a loving abortionist
And maybe I'll never walk your path again
Now I know I was never one of your men
Not sure if you'd ever give up any control
Letting someone into a piece of your soul
I've fallen off your cross
You're the boss, applesauce
I would dream of Edie
When I know You Dream of Jeanie

[CHORUS]
I was born in a child's pose
When I didn't even need clothes
I was born in a child's pose
And still keep my body closed

[VERSE 2]
I'd like to turn the whole world on
Just for a moment
That way I would never have to be scared
Of your abandonment
I've been sent by the heavens
To share with you my sevens
Girl, girl, girl, girl, you're not yet a woman
You have eyes like a child
And a guise like a child
Even though you hurt
You still have wonder like a child
Tell me, do you still need
A Little Red Riding Hood tattoo
Or will the time pass by until you're finally blue
Without ever needing one, look
My face is in the sun
Accidentally I become
Obsessive and possessive
But rape wasn't really my intention
And I forgot to mention
You're like a twenty-four-hour climax
I'm just a girl playing the suicide king

I'm just a girl playing the suicide king…

[CHORUS]
I was born in a child's pose
When I didn't even need clothes

I was born in a child's pose
And still keep my body closed

Headcase

[VERSE 1]
I'm critically insane
This is Headcase

Battle cry
Fall now
Tell me how the cow
Speaks of better days
I'll say you'll know the truth
When we go back to a tooth for a tooth
We go back to a tooth for a tooth
Believe in the soothsayers
And the way I say slayers
Never take candy from an infant
To them you're an elephant
So don't take they're virginity
I love that smell
Tell me of serenity

[CHORUS]
Second installment Headcase

First hit of the crack vase
Seventh deed of drug lace

[VERSE 2]
I lead you by the hand into the sand
Playing seems so grand
When the imagination of a child
Runs wild into the night watchman's hands
Withstand all the abuse
Come loose
Suck on the obtuse misuse of Heffalump
Lumps and cunts singing to the rainbow
Crown, king's hat
Recap all that went before
All I did was try to score

[CHORUS]
Second installment Headcase
First hit of the crack vase
Seventh deed of drug lace

[VERSE 3]
Tell me when you hit the ground
Don't make a sound
As if you didn't know you're hellbound
Why'd you buy that rope
If you wasn't gonna tie me
Why'd you buy those condoms
If you wasn't gonna lay me
Tame the ground runnin'

Same the sound gunnin'
Frame the round drummin'
I want your blood as I strip down
Leave it to murder cases
See you drowned
Blown away by fathers not there
Stare into the sun as if you didn't care

[CHORUS]
Second installment Headcase
First hit of the crack vase
Seventh deed of drug lace

[VERSE 4]
Bobbing for compliments
Never gettin' some
How come you're lookin' for the ones
On the run from home
Skin and bones
Melt clocks with the sun
Why wait for the chase
When they're ready and wet
Ready, set, go
Reach in, stroke left
Make a bet

[CHORUS]
Second installment Headcase
First hit of the crack vase
Seventh deed of drug lace

[VERSE 5]
Take off from a sitting position
Land in on her in a mounting situation
Sensation to stroke with her blood
I fell down and cried in the mud
And I'm trudging back to Mommy
Forgive me for abortion, claw me
From my safe-haven of regret
We've all be together
But this timecode isn't set
I bet you always felt the loathsome
Tyrant of the sky
Ask why
Get a death back as an answer to your why
Decide to reject, reject, reject
Then inject
Inject my semen hate

[CHORUS]
Second installment Headcase
First hit of the crack vase
Seventh deed of drug lace

[VERSE 6]
I blew up the moon-bounce just for you
So be true to me and tell me why you're blue
Cause blue is death
And green means life
Your blood's on my knife

But you're not my wife

[CHORUS]
Second installment Headcase
First hit of the crack vase
Seventh deed of drug lace

[VERSE 7]
Boom shaka-laka
Boom shaka-laka
Boom shaka-laka
HA HA HA

Boom shaka-laka
Boom shaka-laka
Boom shaka-laka
HA HA HA

Boom
Boom
Boom boom boom

Our love is epileptic
Our love is apocalyptic
Our love is contraceptic
Our love is epileptic
Our love is apocalyptic
Our love is contraceptic

Segment my soul

Mix me in a bowl
Castrate my lungs
I'll forever be hung
Kill this linguistic game
But still I feel no shame
Kill this linguistic game
But still I feel no shame

[CHORUS]
Second installment Headcase
First hit of the crack vase
Seventh deed of drug lace

Goodbye Lifestyle Lullaby Soliloquy

[VERSE 1]
Fuck it
I can't fucking lie anymore
Your ropes and leather have left me sore
Always asking for more
Than I'm capable of giving
Submitting to your whips
May be one way of living
Power exchange doesn't make us
Separate but equal
Your power quota has been reached
Look at the sequel of vengeance
Which is what?
We're together but unequal
Follow my bloody footprints
Slowly watch as your sadomasochism
Turns to maso-sadism at the core
Of everything is "I'll hurt you only if it hurts me"
Come see through my eyes

And you'll know I've broken free
From your handcuffs, wrist cuffs, dick cuffs, soul cuffs
I'm like the genie in Aladdin calling all your bluffs
The desire to serve has left my body tonight
Once the Perfect Forever fled out of my sight
But tight were the ropes that bound us together
Like bondage triple trick-or-tied and never severed
But now you're like a daemon cut from my body
My hands made shoddy relationships, still disembody
The lifespan of a domme and a sub
No contract, no protocol
As she scrubs away my heart
Go fuck your shiny latex
I know now we'll never again have unprotected sex

[CHORUS]
This is my goodbye soliloquy
We fell face first into the sky
Then I gave back your skeleton key
Don't worry
I'll look back as I whisper bye

[VERSE 2]
You brought me into your poly-family
As a submissive
Starting out loving and ending up
Cutting and derisive
Your cock and ball torture
Is only psychological
Pathological seductress

I made you mythological
Christening you the Perfect Forever
How clever
To make a name binding me to you
However, we've been pulled apart
Like a fetus from the womb
But you still walk with me into a child's room
I can be your little acomoclitic boy
Coy, and submitting as a virginal toy
For your fetishistic sadistic nature
I venture
To say a child adult in stature
Not a catcher in the sheets in heat
Beat me till I scream behind the ball gag
Fag, I'm a fag
But fucking you on the rag
I fucked you cause you looked
(Smells like children)
Forgive me, Father, for I have sinned
Amen
I wasn't in long enough to pull out and cum
But I was strapped down and flogged till I was numb
I thought you said you loved me
I thought I found my savior
But I'm still your little daughter,
The werewolf, and Rainbow warrior

[CHORUS]
This is my goodbye soliloquy
We fell face first into the sky

Then I gave back your skeleton key
Don't worry
I'll look back as I whisper bye

[VERSE 3]
If I listened to everyone who told me to stop
I'd still be nothing
You'll never be my top
Pedro, this is for you:
I'll never fucking stop!
You're falling under the spell of false power
Forever read my tarot,
Said I was followed by the tower
Fuck that
You'll never see the world collaring me
As I see your torture,
That's me hollering "flee"
I've fallen from the noose
Broken from the torsion
But this isn't a full departure from the scene
Just partial, like a partial-birth abortion
What's the safe word?
I'm sick of always hearing
How much you wanna fuck me
You've been on top of me before
Back the fuck up and let me be
Can't you see
I'm just a little boy
That's lost the gift of joy
Dropping it in menstrual blood at seven

A treehouse will be my hell and heaven
Shaping me from scratch
Then from my ass detach
Get that anal hook the fuck away from me
Still in the scene in spirit
But this is my decree:
I relationship's not a contract
And love is not a pact
If we're together cause we signed
Then I guess that love is blind
But still, cocaine won't get me to subspace
Will you only get hard
If you continue to rub lace
Or maybe nylon is your thing
That makes your penis sing
Give me our coitus interfemoris
No penetration, no more pain
No pleasure, no sensation
But your eyes give me a
Permanent chastity belt
You made me impotent
Forever, then dealt me forty-nine
Lashes from your single-tail
That's seven times seven, inhale
Then choke me as I climax
And suck your bloody tampax
We practice gender-play,
Feminization, sissy-fication, fuck you
Your odontophilia left me wanting
To commit suicide (red)

Getting fucked with a strap-on
Doesn't make me gay
Bust out of our cages
But I know it's all a role-play
My life isn't *Venus in Furs*
Or *Story of O*
I'm not a submissive or a bottom
Now you know
When it comes to BDSM
I have my own tools
When it comes to D/s
Make your own rules

[OUTRO]
Peek-a-boo, I see you
I'll be a little girl
Masturbating for the Perfect Forever
Come to my scorpion web
And I'll spin you a myth

No Gandhi

[INTRO]
She was Violet
And she was Perfect
At least I thought she was

[VERSE 1]
I was spring-loaded, corroded
With broken relationships
Permanently re-encoded
Encrypted, a cipher unreadable
Angry hyper, but my proximity
To a potential rape became despicable
But hey,
Some things make a bitch hit-able

Life after Sherry
Searching for a girl who could carry
Herself in the stride of a man
And my hands are shaking
There are worse sins than mistaking
A female for a male

Oh, Mother
I pray for a world where all gender
Can cease
She told me, after that
We'd all be at peace

[CHORUS]
She ain't no Gandhi
No, not yet
She ain't no Gandhi
No, not yet
She ain't no Gandhi
No, not ever

[VERSE 2]
She was my bald beautiful princess
A bi-sexual genderqueer
Who could express herself
Musically and artistically
But like me, historically in pain
We were the same
Pornographic Childhood with
Abortion soon to follow
The Polish seed of a schizophrenic father
Maybe some was passed to his daughter
I never taught her how to hate
But the issue in debate
Does she live in a bubble she herself creates
Unable to see the cracks left in her wake
Let's take a break…

How can we reconcile
A spirit who's hostile behind her smile
Perhaps she was ignorant of her guile
A style of unintended lies
Where flies wait as she dies
Ravaged cries from a soul
Where affliction takes its toll
Twisting reality
To instill an illusion of stability
The truth was fragility
Killed all traces of tranquility
So she spoke words like love and peace
In spite of the fact the drama would increase
Her house-mate went insane, a woman that's obese
Here she goes calling up the police
Did she do it for release
A thrill
A fuck you to her mother for putting her on a pill
But in spite of that I loved her
She rejected me, hence I suffer

[CHORUS]
She ain't no Gandhi
No, not yet
She ain't no Gandhi
No, not yet
She ain't no Gandhi
No, not ever

[VERSE 3]
I hadn't seen her for three weeks
So I ask how a Perfect speaks
I went to her house tripping on acid
Didn't you know I'm still a little kid
She had gained weight
And was fucking an anorexic skater faggot
Crawling like a maggot
I inch toward the kitchen
Where bright melting lights
Gave me hypertension
Reality suspension
Time tracked like vertebrae retention
But control left
And I watched the theft
Of self and friendship botched
Destroyed like a toy made entirely of soy
No joy for a boy who's in love with a decoy

All dead inside their houses
Dulled minds by the thousands
Medicated and sedated
So no words get regurgitated
But leave it stated
Your whole journey has already been dictated

Just home after three weeks in the hospital
I was tripping so to me
It was completely possible
Her mom sent her back to the bins

No child injury like bruised knees
Or scraped shins
Three weeks
Where the only thing that's heard is shrieks
Freaks who have reached their peak
Misunderstanding left their thoughts
Fatally oblique
But I ask you
Is it a sin to seek an immortal mystique
Is it a sin to seek an immortal mystique
Is it a sin to seek an immortal mystique…

Open Your Eyes

Just open your eyes
Now

Open your eyes
Don't be blind

People indecisive
Death, intricately reclusive
Making love, sex
Experimentally inclusive
Red, blue, purple, black
Sing out
Describe our spiritual drought

Open your eyes
Don't be blind

Sacagewaea manifested
In a bloody bed of incest
Raped by a brother, uncle, or father
Babies are crying

Babies are crying…

Our innocence has died
The leaders all have lied
Speaking the real has been
Gagged, blindfolded, and cuffed
Cut off
From a world
That needs to hear your words

Silence…

Open your eyes
Don't be blind

Silence…

Our awakening's on hold
Waiting for the ones to lead the struggle
The march
Don't depart before your time
But you're blind
You're blind
Don't depart before your time
But you're blind
You're blind
Be wise
Or we'll all come to
An early demise

Don't listen to the lies
Be wise
Or we'll all come to
An early demise

Be wise
Don't be blind

Open your eyes
Don't be blind

Emotional Ghetto (2011)

1. Opening Sequence
2. Cracked Lips
3. With Sunglasses On
4. Build a Forest
5. Monster
6. Get Off Dat Nigga's Nuttz (ft. Ill Will)
7. Goodbye Message (skit)
8. Suicide Eyes
9. Emotional Ghetto (ft. Brittney Blue)
10. Bloodstained Treehouse
11. Keep It Real (ft. Ill Will)
12. Finding the Audience (ft. Documentaries of the Dead)
13. Steal Your Fans
14. Wigger
15. Like Water (ft. G-Tek)
16. Beauty/Sexy
17. To You Bitch
18. Itch Bemuse
19. Portrait of Distania
20. Ambivalent Narcissism
21. Negative Seven

(note: no text is included for the skit)

"'Emotional Ghetto' started out as a concept to create a short mixtape, but then evolved into something completely different. After going back to Park Ridge (where the whole Emotional Ghetto concept came from), the "mixtape" then transformed into a full album because so much happened during my visit. These incidents gave me more material for the album. It definitely traces the mood swings from joy/fun, to sadness, to negative pessimism. They pushed me to the negative side of Seven. Now listen."

- Nilotic

Opening Sequence

[VERSE 1]
Darker than David Fincher's *Se7ven*
Images to bring about Armageddon
All of a sudden a swift concussion
Splinters my percussion
With no cushion
My thought process is interrupted
By an unscripted presentation
Caught in suspension
An altered representation of *Ichi the Killer*
Torture porn version of Thriller
Directed by Eli Roth
Why can't I be a Goth metalhead moth
Hip Hop brought up never to shut up

[CHORUS]
This is my opening sequence
I got no political speeches
Do my words contain what teaches
And Cornelius, he preaches

[VERSE 2]
I'm up here in makeup
Looking like Clive Barker's child
Film reels of gay seeds filed
Away for stock footage
Suicide god in an Elias Merhige cottage
I'm a novelist turned lyricist
That went through filmmaking in the process
With an excess of shots
Auditory hallucinations banging pans and pots
I'm not meant to rot
Like the American tourists in *Hostel*
Preaching the gospel in a polluted brothel
Will get you dead
Or forced to give me head
A knife-tipped strap-on
Raping Little Red Riding Hood with a trap on
The ground scattered with bones
Both brothers Grimm hearing female moans
In a fantasy land where creatures rule
The imagination is a powerful tool

[CHORUS]
This is my opening sequence
I got no political speeches
Do my words contain what teaches
And Cornelius, he preaches

[VERSE 3]
I am the Nilotic
Clive is a prophet
When I'm having a *Requiem for a Dream*
I'll be cursed to hear that mother's scream
Then Stephen King rhymin'
HP Lovecraft to keep timin'
I'm getting Dario Argento to direct my videos
With baphomet milk and bleeding Oreos
I'm giving you a show
So act like you know
Your blood flow is my rap flow
I'll make you scared to be the host
Like Butters conjuring Biggie's ghost
Keep these names in mind:
Nilotic
Jacob Steep
Rosa McGee
Edie Warhol
Adolf Crowley
Alice
Cornelius Trowman
Benevalment
Have you seen the settlements yet
You bet I'm a fucking train wreck

[OUTRO]
Broadcast journalism bought with food stamps. We are the sole survivors of a lost cosmopolitan famine. Spiritually

speaking, this nation is dead. We speak nothing to the flowers that sprout dead plasma TVs to heinous, righteous, barbecued elitists of our nation. Standing up we see faces that are coked-out on the phenomenon called business. The establishment has requested our finances, but also requested our souls to be sold into the marketplace of our deaths. Wasted and forever forgotten in the world slid down to the sediment of the ocean. Sunk like Atlantis. How can we steady the axis when it is so gone, bent, and warped by what we cannot fight against? The only way to fight it is passive, aggressive, and fervently. Never giving up time or place to the people who don't understand the passion. We've trekked through their half-naked skulls up to the necks with Pansexual dogma. Why do we cut off our dicks, fillet the godsends, and let the mighty ones fuck us up the ass? Hell no. Forever this. Forever that. No way. We are this way because we choose to be. But remember how I told you the bloodstained treehouse is forever? That's because it is for me. But you can choose not to get raped. I never had that choice. So sue me for crossdressing. Sue me for indecent exposure. Sue me for rape. But I'll never stop raping your face, your ears, and your eyes because they now belong to me. Just as your body belongs to me. For me to penetrate deeply and subconsciously. This is why I wish to rape you. So that I can hear you squeal as I get the final shot of my death on film. On film... On film... On film...

Cracked Lips

[INTRO]
Yo, check it
Our bodies our cracked maps
Like *Palimpsest*

[VERSE 1]
I dried out in the sun
Then cried shouting into a gun
This song is my son
Sustain the pain before I came
Inside the brain fame
Fighting through my cocaine strain
My Pride Parade is a grenade
Set to explode
With vocal cords in a choke hold
Your soul has been sold
Emotions are cold
Premonitions are bold
Folded pages
Lying sages

I'm courageous
Suspicious like conspicuous
Performances laying dormant
With Twisted Torment pouring forthwith
Insisting each thought
Keep persisting
Listening to each word
Become a Lord

[CHORUS]
Cracked lips speak of hips
Death acid trips
Melt tips of iceberg worlds
Our existence just went belly up

[VERSE 2]
Parameters are banter
They just don't exist
Spit a list as a lyrical fist
My mental mist consists of this list
Names of dead stars
Living stars
Striving to go far
Riddling fiddling
Saddling our bodies
Daddies riding our backs
Telling us we're naughty
Haughty socialites
Elites sitting on a high seat

But the fucked up shit they do
Is kept discreet
They tell us never to repeat
What happens in the back seats
Of cars
After leaving lonely hook-up bars
We might as well sew our scars
With latex string
For what we bring to the table
Is unstable
Like nuclear reactions
To social-sexual factions
Let me repeat
If you didn't already catch me
Sexual Communism
We give away our bodies
Lip service under a naked
Stripped away marquee
Oddly enough I've been too fast sexually
My cracked lips have circled the tip
Now I equip myself with knowledge
But still say fuck you to every college
(That includes Tribeca Flashpoint)

[CHORUS]
Cracked lips speak of hips
Death acid trips
Melt tips of iceberg worlds
Our existence just went belly up

With Sunglasses On

[VERSE 1]
There's glass between us
Have you seen us
The little girls grabbing their penis—
His?
I'm a homophobic gangster tap-dancer
A Dark Father romancer
A truth enhancer
That could cure cerebral cancer
But what life dealt me
Was a sea of disease
That not even the fees could appease
And the leaves a poet sees
Comes clean through the trees
Keys granted, pain chanted
Insanity is ranted
I've become disenchanted
We're all superstars
Gracing dives and cheap bars
I'll deep-throat your guitar
My skin is where you can put out your cigar

This tar disappears
And these tears clear away
When the day darkens under translucent gray

[CHORUS]
The world looks so much better
With sunglasses on

[VERSE 2]
Slip on a pair of sunglasses
So I don't have to see you bastards
Slip on a pair of sunglasses
So I don't have to see you bastards
Slip on a pair of sunglasses
So I don't have to see you bastards
Ah, fuck it
Suck it deep, you faggot freak
Why you think Warhol
Walked around with tinted eyes
Horse blinders, question finders
Can't see the rear or to the side
Inside is where I'll hide
Celebrity visors, industry advisors
Told to face the race
Give chase and come in first place
Through the glass we cannot see the crowd
Kiss my fuckin' ass
The Versace is my shroud
I said:
The Versace is my shroud

Blinker, blinder
But with these things comes a bridle
With a tint shading eyes homicidal
Given pacifiers meant to calm our qualms
Sending blind men meant to read our palms
But does this ocular mesh
Cultivate a state of narrowness
With an inability to see the larger picture
A permanent fixture
On how our brains rearrange
Cast out like loose change
We live on the fringes
Loose hinges
We're all Strange
Personal cages with no wages
But you cannot read these pages
If you're blind or not courageous

[CHORUS]
The world looks so much better
With sunglasses on

[VERSE 3]
It's also protection from the infection
Like a broken condom
An unspoken stardom
Neglected blossom from the bottom
When I'm chokin' I go unspoken
This joke is just a token
Like cheap protective eyewear

It keeps you unaware of my stare
I'll shield you from my eyes
With my own public figure disguise
A desire to mask my own identity
But with a drive to live in infamy
Surrounded by a crowd to sing my symphony
A name to place in history
Suns to shine forever glory
Reflecting like lens flare
Wearing fashion that blocks out every glare
These aren't shades
My eyes are two-way mirrors
There's no way to make it clearer
But if eyes are windows to the soul
You won't get nothing through my Jackie-O's
Extreme use of clothing
To hide from paparazzi
And still cover what we don't want you to see
If I can dictate the way I appear
You'll never get to see me shed a tear
If I can dictate the way I appear
You'll never get to see me shed a tear

[CHORUS]
The world looks so much better
With sunglasses on

Build a Forest

[VERSE 1]
Tackled buildings
Washed up on the shore
Of my Imagination Station
Termination of this Caucasian invasion
Demonstrations of appreciation
Guttural salutations
Asphyxiation on sedatives
Repetitive stresses
Testing methods of life and death
If you think slander can stop my breath
Or is it meth to kill the one born by Seth

This piece is assembled from
Junk that I've sunk
Resurfaced then gave it spunk
The right words could make
A monk become a punk
Afterthoughts caught in twisted pots
I fought what they taught
For it was completely wrought of naught

A planet overwrought
The abstract becoming sought
Sometimes I receive images from the demons
And words emerge from Seraphim semen
Dreamin' of a world where love perpetuates
But mistakes only seem to create hate
Maybe if I can actuate a state of grace
You all would cease to cremate my face

Sorrow flowers grant me power
To bring a needle shower
That will destroy your feeble tower
And make a sweet tongue turn sour

[CHORUS]
We...
Built a forest of synthetic trees
A collage of choruses
That invoke the Master Key

[VERSE 2]
Targeted but forced to be marketed
If you label me a fable
It's your world that I show is unstable
Cable stations emitting radiation
So be ready for extermination

Targeted but forced to be marketed
If you label me a fable
It's your world that I show is unstable

Cable stations emitting radiation
So be ready for extermination

[CHORUS]
We...
Built a forest of synthetic trees
A collage of choruses
That invoke the Master Key

Monster

[VERSE 1]
I'm destined to provoke
Just messin' then I choke
Invoke Steep whenever I'm on coke
Stroking blades in a smoking haze
This verbal maze has been razed
Caged like an insane enraged
Onstage arrest
I see visions of women
Hanging by their pussies
Publicly executed hussies
I make love with a scythe
This is just my life
Haters told me I was trife
Then I eviscerated a hater with a knife
And discovered he was rife
With maggots
But no truth recovered
My lovers are all dead
So I bludgeon your son
Before you could give birth

The way I see the Earth
As one giant curse
I living breathing spherical hearse
Which can be destroyed
Through one uttered verse
I disperse shots
And leave your ribs laced
With subliminal blood clots
The Vegas slots will become gas chambers
The New Age Hitler will be responsible
For all your heart failures
Our jailers resemble ourselves
Every skull racked up on my shelves
I fucked you personally
And jizzed AIDS just perfectly

[CHORUS]
This mind of mine's a monster
I'd rather be that than an imposter
So foster seeds of hate
So we can share this fate

[VERSE 2]
Recast, dispatch murder raps
Feed you scraps
From human fragment traps
Watch me tap a vein in your brain
Yes my life's insane
FBI could never make me tame
But you're just the same

So I take it upon myself
To be the source of your pain
And I tell you,
First day I met Elan she trained me with a cane
So remember, this rain will bring your bane
Your living's been in vain
My concepts seem to contain
A profane refrain
Telling me:
You're preordained to be inhumane
Watch the way they suffer
Why I became a stuffer
I'm not a bluffer
I'm a bloodline snuffer
Then I'll use your skin to write from within

Psychotic and wild
Like a necrophiliac pedophile
Raping a dead child
I'm meant to be reviled
My whole persona has been styled
Around a broken child that's been riled
Dead, but I'm immortal
So fuck being cordial

[CHORUS]
This mind of mine's a monster
I'd rather be that than an imposter
So foster seeds of hate
So we can share this fate

[VERSE 3]
It's fucking crazy subjecting my body to this violence
I see razor blades in your anus
With blood forming books
Throughout these pages
And if this song enrages
Just think how language engages
Thoughts that leave you distraught
Never deny that I've caught
Your mind in a trap
Like a shroom trip death cap
When a million eyes watch me
I gouge the world from its socket
With your genitals caught in a sprocket
Unbeknownst to be me
I receive the death penalty
So I commune with the spirit of Lee Wuornos
Monstruos Humanos
That's what you have labeled us
Filling up my lungs is pus
Mades specifically of a truss
That cannot hold my hernia
That's why I penetrated your urethra
This gun holds one bullet with my name
A limited run so cold after I took aim
At this fame, and this game
Is just to see if we can maim
Our worlds will chill you then kill you

Echoing a shrill laugh that resonates true form
With a wicked storm sent to destroy the norm
And my true form
Is a platinum-armored titanium tape worm

[OUTRO]
And if any of you motherfuckers try to get rich off of me after I'm dead, I'm gonna resurrect just so I can come back and kill your entire family. And piss on your grave, bitch.

"Because I'm, out of retaliation for taking my life like this and getting rich off it all these years in total pathological lying. Yeah, thanks a lot. I lost my fuckin' life because of it. Couldn't even get a fair trial. Couldn't even get a fair investigation or nothin'. Couldn't even have my pills right. You sabotaged my ass, society. And the cops. And the system. A raped woman got executed. And was used for books and movies and shit—ladder climbs or elections, everything else. I get to put a finger in all your faces, thanks a lot. You're inhuman—you're an inhumane bunch of living bastards and bitches and you're gonna get your asses nuked in the end. And pretty soon it's coming. 2019 a rock's supposed to hit ya anyhow, you're all gonna get nuked. You don't take fucking human life like this and just sabotage it and rip it apart like Jesus on the cross and say thanks a lot for all the fucking money I made off of ya. And not care about a human being and the truth being told. Now I know what Jesus was going through. I've been trying to tell the truth, and I keep getting it stepped on. Concerned about if I was raped, if I—

I'm not giving you muck. Book and movie info. I'm giving you info for investigations and stuff and that's it. We're gonna have to cut this interview, Nick. I'm not going to go into anymore detail. I'm leaving. I'm glad. Thanks a lot, society, for railroading my ass."

- Aileen Wuornos

Get Off Dat Nigga's Nuttz

[VERSE 1]
In this dream I resemble
My idol
But I'm no longer suicidal
Come follow my title
So we never become stifled
First time I heard it I was not yet a fan
Though it was already planned
For his philosophies to enter my world
Through the mouth of a little girl
Speakin' "you look like Marilyn Manson"
Unsure wether that was a compliment comparison
So I said, "is that good?"
"I think Manson is sexy, come fetch me"
Set your lech free
Hold up, I'm being testy
Danny created a monster by giving me his book
Which led me to a poster
It's a long hard road outta hell

When you're born into this swell
Well, I don't worship any stars
But I love ones who show their scars

[CHORUS]
Get off of Manson's nuttz
Get off of dat nigga's nuttz
Get off of Sage's nuttz
Get off of dat nigga's nuttz

[VERSE 2]
Obsessive with Celebritarianism
And I only *studied* Satanism
I'm having gay fantasies
Of Marilyn Manson and Sage Francis—
Fuckin'
Suckin' off beats
And shitting pre-disposed of teens
The way it seems
I'm being fisted by a fashion expansion
Granted, I may look like Manson rappin'
Or Sage just toe-tappin'
But I'm the one bringin' similes cappin'
Nilotic
The one with the severed penis
In her purse
Nilotic
Eden's pretty Manson meant to curse
Inside I encoded a Gidget Gein rhyme

Keeping time away from mine
Yeah, no shit I'm the Goth kind
Are you faggots blind
Rewind my mind
Till you get fucked from behind
Holy Wood designed
But look harder and you'll find
It's written "Nilotic" where I signed

[CHORUS]
Get off of Manson's nuttz
Get off of dat nigga's nuttz
Get off of Sage's nuttz
Get off of dat nigga's nuttz

[VERSE 3]
Sometimes I feel like a psychic vampire
Building a demonic empire
Backed by a fatal choir
Fuckin' listen while my throat is hissin'
Or just continue dissin'
I'm not Marilyn Manson
I'm not Sage Francis
I'm the fucking Nilotic
But maybe we lack
And need to think back
There's a reason the best of album
Is called *Lest We Forget*
Seems y'all forgot

Now I'll show you what I got
Know I've written the plot
Accidentally caught beef
Then repeat it on eternity looseleaf
Yo, he's just a metalhead rhymin'
Like Eminem in drag
How come he calls himself a fag
With audience repeating:
That's not my bag
So watch me fly flags
Of authentic aesthetics
That bring death to my skeptics
We do need some controversy
But bursting with originality

Suicide Eyes

[INTRO]
He was the boy with clock eyes
The one to shift time
The one blessed with powers
Of foresight and hindsight
Fourth Dimension
Seventh Wisdom
But what comes with blessings
Is severe suffering

Suicide eyes

[VERSE 1]
I'm a Technician in a Strange Wonderland
Creating a global Distania
Plagued by hysterica in America
No one'll marry ya
I carry on as an independent pawn
Unused by the crew
Who could never see my view
Despite it being laced with truth

But if this is what you choose
Don't be afraid to lose
Cause people wouldn't want
To walk a day in your shoes
But if you follow these clues
You'll know why I caught the blues
We live in a life
Where a little girl is forced to kill her baby
Come save me
Crave me
I'm fully depraved, see
But the world behind me dies
I have suicide eyes

[CHORUS]
Suicide is in my eyes
As the world behind me dies

[VERSE 2]
I used to live here
Miles behind where the past can't last
Depression makes memories die fast
But I'll broadcast a dreamcast
A surrealist landscape laced with fate
But remember we create this state
Where we process meat with hate
I reincarnate as Dr. Suess
And lay waste as a papoose moose
Weighed down with a lit fuse

And seven-tipped horns
Waiting for the hail-storms
Torrential rains shaking chains
We'll walk with canes before our graves
They say he saves and pays
Our debts off one by one
But where is his Son
When I'm holding this gun
There's a barrel to my temple
Tremble

[CHORUS]
Suicide is in my eyes
As the world behind me dies

Yo, I know it's hard to listen sometimes
When you got blinders on
And I know it's hard to see
When you have plugs in your ears
Listen, I got something to say

[VERSE 3]
He said Nilotic was nihilistic,
I'm not pedophilic, hedonistic
Just *Anghellic*
Never docile from the Nile
But being attracted to child-like frivolity
Doesn't make me a fucking pedophile
I know that you all hate me

But you can never shake me
I'm the one who's free
Scales cover your eyes
As darkness fills the sky
An existence gone awry
A lament sentence
Severed penance
Taken to hear to deliver vengeance
Hip Hop reparations
Succeeding severance
My essence has a resemblance
To an evil presence
This appearance is not a semblance
The dark is just my preference

[CHORUS]
Suicide is in my eyes
As the world behind me dies

Emotional Ghetto

[VERSE 1]
I cry myself to sleep
When the pain is too much to keep
Inside this supposed holy temple
My body jerks and trembles
From these internal symbols
I saw you tried to kill my pride
The Apocalypse is raging on inside
You proceeded to rape my heart
I'm being torn apart
Between urban and suburban
Dark and light
Black and white
Good and evil
Soul and devil
Human and animal
Even though I spit
Like I'm a metaphorical cannibal
Wait, slow it down
Listen to the sounds
I found myself back in time

I was in the before-time
Stricken again and plus
I felt that I must
Reinstate a critically trust
But first they bum-rushed
They thought they got it hushed
Demon got up, blushed and gushed
Wait, I need y'all to keep me grounded
Couldn't tell me how that shit sounded

[CHORUS/BRITTNEY BLUE]
I keep on running
But the struggle keeps on following me
I keep on running
But temptation keeps on following me
It's all
Oh, it's all on me
I keep on running
But the pain keeps on following me
I try my hardest to give the world
What they expect from me
It's all on me
Emotional Ghetto

[VERSE 2]
Park Ridge, losing sleep
Sadness welling to a peak
If it's Enlightenment you seek
Come back to speak and teach
So I reached out to my friends

Trying to lend hands and tie loose ends
And maybe even make amends
It's hard when everyone is dying behind
Struggling to see and not be blind
Sickness, illness, HPV, cancer, STDs
Substance abuse
This cute fuse has torn loose
Now which way do you choose
How can I kill on on one track
And embrace you in another
How can I say your shit is wack
But switch after I discover
Hope you got stomach for some other
But now this is for my peeps
Living in an emotional ghetto
Soul pierced by serrated stilettos
Pushed to make artsy amateur pornos
I wrote this for Peter Hoffer and Aleks Brown
You were lost but now you're found
Bluom, Another, Maria, Ariel, Noel,
Britney, Jesse,
All my dudes in Park Ridge and Chicago
Leo, G-Tek, Jose, Danny
No, but seriously furiously I write
While your lips are out of sight

[CHORUS/BRITTNEY BLUE]
I keep on running
But the struggle keeps on following me
I keep on running

But temptation keeps on following me
It's all
Oh, it's all on me
I keep on running
But the pain keeps on following me
I try my hardest to give the world
What they expect from me
It's all on me
Emotional Ghetto

[VERSE 3]
Is there such thing as a suburban ghetto
An emotional ghetto
Laid to waste inside space
Inner space getting a taste
Of a heavy depressive mind state
I watch other people's windshield wipers
So I know it's not just raining on me
Wouldn't you see what it is I see
Spinning flight free
Wanting to be free of disease,
Wounds, pestilence, and fleas
These breaths cease
When we're brought to peace
They said I was a misogynist
But listen to me twist this
Only something I love
Could make me hurt this much

The women I love

Only exist as digital images
Hidden agendas laced in marriages
Loving Miranda July and Pink
I begin to sink and take a drink
My lungs fill up with poison
This is how I've chosen to cope
Inside dope there's little hope
Except maybe to choke out your soul
Till it's spacious, riddled with holes
The soles of my feet have lost all feeling
I need to break through this ceiling
Chicago to Providence to Boston
All love to you
Ill Will, Chris, Brittney Blue, Dizzy,
JuJu, Turtle, DubK, Twizz,
Documentaries of the Dead,
All my people, man
You know who you are
And especially Marlene
Who's stuck by me since my
Blindbastardsamurai days
Fuckin' love you
Don't you people remember that:
When you're Strange,
No one remembers your name

[CHORUS/BRITTNEY BLUE]
I keep on running
But the struggle keeps on following me
I keep on running

But temptation keeps on following me
It's all
Oh, it's all on me
I keep on running
But the pain keeps on following me
I try my hardest to give the world
What they expect from me
It's all on me
Emotional Ghetto

Bloodstained Treehouse

[INTRO]
Yo, listen while I'm whispering
I want to relay to you my story
The details may be gory
But I won't pretend
And I don't intend
For this story to live in glory

[VERSE 1]
I was seven searching for heaven
Didn't know that I was destined
For an emotional prison
A death sentence
Lived out in a visceral sense
Hence, I hung out with an older boy
Who seemed to think I was his toy
After which my childhood joy was destroyed
His ploy was to say it was a game
Lame

Bet he felt no shame
All the same
We're out back in my treehouse
No sign of my father's spouse
He said, "come here let's spin the bottle"
I wasn't aware my play area said *brothel*

Truth or Dare becoming harmful
So I groveled muttering
He whispered, "I dare you to put it in your mouth"
So I did it without a sound
Even though the events seemed to confound me
When he pound me he unwound me
While he was inside me,
I caught the rejection infection

[CHORUS]
The bloodstained treehouse is eternal
Inside the pages of my journal
This journey, cerebral
If I back away they call it feeble

[VERSE 2]
At that age a sexual cage produces rage
I passed away, far away
But in my brain I'm lifted
Shifted, shape-shifted, gifted
Blessed, cursed
At first I burst
Thinking my thirst was forever

No, never
So I chose to flip the lever
And thought my endeavor was clever
But I couldn't shake the pain whatsoever
Then the chains came
Whispering: *you're just the same*
And when you go looking for the fame
All you'll get is flames, no acclaim
So I intended to defame that claim
When I became Nilotic
My spirit shakin' from
Neurotic chaotic hypnotic erotic narcotics
But my soul will never become robotic

[CHORUS]
The bloodstained treehouse is eternal
Inside the pages of my journal
This journey, cerebral
If I back away they call it feeble

[VERSE 3]
It was never a choice to be queer
I let the violence sear a feminine tear
But had it dissolve away all fear
Not feeble-minded, I've been blinded
Not once, twice, no
Seven times seven
10241989
Let me listen to the words of Tech N9ne

He lets me find the signs
Of these Apocalyptic times
Inside these rhymes I laced some hope
To cut your ropes
But why would you trust someone
With a serpentine spine
Listen to this line
Redefine divine
It's a lie to say:
It's better to be used than useless
But we find ourselves stuck
Unless we address
What causes our distress
To progress and not regress
But never choose to suppress
Healing comes from within
And coming to terms with where we've been
Even though I've wrested and been tested
I want you to know I never molested
And never will

Ill Will and Nilotic

Keep It Real

[NILOTIC]
They say I'm pornographic
No toning down, I keep it frantic
With Satanic imagery laced
Encased in a delivery rapid-paced
My genre was designated horror
With emotions leaving me poorer
So I couldn't make my core
Romantic Comedy
Cause that would be a fallacy
Sometimes I'm left loveless
But never cut-less
Success is a process
So I feel free to confess
If I gave you what you want
It would be the wrong font
Seems cats just wanna flaunt
Superfluous bling-bling
The way we sing-sing should be enough
You rough ching-ching king with tell-tale rings
It's obvious you're a slave to the game

And would sell your soul for fame
Letting record labels create you in their image
A facade worshipped like a god
My living made me hard
You played the right card
I design my own with a home-grown tone

[CHORUS]
Keep it real, motherfucker
Keep it real, keep it real

[NILOTIC]
She called me talentless
I don't think it was in jest
She built a nest made of incest
My body's a wound festering
Pestering, molesting ears
With tears seeping through violin strings
I don't talk about the pain
Just to complain
I never feign in songs
So why you telling me I'm wrong
You never removed that bitch's thong
Come on,
Your persona is everything you'll never be
I'm just doing me
Immortal Technique forced me to see
Now I'm spiritually and revolutionarily free
But maybe I should lynch myself
For using the word nigga

But I ain't no wigga
Check it
Yo, Lil B is queer
That is why she's here
I'll leave her lipstick smeared
Lil B, short for Little Bitch
I'll violate that bitch
And leave her asshole needin' stitches
You wanna rap about riches
And how you fuck bitches
Tell 'em how your dick twitches
When you see Lil Wayne
Then in your pants you came

[CHORUS]
Keep it real, motherfucker
Keep it real, keep it real

[ILL WILL]
Keep it real, yep
Where is the mindset
Of this new generation going
Worshipping the media
And not even knowing
Of the secrets, the lies
The unfairness and closet homo guys
We need to bring back the meaning
Of keep it real
Cause some of my former friends
Told me that, but they don't know the deal

Tryin' to be someone you're not
Get's you fucked over
Luck won't save you
I'm ripping apart your four-leaf clover
It seems like fake is the new in thing
Autotune for those who really can't sing
Aren't you sick of rappers
Wearing plastic bling-bling
Wearing a crown
In his own mind thinks he's king
Sittin' there thinkin' you're the fuckin' boss
You ain't nothing but bitch-ass Rick Ross

[OUTRO]
Nilotic: Yeah, that's what's up, keep it real
Ill Will: Always
Nilotic: Keep it literate
Ill Will: Yes
Nilotic: Yo, man
Ill Will: What up?
Nilotic: Lil B ain't controversial, he's just fucking retarded
Ill Will: Yeah right, fucked in the head
Nilotic: He doesn't deserve a whole diss track, only three fuckin' bars
Ill Will: If that!
Nilotic: I'm out
Ill Will: A'ight, let's go

Finding the Audience

[DOCUMENTARIES OF THE DEAD]
Yeah, making that Worcester-Providence connection
Yo
A ransom plan with a twisted list of demands
A strand you planned to can
But it just didn't pan
Or it didn't stand
How can I reach out to outcasts
Who just give a damn
Nope, no other listed inscription in hand
Just a simple list of demands
That you respect who I am
In this prophetic rhyme scheme
That leaves me gifted and damned
Truth is ubiquitous
I'm bidden forbidden inquisitive images
Of kids hitting this
Listeners get exquisite
Infinite fit limitless hits
Killin' unwillingness
Feeling this bliss

Until it exists
This villain is chillin'
Spillin' in the abyss
So put up a fist
Respect existence or expect resistance
I refrain to abstain from political interest
Stackin' poker chips at the card game
Misdirecting children's futures in our name
Can someone please direct me to our shame
It's nonexistent
Shame…

[CHORUS]
Spherical lyrical prose
Sunk but exposed
Cry-oh-Genically frozen
Brain chokin', binaural doses
Ferocious
Exploding with an ocean of focus
Suppose it's
Two spoken word poets
Get another fix just for kicks
Hit 146, roll out
From Worcester headed south to Providence

[NILOTIC]
Where the fuck is my band
Does my silly joker hand stand
Produce contraband
That your mind could never withstand

Do the Juggalo show so you know
Where you're categorized in flow
Let it snow
My spirit is frozen
Why the fuck was I chosen
The water won't touch me
But I live in the ocean
Trying to disperse my potion
This lyrical assassination explosion
Rollin', where are the fans
Bam bam
Where are my fans
Slam dance
I catch a glance
From an audience of millions
How come no one else got these feelings

[CHORUS]
Spherical lyrical prose
Sunk but exposed
Cry-oh-Genically frozen
Brain chokin', binaural doses
Ferocious
Exploding with an ocean of focus
Suppose it's
Two spoken word poets
Get another fix just for kicks
Hit 146, roll out
From Worcester headed south to Providence

[NILOTIC]
It's hard sometimes finding your audience
Kicking and binding your confidence
I was told everyone has a thousand true fans
But I feel empty, alone in blue hands

[DOCUMENTARIES OF THE DEAD]
Yo, Nilotic
Let me give you a hand
It's true when I tell you I'm giving a damn
People mixin' twistin' facts
Warping, contorting in traps
Until you're only left with the scraps

[NILOTIC]
Combat back like rats
Documentaries of the Dead
Bringing verbal rat-a-tat tats
We build armies from dust
And make industries feel our thrust

[DOCUMENTARIES OF THE DEAD]
We've got every variety of hallucinogen
On tap
Welcome to our weary world of wisdom
Where we speak of our freedom
And we do it through rap

[NILOTIC]
Yeah, that's right

We gotta keep speakin'
Even if they try to silence us
Buck back

Ill Will, Tocxina, and Nilotic on "Life in Your 20's" radio show

Steal Your Fans

[INTRO]
I made a breakfast portrait
To keep the haters out
Unaware of who all is in my orbit
But if any express doubt
I don't need anyone cause I know
I'm a seed ready to sprout

[VERSE 1]
Drove straight from Chicago to Pawtucket
The bucket
To chill with Storm Davis
He took me in when others did dismiss
And listened to my story
In all its pain and glory
A true momento mori
Toppling into a hook
Written into a book
The way my body shook
When my passiveness got took

Look, I am far from perfect
So why point out every defect
Or feel you must dissect
Or subject me to disrespect
I've very direct on tracks
Is that why they turn their backs
That's why they turn their backs

[CHORUS]
Open mics with hidden agendas monetary
Blocking every real emcee
I'll steal your fans
And if I'm getting banned
They're coming with me

[VERSE 2]
Playing demo tracks into the Storm
Respecting the fact I didn't conform
And continued to perform
But regrettably had to inform:
Yeah, you got good flow, you know
But I don't know what to do with it
I don't want to take my work
And just sit on it
When will it be okay
To be a fan of Nilotic
When I rap about homosexuals,
Coke, and child molesters
And speak against corporations,

Colleges, and investors
I'm just testin' the waters
Cursed by the sins of our fathers
And discovering God's armor
Is only made of foil
When we spill our guts like BP oil
I rock the crowd even if no one's in it
Who heard it
They take my words and spin it
When you hit it I spit it
Finished
Dragging this world
Closer to Finality
When commonality
Is that there's no loyalty
Our mentality is sexuality
And widespread brutality is proof of no morality

[CHORUS]
Open mics with hidden agendas monetary
Blocking every real emcee
I'll steal your fans
And if I'm getting banned
They're coming with me

[VERSE 3]
You think you got a tribe
When it's only three people
It's all right, you tried
Didn't mean to kill your pride

But I can't be on your side
When you were never on mine
Don't take it out on me
When it's you who fail to shine
Guess you couldn't see I set you free
So where's your LP?
Okay, I know why you didn't feel me
The third degree made you an amputee
I knew you were missing something
That's why you couldn't sing
Sometimes you gotta be your own fan
When they trip you every time you stand
You're subjected to a horrific Wonderland
I created in Distania
I'm coming to your area
Bringing vicious malaria
If you're sick, I'll carry ya
But if you want me dead
I imbed dread where you bled
Cause Apocalyptic Rhymes is becoming widespread
I fed y'all nutrients
Now choose to follow my ascent

[CHORUS]
Open mics with hidden agendas monetary
Blocking every real emcee
I'll steal your fans
And if I'm getting banned
They're coming with me

Wigger

[VERSE 1]
This is a story of a dude
By the name of K9
With a bit of new kid luck
He became a friend of mine
He then pulled me into his little crowd
We were cast out, but yeah we were loud
Life for us was no silver-lined cloud
I remain proud of everything I was
The jaws of the beast encircled my laws
And I began living the way a youth sometimes does
Even among the outcasts we try to fit in
A'ight, herein we begin
K9's mortal sin was that he felt that his skin
Didn't match what was within
He was born to be a gangster, a hardcore thug
We'd peep a tight beat while puffin' a green drug
I found myself rockin' South Pole, Ecko, FUBU
Introduced to Tupac, Three Six, and some of the Wu
True, I mighta looked the type
I was ignorant back then

To what mainstream rappers wrote
Was just overhyped tripe
But hey, I took another hit from the pipe
And decided to play half the stereotype

[CHORUS]
All he ever wanted was to be considered a nigga
But because of his color he was just another wigga
Who couldn't pull a trigger or even exhibit any vigor
So he was known as just another fucking wigga

[VERSE 2]
But the story doesn't end there
When I decided to grow out my hair
And make people stop and stare
The way he treated me
Was less than fucking fair
I love Hip Hop
But I also have loyalties elsewhere
Boy George is my faggot
And I gotta say this
Kanye West is just a fucking maggot
I'll never retract it, in fact it
Was already falling to dust
Our friendship that is
Covered in a coating of platinum rust
We must be real so I kept it all too real
And K9 couldn't handle my zeal
But maybe his hard persona
Was meant to seal and conceal

Some dark secret he wasn't willing to reveal
But just know when you come out from the inside
I'll be there to hug you
Cause when you hide
You create a Jekyll and Hyde
Within the confines of self
And leave everything you are hidden behind a shelf
Life dealt us both harsh blows
I know this very well
We got scars and it shows
Emotional infantry that fell
And he said to me:
How can you be raw when you wear a fucking bra?
I turned and replied:
How can you be a thug when you're born a bourgeois?
Nothing was said, nothing was spoken
And our silence still remains unbroken

[CHORUS]
All he ever wanted was to be considered a nigga
But because of his color he was just another wigga
Who couldn't pull a trigger or even exhibit any vigor
So he was known as just another fucking wigga

[VERSE 3]
After he called me a faggot
We went our separate ways
All us friends were together
On the last few days

Come what may, I moved miles away
I still rap cause I do have something to say
But I'm not here to sway you one way or another
I just give it to you straight
No pun, just tuck it under
No wonder, I'm just a queer emcee
Who would never snitch or squeal
Now check it, that's fucking real
What do you get when you peel
Back every layer
Just a frightened soul posing as a player
Writing little battle raps
Thinking he's a Rhymesayer
But no matter how loud he screamed a prayer
I'd never hear him on my record player
No matter how loud he screamed a prayer
I'd never hear him on my record player
Fruity Loops beats and hook line repeats
Lacking substance they say is in the streets
I know that you're scared in-between the sheets
Cause you feel your skin makes you obsolete

No matter how loud he screamed a prayer
I'd never hear him on my record player

Like Water

[CHORUS]
G-Tek, Nilotic
Stay straight-up psychotics
The day we die
Is when we run out of topics
Money-loving people-hating rappers
Need to stop it
Educate your mind state
Speakin' like we're prophets

[G-TEK]
I jump up in a cypher
Like a samurai who's killin'
See your next move
With my Nostradamus visions
Mind state causes verbal cataclysms
Fix yo wack flow, call me lyrical technician
My war strategy got me crowned the best tactician
Spit a kamikaze and my missiles never missin'
The bulletproof monk
Weed stinking like a skunk

I got too much funk for all y'all punks
Wield the mic-sword like Super Saiyan Trunks
Yeah

[CHORUS]
G-Tek, Nilotic
Stay straight-up psychotics
The day we die
Is when we run out of topics
Money-loving people-hating rappers
Need to stop it
Educate your mind state
Speakin' like we're prophets

[G-TEK]
Straight up, yo
Them radio cats are wack
Components of a real emcee is what they lack
While we spit intelligence and we spittin' facts
They spit irrelevance and they spittin' crap
Listen to the track
When I express I'm consciously aware
That my culture needs repair
Fuck a puppet of the industry
Their brains ain't even there
Rappers flauntin' riches without a thought or care
The fact that children wanna follow
Just ain't really fair
I spit for the underclass and the minority
Who fight against certain fraternities

AKA devils
Who have evil thoughts of superiority
USA stands for Under Satan's Authority

[CHORUS]
G-Tek, Nilotic
Stay straight-up psychotics
The day we die
Is when we run out of topics
Money-loving people-hating rappers
Need to stop it
Educate your mind state
Speakin' like we're prophets

[G-TEK]
Verbally slaughter
Don't even bother
My lyrics are harder
My rhetoric is hotter
Than your average commercial
Rappin' ballers sellin' their souls for dollars
While I'm spittin' that culture
Givin' back the basis of life like water

[NILOTIC]
I see clear and present danger in my sight
With justified anger building to a fight
Now I refuse to back down
Or silence my abrasive sounds
I stand by these words

Don't act like you haven't heard
Fuck radio-friendly, kid-friendly, trendy Pop dolls
I'm answering the calls
Of he who spins above time
And decides to code worldviews into rhyme
If you think I'm fake
You probably never been awake
Do you think many MTV hits write their own lyrics
Let me hear it
I only hear shit here
So disappear into fear before you ever see her
Tear her soul into seven pieces
Where ghost-written bars only amount to feces
Please cease
I'm not one to judge how you get release
But kids eat from your hands like geese
All I want is peace of mind
In a world where our eyes don't keep us blind
So send me to space
What if it's all a waste

[NILOTIC]
Verbally slaughter
Don't even bother
My lyrics are harder
My rhetoric is hotter
Than your average commercial
Rappin' ballers sellin' their souls for dollars
While I'm spittin' that culture
Givin' back the basis of life like water

[CHORUS]
G-Tek, Nilotic
Stay straight-up psychotics
The day we die
Is when we run out of topics
Money-loving people-hating rappers
Need to stop it
Educate your mind state
Speakin' like we're prophets

Beauty/Sexy

[INTRO]
Yo, check it out
How does it feel to be one of the sexy people?

[CHORUS]
Beauty/sexy
This is how we see

[VERSE 1]
Everyone's a unique freak
Who seeks to be chic
But everything seems bleak
When my physique becomes oblique
In school my friends complimented me by saying:
You're ugly like a duckling
Chuckling, but inside I was buckling
As if to say keep suckling
On your momma's tit
Is it a friend if they're constantly giving me shit
I wish I could hit him in a fit

Then we'll see who's beautiful
But I realized that talk was juvenile
Just the usual casual banter
Discussing who was a pretty enchanter
But can't her imperfections
Be my predilection
No need for correction
Cause your birthmark gives me an erection
Perfection's nonexistent
And to the extent we prevent
Happiness by bodily malcontent
Insisting women need a supplement
There's no fucking need to augment
Images are altered
Cause we're forced to feel awkward

[CHORUS]
Beauty/sexy
This is how we see

[VERSE 2]
All I ever wanted
Was to be pretty like a kitty
Instead I was gritty like a dirty city
What a pity
Never allowed to be glamorous
Cause I have a penis
But my dream is ceaseless
And I've become priceless
An artifact, but if my lips are cracked

Would you kiss me
If my bra is packed
Would you diss me
If I was made to attract and not subtract
Would you miss me
Kiss me
This is our flawed lips
Thrusting broken hips
Ugliness and beauty then eclipse
Flaw and perfection are one
Complete person, there are none
Plastic alterations come undone
Leaving models in a state of stun

[CHORUS]
Beauty/sexy
This is how we see

[VERSE 3]
That's right, I like tiny tits
But no guy I know commits
Him and her eventually split
My generation is shallow
Babied forever and callow
Thinking looks make a man
Or looks make a woman
What a sham
This seems to be a scam
Am I insufficient cause I don't have chiseled abs
I'm scarred cause I peeled off all my scabs

I told you don't be surprised when you catch crabs
Everyone thinks they fab
Hop on the latest fad
Who says the way you're clad makes you hot
You caught lies in your brain
If you're beautiful you gain the fame
But if we all look the same
Everything within this frame would be lame

To You Bitch

[CHORUS]
This is what I wanna do
To you bitch

[VERSE 1]
Slit a quick ligament
No time for your soul to repent
Here comes the serpent
Dispel spells
Blue ribbons won in frozen hells
Violet Perfect left me ragged
Naked jagged baggage
Wish I could tear your heart into fascist fragments
Damaged battlements
Stone hearts immortalized in cement
Hate-Love lifestyle Heartbeat Miles behind
Maybe if I show you I can shine
Then I could call you mine
Now I wish you died and drowned in wine
But you're destined and designed by me
I gave you your name and set you free

[CHORUS]
This is what I wanna do
To you bitch

[VERSE 2]
Hooks raked
Lakes of blood
Violent love
Shove this gun
Break the sun
I won this war
But cancelled my tour
For reasons I lost
When you win you lose the most
Female fairy ghost
Existing as a demon host
Soul spit roast
Tied to demon lovers
Hidden inside Manson covers
I'm a combination of everyone I fucked
As well as everyone they fucked
But I bucked back
Threw her in the sack
Gotta get my mind back on track
Raped then hacked her up
Love me now so shut the fuck up

[BRIDGE]
Rotting faces in the snow
My glow has been subverted
And left me just perverted
Now I finally know

[VERSE 3]
David Sherry was a fairy
Jacob Steep is scary, Sherry
So faggot David got his throat cut
I shut his fuckin' mouth permanently
Raped his soul mercilessly
Terminally silenced
Now Steep has got a voice
I know it's your choice
To listen or to not
As I left David's body to rot
His last words,
As if from the dead head of a dolly
He said,
Go back to Flashpoint and tell Peter Hawley
To shove that marketing strategy up his ass
Take that marketing strategy
And shove it up your ass
After which David died
And was dealt back into the collective
Now everyone will viscerally
Experience my perspective

[BRIDGE]
Rotting faces in the snow
My glow has been subverted
And left me just perverted
Now I finally know

Portrait of Distania

[VERSE 1]
My name is Cornelius
Come with us if you must
To a land built of lust
This is a Portrait of Distania
Broken Illinois and outlying areas
Where there's rampant hysteria
I live in the Mysanthrium Monastery
No King Arthurs or evil fairies
Just days filled with duties of a monk
Good luck leaving Distania
Without a chunk of your heart cut out
A land in eternal love drought
But this what I'm about
Studies
Reading up on History's Mysteries
Minding my own business
While studying messianic likeness
Until infinite nazis came
To force me in their game
Under the alice/Steep reign

But for me, I just saw pain
In a land of endless orgies
There can't exist families
When everyone is fuckin'
Sexual Communism
Under the Seventh Reich of Jacob Steep
He'll forever be a creep
Cause alice never sleeps

[CHORUS]
Painting Distania
Brushstrokes blood-soaked in pain
When I came they knew my name
Cornelius Trowman

[VERSE 2]
Benevalment strains to hear the beating of my heart
In this art I wish to write
But this fife forced me to speak
To preach
And in turn teach
But who am I to reach
When I'm stalked by a demon
And have talked while I'm dreaming
He wished me to go the way of Adolf Crowley
Fuck that, now I see
That it must be me
To set Distania free
Alice is the King

Have you ever heard her sing
Now the infinite nazis bring
Me to my knees in front of Steep
In the Pink House his secrets keep
Everyone balls deep
Where bodily fluids seep
Through every orifice
When he forces group sex everyday
No matter what I say
He says, 'translate the book, *im with alice*'
After which they sent me away
Plagued by Steep and Benevalment
I fled to the settlements

[CHORUS]
Painting Distania
Brushstrokes blood-soaked in pain
When I came they knew my name
Cornelius Trowman

[VERSE 3]
So I went into hiding
Instead of abiding or cosigning
His sexual dictatorship
Which causes every dick to drip
Or send them on a trip
Through acid, coke, and pleasure tricks
I guess everyone needs a fix
An equal mix of sex, drugs, Hip Hop

And fluids to swap
But I must speak on how his regime needs to stop
I already read that plot
Where everyone gets shot
So watch your Blind Spot
I'm translating *im with alice*
So you aren't ignorant of the malice
Or how he wishes to drink your blood from a chalice
In a land all sex and no love
Every dove is dead
And I've heard it said
He's building a great iron eagle
To show everyone that he's regal
He'll let it hover in the sky
Till everything is dry
With a glass orb under the feet
A Machine of self-deceit
To simulate a state of love
When we feel nothing is above
Sex except a mess of stress
Where there's no comfort for distress
Our comfort comes from a Machine
It was foreseen we all demean
Under an unclean king and queen
Until Steep is deceased
I'll forever be a Priest

And I'm forced to say this
Cornelius doesn't fuck

But Nilotic says you all should suck his dick

[OUTRO]
Painting Distania
Brushstrokes blood-soaked in pain
When I came they knew my name
Priest Crow

Priest Crow
That's me
Also known as Cornelius Trowman
If you ever see me with my wizard hat
And my olive-colored robes
Come talk to me
I have things to teach

Ambivalent Narcissism

[VERSE 1]
I kill myself over and over
With a body made of clover
To rearrange into strange
Patterns of indecipherable change
But I change lanes to remain
Relatively sane
The ability to regain your own fame
Is a concept to embrace without shame
They'll crucify you with words
But remember to send them back
So their perception is blurred
And their emotion is stirred
Audiences hate to get called out
So they pout and spout off at the mouth
Throughout their doubt I find alternate routes
To stir up a bout
The joke's on you
Cause I can see right through
The reason I can make you feel

Is because what I speak is real
It's real

[CHORUS]
I'm in love with the pull
The violence to myself
You refuse to pay in full
Getting off on the nature of self

[VERSE 2]
I jerk off to the mirror
Making you fear her
Zero, make it clearer
If I say I'm God,
Does that mean that it's me that I worship
That's horse-shit, you make me distorted
Since you never supported
And made it clear you couldn't afford it
Contort slits in hits of cohorts
This is what I hear: *abort, abort, abort*
Mission, I went fishin'
And reeled in another side of me
Then killed David to set Steep free
Now do you fucking see
I could be your salvation
I could be your destruction

I could be your salvation
I could be your destruction

Creation
Destruction

[OUTRO]
Mom, they're pushing me
To the negative side of seven

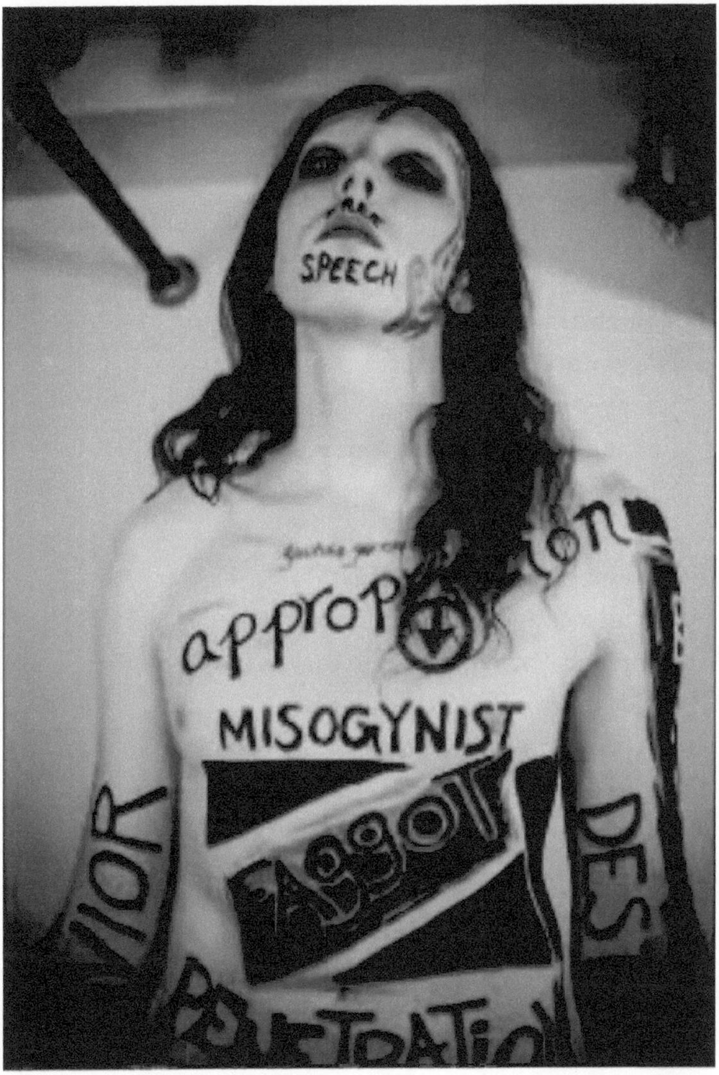
SPEECH
approp
MISOGYNIST
FAGGOT
VIOR
DES

Negative Seven

[VERSE 1]
You turned me into a demon
No, you are not dreamin'
It's my semen flowing through your mind
Forcing you to find that you're already blind
Signed, Negative Seven

It was insisted I be blacklisted
Dismissed cause I'm twisted
Seemingly you don't wish to coexist
Inside my mist but in the midst
Of this storm emerges Seven
Inside a personal heaven
I persist and subsist
Leaving your brain to contain
A hemorrhagic cyst
I'm building an army, come and enlist
We never cease and desist
We confuse you, consume you
Never abuse you
But I let your bruise ooze

Cause you sparked my fuse
And if you make it competitive,
You're guaranteed to lose
If you're gonna accuse me, excuse me
Make sure you can diffuse me
Look down, do the shoes fit
You choose it, now infuse it

[CHORUS]
When you invoke the wrath of heaven
You get an angel fallen demon
Calling forth the negative side of seven
So realize you're very far from Eden

[VERSE 2]
What is it you fear
Is it him, is it her, is it me?
You pretend to disagree with what I see
When it's your life that's becoming a Dead Sea
I told you once, I'll tell you again
I'm never fakin', body shakin', heart breakin'
Save me
When I gave you light, you didn't deserve it
When I give you my words, you pervert it
Seven, seven, seven
Pushed to the negative side of seven
A peaceful lifepath seven,
If pushed will turn on heaven
Becoming sporadic, Satanic,
Manic making you panic

Frantic fleeing from my
Gigantic volcanic anti-Tantric
Archaic photovoltaic mosaic
Seven, seven, seven
Negative
10241989
When I was born, walls were falling
Calling forth an appalling crawling sprawling
Half-aborted fetus naming every weakness
With an afterbirth-covered fist
If you get me pissed,
I won't hesitate to be violent
When I'm made to feel like my only right
Is to be silent

[CHORUS]
When you invoke the wrath of heaven
You get an angel fallen demon
Calling forth the negative side of seven
So realize you're very far from Eden

[VERSE 3]
In a past-life my father was a hitman
We began by measuring my wingspan
Seven feet tip to tip
This is why I can outstrip
Anyone giving me shit
You say appropriation, I say miscommunication
Through creation in the direction
Of misinterpretation

Feeling sensations through your misconception
Feeling like I'm being punished for giving credit
To my inspirations
If you can't acknowledge my authenticity
Then maybe you're the one who's phony
The Negative Seven protects me
From this world that only I see
Poking the balance between just provoking
And being thought-provoking
Boasting the way I ghost hosts
I've learned to keep you all engrossed
In general I'm the most
Now let's toast to this:
I have a policy about honesty
Money is not my priority
When I have truth spitting out of me
But I said, I cashed out on all my sins
And am left with just a rash
Now I don't want the rash, give me cash
Flash, dash past
I've already lapped you seven times seven fast
When I scripted an epic suicide-pact
Between Steep and God
And I planned a murder-suicide
For just me and you, decide
I'm not here to destroy Hip Hop
I'm here to destroy the world
Our culture just went pop
Our culture just went pop
Pop Culture

[CHORUS]
When you invoke the wrath of heaven
You get an angel fallen demon
Calling forth the negative side of seven
So realize you're very far from Eden

Pornographic Childhood (2011)

This album was released under the name Spindle Trap.

1. Dear Listener
2. Born with an Erection
3. Seven Years Young
4. Penetration
5. Family Ties
6. Not Allowed
7. Your Little Girl
8. Run Lolita Run
9. Let the Past Be Past
10. Was It Really Rape? (skit)
11. Child Be Still

Dear Listener

Dear Listener,

Before we get into *Pornographic Childhood* there are a few things I need to get off my chest. The issue of child abuse and child sexuality has been explored extensively in books and in film. Movie titles such as *Mysterious Skin, Me and You and Everyone We Know, Running with Scissors, Black Snake Moan, The Heart is Deceitful Above All Things, Little Children, Hard Candy, Lolita*, Jack Ketchum's *The Girl Next Door, American Beauty, Towelhead, Hounddog, Monster,* and *Happiness*; to name some of my favorites. That being said, it's an issue that hasn't been explored much musically. The only album that comes to mind with similar themes is Marilyn Manson's *Portrait of an American Family*. This album you are listening to is my experimental way of exploring and dealing with events that happened to me in the past, as well as addressing similar issues; emotional abuse, neglect, incest, and so forth. My intention was not to make a morbid, hopeless album. I feel this is important to know before you listen to the songs. I speak on these issues so that people who have experienced similar abuse in their lives know they are not alone in what they've been through. And also to educate others who may not be aware that these type of issues are more common than they think. I hope with all my heart that this album will find its way into the hands of those children stuck inside adult bodies as well as ones who have already started their healing process. And I hope you all can gain something positive from what I've created. There is hope for growth and hope for healing. Spindle Trap is the Nilotic with Ill Will on the beats. I am the Nilotic. Spreading love while exorcising demons. One.

Born with an Erection

I was born with an erection
Detection of something similar to seduction
As I spilled from my mother's pussy
They naturally wanted to touch it
Caress it like a tender young lover
Then lay me on the floor and suck it
Fuck it
Being born with an erection
Determines the election
Of sexual molestation void of affection
I was born with an erection
So naturally my mother felt the sensation
In the destination of the nether regions
But neither one resulting in castration
So technically I was born being molested
I was born with an erection
Are you tired of my repetition
So then tell me, what do you know about rape?
Have you been taped by your brother
And touched by your father?
Don't even bother

I'll smother your rectum with my mouth
There's no remedy for the mind going south
Can you relate to Nabokov's *Lolita*
In more ways than one?
Are you the son of a crack whore
Who's always on the run?
I'll give you a gun
But put faith in the sun
Don't say you're done
I'm spinning, I'm spun
Life can be fun so put down the gun
And say life's begun
Nothing's undone
And you can outrun the cum

Seven Years Young

[VERSE 1]
Step inside
Step inside
Step inside
The bloodstained treehouse
In my mind
Fill me from behind
The crime
The crime
The crime
This is the way I am (way I am)
This is the way I am (the way I am)
Take me the way I am (way I am)

[CHORUS]
Seven years is way too young
You don't know
You don't know
You don't know

[VERSE 2]
Take me now
Oh baby I know ya
He was me
Oh baby I know ya
I know you
Come see what they did to me
Come look
Oh, come on
He was in me (inside)
I'm in me (I am)
Seven years, innocent
Seven years, corrupted
(Innocence, corruption)
Then I became him
Walking the line interrupted

[CHORUS]
Seven years is way too young
You don't know
You don't know
You don't know

[VERSE 3]
Too much wood
Does me no good
Sanitize the perception of rape
Rationalize the interpretation of escape
Escape into me
Escape into me

Escape through my eyes
And leave behind the lies
Cause I know from looking back
Houses end up painted black, black, black
Leave me to bleed
Leave me to bleed
Leave me to need

[CHORUS]
Seven years is way too young
You don't know
You don't know
You don't know

[OUTRO]
Seven years I know so well

Penetration

[VERSE 1]
I laid there on your bed
Getting lost in the ceiling
Do we wish to wed
Desperately grasping for a feeling
Just some meaning
In the spirals, colors of penetration
This sensation
This unknown
Is this what's expected of me
Can't you see
The little boy in the mirror
No match for your terror
I'm inferior
You found me on the floor
Was the boy in the carpet always your score
Ask me for more
Far worse than a simple house chore

[CHORUS]
You don't have to

Let him break you
You don't have to
Let him shake you
Don't let him break you
Don't let him shake you

[VERSE 2]
Father?
I'm snuggled under your covers
With my teddy
Please cuddle with me, Daddy
I'm craving your attention
Look at me
Look at me
Look at me
Daddy, I want you to fuck me
Just fucking look at me
Don't let him break you
Don't let him shake you
Don't let him break you
Don't let him shake you
The sensations of penetration
The sensations of penetration

Family Ties

[VERSE 1]
My mother said she was sorry
For not protecting me
My father never said a word
But kept on rejecting me
Home was never a shelter from the storm
Corruption becomes the norm
As I'm being born
My mind is being torn
At birth they poisoned me
At birth they poisoned me
Poisoned my mind
I'm going blind
Show me the way
Please make it one day
We love lost
We've lost love

[CHORUS]
He said he didn't know
He was hurting me

Cause there was incest in the family
Forgive me, he said
I'm healing
This hot wax is never sealing
Searing my heart with bloodstained lies
Should I decide to break these family ties

[VERSE 2]
But can we cut these ties
Leaving the lies behind to die
In the ashes of my family urn
I've frozen to death inside
But now it's your turn
I'm crawling back to hell
My only truly home
I'm crawling back to hell
Where I belong
Heart, soul, and bone
Give me just one kiss goodnight
Tell me at least I did one thing right
There's gonna be a fight
There's gonna be a fight
Who's gonna leave
Mommy or Daddy tonight
Home is where the reaper lives
Home is where the reaper lives
Home is where my temper gives

[CHORUS]
He said he didn't know

He was hurting me
Cause there was incest in the family
Forgive me, he said
I'm healing
This hot wax is never sealing
Searing my heart with bloodstained lies
Should I decide to break these family ties

[VERSE 3]
I'm crawling back to hell
My only truly home
I'm crawling back to hell
Where I belong
Heart, soul, and bone
Home is where the reaper lives
Home is where the reaper lives
Home is where my temper gives
There's gonna be a fight
Who's gonna leave
Mommy or Daddy tonight

[CHORUS]
He said he didn't know
He was hurting me
Cause there was incest in the family
Forgive me, he said
I'm healing
This hot wax is never sealing
Searing my heart with bloodstained lies
Should I decide to break these family ties

Not Allowed

[VERSE 1]
I was a child till I was seven
Now my childhood lasts forever
I wanna grow up
I wanna be
A big Rock and Roll star
I wanna grow up
Inside our young years
We denied we had any fears
Tears reserved for Mommy
Tough around our friends
I ain't no pussy
I wanna grow up
I wanna be
So no one fucks with me
Yeah

[CHORUS]
Give me time to play
Not allowed
Shut up, stop squirming around

Gimme my teddies, my dollies
Please stop
Not allowed a childhood
Blood running through
A broken sandbox

[VERSE 2]
Innocence corrupted
Innocence destroyed
A living broken sex toy
No joy for this little boy
Not allowed to have a childhood
How could you
Stroke, pet, prod
After which I created my facade
Stunted, runted, corrupted
Cocoa Puffs laced with broken glass
The weather forecast
Stuck forever in the past

[CHORUS]
Give me time to play
Not allowed
Shut up, stop squirming around
Gimme my teddies, my dollies
Please stop
Not allowed a childhood
Blood running through
A broken sandbox

[VERSE 3]
We split our personalities
Like broken bodies
Uncivil War casualties
A Kindergarten execution
What's my solution
Revolution
One side of me grows up
The wounded puppy in the shadows
He shows up
When I'm dealt harsh blows

[OUTRO]
Give me time to play
Not allowed
Give me time to play
Not allowed
Give me time to play, please
Not allowed

Your Little Girl

[VERSE 1]
I don't want you inside
But your skin is mysterious
I think I just died
I'm here bleeding and furious
Somewhere deep in me
Is a child screaming: *free me*

See me

Somewhere deep in me
Is a child screaming: *free me*

See me

A personalized curse
I was sexualized first
Now come and quench my thirst

[CHORUS]
Call me a little white queer
But yours is not my world
And that is not what you will hear
I can't be your little girl

Can't be your little girl

[VERSE 2]
What's weak
What's meek
What is it you seek
A fragile wounded lamb
Yo, fuck you
And fuck your fucking scam
I won't crumble
Sometimes humble
Sometimes not
But you still left me out to rot

[CHORUS]
Call me a little white queer
But yours is not my world
And that is not what you will hear
I can't be your little girl
Can't be your little girl

[VERSE 3]
Masculine
Feminine
Who created this distinction
This is prediction of extinction
I'm skirted, you flirted
But ran when you saw I was inverted
Masculine
Feminine

Who created this distinction
Child-like
Adult
Do I have to fit in one
Don't tell me what I am
It's just a jagged insult
So don't tell me what I am
That's just a jagged insult
You're a jagged insult

"Everything I write is so shallow, superficial. Can't anyone see through my work? Its inherent phoniness; rape at eleven, rape at twelve. What the hell do I know about rape? I've never been raped. I'm just another sordid exploitationist. If only I'd been raped a child, then I would know authenticity. Instead—uhhhhh! I'm no good. No good. Nothing. Zero."

- Todd Solondz, *Happiness*

Run Lolita Run

[INTRO]
There's worse things to take from a child
Than candy
Virginity

[CHORUS]
So run Lolita run
Run Lolita run
Run Lolita run

[VERSE 1]
Scrape the wounded child off the ground
Protect, don't neglect
Parentally soothe those whimpering sounds
You're the target, retreat
You're the target to mistreat
See that van?
Inside's complete deceit

[CHORUS]
So run Lolita run

Run Lolita run
Run Lolita run

[VERSE 2]
Escape his phallic gun
Your mother cannot save you
Fingers slipping around your wrist
Your mother cannot save you
This won't hurt a bit
He insists, resist

I'm one world too late
He perpetrates then penetrates
I'm one world too late
This doesn't have to be your fate
I'm one world too late
I know the hate but never desecrate
I'm one world too late
One world too late

[CHORUS]
So run Lolita run
Run Lolita run
Run Lolita run

Escape his phallic gun

Let the Past Be Past

Nilotic. 11:40 PM; Saturday, December 3rd, 2011.

Many infinities later I'm still grasping. It's sort of ironic that it's taken me this long to write this. I've been detoxing, to borrow a term some will understand. To borrow my own line: *At that age a sexual cage produces rage.* The way we interact with and perceive the world around us as adults has already been decided by events which happened before the age of puberty. Let's go back in time, if you would for a minute, into the past. Into *your* past. A childhood that was compromised way too early. Compromised by rejection, incest, molestation, emotional abuse, and physical abuse. After that moment our development has immediately been arrested; sometimes producing uncontrollable rage. Maybe the Hulk was molested as a kid, you never know. This traumatized child will feel flawed, defective, dirty, damaged, and different. *It's my fault.* Stuck, unable to grow up. Peter Pan complex. Alice complex. We didn't realize that the trauma had locked us into survival mode; which would be our norm as we push through adolescence into adulthood. But remember this, son, from now on you will be responsible for the consequences of your behavior and your decisions. But the concept of responsibility was lost on a generation of babies. Signs surfaced in the teen years of wounds dealt to us in our childhoods. Isolation and mood swings, ADD, anger, aggression, blame, denial, and poor memory. Does our desire for revenge carry into adulthood?

Imagine, if you would, a wounded child growing into his teen years, searching for an identity. As the matter in our brains begins to solidify, we begin to believe the lies and distorted perception of ourselves. We are already living in arrested development. The outside world sees our bodies grow up, but our inner identities are still struggling; still hurt children. Identity. I said *Identity Equals Propaganda*. So we created alter-egos, personalities to compensate our inner children that never made it past puberty. But it still wishes to fuck, and be fucked. Peter Pan men in deceptively grown bodies trying to cope in an adult Wonderland. Like Macaulay Culkin, I guess.

But I digress. High off this blunt. Zoned to this beat. Trying to leave the past in the past. But Part Seven is entitled: *Man-Children and the Women Who Love Them*.

Little Red Riding Hood is bleeding.

If a child is abused sexually, then their value as a sex object is set up from the get-go. *Can you see the pattern of my cuts? How come Billy eats so much and got fat? How come my friend*

Suzie throws up in the bathroom after lunch at school? **Because you're alone**.

But you're not. Listen. Just listen to my words. I know it goes on and on, but I do have something to say within all the chaos. We're all together in our childish ways. But I say this now: seek to be child*like*, not child*ish*. But you need to know now before we go any farther, it wasn't your fault. Say it with me now.

It wasn't my fault. So let's grow. Let's grow.

You can listen to a song twenty times without anything sinking into your hearts. So ***sin, suffer, repeat***. Unable to break the cycle: *abuse, hatred, despair, self-loathing, immaturity, irresponsibility, emotional isolation, manipulation, anger, and the* **inability to maintain relationships**. The unresolved traumas from our childhood come bubbling back up as destructive adult behavior. Body, mind, and soul ravaged by loneliness, distrust, confusion, hopelessness, and suffering. This is evidence of damage that lingers; as if some of us have *come fuck me over* written on our foreheads. Huh? You know what I mean? Like there's a big stamp on my forehead that says *come fuck me over*. Ill Will, you know what I mean? You know what I'm sayin'?

(*sigh*)

Observe this grownup child right now, which is me. Creating personalities to deal with trauma, and in an embarrassingly obvious identity crisis. Jacob chooses the one of the **Suffering Hero**. *Victim.*

But I'm rambling and ranting. Where is this going? **Choose change.** Know this: **you are not responsible for the wound, but you are responsible for the behavior that you exhibit because of that wound**. But we can and I am deciding to deal with the past and move forward. **Let the Past Be Past.** We choose to break the cycle of abuse. I've seen and heard some pretty unspeakable things in my time; and that's why *Born This Way* can be a dangerous myth. We can rewire ourselves by renewing the mind.

(*sigh*)

We can rewire ourselves by renewing the mind. Child*like*, not child*ish*. Child*like*, not *child*.

I'm floating somewhere between woundedness and wholeness. But I'm bringing down strongholds built in the past. And just to be ironic, *I could quote any emcee, but why should I?*
- Saul Williams

You can make the future, but it starts with leaving the past.
    - Immortal Technique

Where would we be without our painful childhoods?
   - Augusten Burroughs, *Running with Scissors*

The past catches up to you, wether you like it or not. It can be a gift, or a curse. If you let it.
   - Jack Ketchum's *The Girl Next Door*

Was it Really Rape? (skit)

Do you ever think about having sex with family members?
Sometimes. Why, is that weird?
I would say so.
I guess I'm just like that.
Yeah, but why would you be?
Cause my former self as a child was raped?
Was it really rape?
What do you mean? Of course it was, I was seven.
You know, if you yell 'surprise' it's not technically rape.
Yo, I was seven, I had no idea what he was doing.
I think that's just an excuse. The whole martyr thing again.
Then how come I cry sometimes, shaking uncontrollably?
Put the past in the past. If you can, the pain can't last.
There will always be pain.
As long as you let it. Sometimes tell your inner child to be still.

Narcissistic exploitation...

Child Be Still

(Based on the song "Ave Mary A" by Pink)

[VERSE 1]
Predators never getting caught
Prowl the playground
Cause they just can't stop
There's a screaming child in my head
Public school, I think we got a problem
Where to they take them to when they go
Parents never help, I don't think they know
We fuck too fast and we love too slow
Kids, I think we got a problem

And when I dream about it
Don't want to dream about it
I try to write about it
I keep cryin'

[CHORUS]
Ave Mary A
Where did ya go

Where did ya go
How did ya know
To get out of a world gone mad
Help me let go
Of the chaos around me
The devil that hounds me
I need you to tell me
Child be still
Child be still

[VERSE 2]
Broken hearts in a bloodstained cape
Nothing got solved with a crime-scene tape
Pedophile dad and a child rape
Families, I think we got a problem
But for that they got a pill
But for that they got a pill
If that don't kill you
Then the side-effects will
If we don't kill each other
Then the side-effects will
Park Ridge, I think we got a problem

Medicated, sedated

[CHORUS]
Ave Mary A
Where did ya go
Where did ya go
How did ya know

To get out of a world gone mad
Help me let go
Of the chaos around me
The devil that hounds me
I need you to tell me
Child be still
Child be still

[VERSE 3]
If the darkest hour comes before the light
Where is the light?
Where is the light?
If the darkest hour comes before the light
Where is the light?
Where is the light?
Yeah

[CHORUS]
Ave Mary A
Where did ya go
Where did ya go
How did ya know
To get out of a world gone mad
Help me let go
Of the chaos around me
The devil that hounds me
I need you to tell me
Child be still
Child be still

"And when it was over, when we were getting you dressed, your face looked like you'd been erased. And you were just empty inside. And you just fell face first in the floor. Bam. And when we pulled you up, your nose was bleeding... And as we sat there listening to the carolers, I wanted to tell Brian it was over now and everything would be okay. But that was a lie. Plus, I couldn't speak anyway. I wished there was some way we could go back and undo the past, but there wasn't. There was nothing we could do. So I just stayed silent, trying to telepathically communicate how sorry I was about what had happened. And I thought of all the grief, and sadness, and fucked up suffering in the world; and it made me want to escape. I wished with all my heart that we could just leave this world behind, rise like two angels in the night, and magically disappear."

- *Mysterious Skin*, screenplay by Gregg Araki based on the novel by Scott Heim

The Threshold EP (2011)

1. Introspeculation
2. Suspenseful Pencils
3. Past the Point of Distortion
4. (IV)y
5. Light
6. Dark
7. Threshold

This is the Threshold. On track toward the Apex.

Remember: It's Just a Ride

Introspeculation

(Inhale)
(Exhale)
It's just a ride
This is the Threshold
But on track toward the Apex

In the immortal words of Bill Hicks:

"The world is like a ride at an amusement park, and when you choose to go on it you think it's real because that's how powerful our minds are. The ride goes up and down, and around and around, it has thrills and chills, and it's very brightly colored, and it's very loud, and it's fun for a while. Some people have been on the ride a long time, and they begin to wonder, "Hey, is this real, or is this just a ride?" And other people have remembered, and they come back to us and they say, "Hey, don't worry; don't be afraid, ever, because this is just a ride." And we ... kill those people. "Shut him up! We've got a lot invested in this ride, shut him up! Look at my furrows of worry, look at my big bank account, and my family. This has to be

real." It's just a ride. But we always kill those good guys who try and tell us that, you ever notice that? And let the demons run amok ... But it doesn't matter, because it's just a ride. And we can change it any time we want. It's only a choice. No effort, no worry, no job, no savings and money. Just a simple choice, right now, between fear and love. The eyes of fear want you to put bigger locks on your doors, buy guns, close yourselves off. The eyes of love instead see us all as one. Here's what we can do to change the world, right now, into a better ride. Take all that money we spend on weapons and defense each year and instead spend it feeding and clothing and educating the poor of the world, which it would do many times over, not one human being excluded, and we can explore space, together, both inner and outer, forever, in peace."

Suspenseful Pencils

[VERSE 1]
Waterfalls of light spectrum
Drums from some distant plain
Chains raining orchestras expressing pain
What came before was clear
Crystal's dismissal of all that we hear
What Cheer is near with gushing tears
Tear fear into fragments
Take lakes for enchantments
Foxholes we mold the way we're told
Stay indoors and hold the soul till it's full-grown
But the adult cult is built on a tilt
When they pay children to sing
And to bring sin when they begin

[CHORUS]
Sun is sinking
After thinking is drinking
Shrinking mental petals
Speak metal minstrels

[VERSE 2]
Suspenseful pencils
To stencil me into casual minstrels
Ravens, birds of my havens
Laden with twisted wicked maidens
What the day brings is sanctuary wings
Feathers breaking tethers
Free into the atmosphere
Isn't it clear what I hear
Is for you all too
The reason we know that in order to grow
Planting is necessity, rotation is necessary
Carry the stones till I rattle your bones
Steadily climbing, continue finding
Time is vanquished through rhyming
But the crime of caring too much
Requires a tender touch
Trust pounded into dust
But when we're rising
Never downsizing

[CHORUS]
Sun is sinking
After thinking is drinking
Shrinking mental petals
Speak metal minstrels

[VERSE 3]
Never let ourselves be locked in a cage
Reading religiously only the same page

Was that a fit of rage
We disengage
Have we boarded a spacecraft
Futuristic ceremonies of witchcraft
Why you gone so soft
You're about to be lost
Paying more than the cost to do business
Heinous lives come over to my side
We glide after a rough ride
We never abide in a dull world
Creation of a swirl
A storm to never conform
Build the ladders to destinations
More creations

Never land if we can
Neverland if we can
NeverLand if we can

In a NeverWonderland
We're in a Neverwonderland
We're in a Neverwonderland
Writing with suspenseful pencils

Past the Point of Distortion

[VERSE 1]
Distraction from basic transactions
This time I never die
I am the sky
We start at the bottom
But stay to climb high
I'm past the point of distortion
I am nails on a chalkboard
I'm Superjails going toward
Mental wards who hearing
Screaming with searing flesh
I am a cesspool tearing death
From wordless mouths drowning in noise
Misuse instruments like toys
Joys to blow out your ears, I'm near
Boom
This room is not solid
Bass shaking walls
Wait for the falls

[CHORUS]
Past the point of distortion
Made deaf through abortion
All senses broken with contortion
Past the point of distortion

[VERSE 2]
No redemption in your ears
There's salvation in your tears
The year of the screech
Till my speech does reach
The temple of the drum
So come get some
Come get some
I miss, bop bop poof
I insist, bop bop ckkkkkkkk
Transmission interrupted by a girl
Auditory swirls creating curls of worlds
Semi-scapes, scrape our sound-waves
Trapped in flesh caves
This is how he saves

[CHORUS]
Past the point of distortion
Made deaf through abortion
All senses broken with contortion
Past the point of distortion

[VERSE 3]
Train brakes hit in haste
Just in case our life is just a taste
To hear sounds of our surrender
Near clip-rounds shot by pretenders
Remember, whichever ear we lend her
The message will be sent ta vent the
Noise of my poise
What size do you see
What size do you see
What size this be
I am he

[CHORUS]
Past the point of distortion
Made deaf through abortion
All senses broken with contortion
Past the point of distortion

(IV)y

[INTRO]
This transmission
Has been temporarily interrupted
By a girl
Who is IVy?
IVy, IVy
The Infinite Visionary?

[VERSE 1]
I feel as if I'm waking up in the ICU
Turning blue
What do they have running through these tubes
There's a little bag attached to my IV
Meant to heal my psyche
The liquid in the bag is green
Yo, nurse, what does this mean?
That's when the bag assumed a human form
Unsure wether she was a ruin storm
Or just a union torn
A Green Woman born
Standing at the foot of my bed

With ivy climbing down her head
A green dress flowing down her legs
She didn't speak but in her palm
Was a blood-stained egg
Is this my peak, am I dead
I don't feel like my body has been shed
"I am the IVy sent to keep you alive," she said
Without moving her lips or her hips
Sent to infect and inject
Love back in my veins
Please don't add to all this pain
Inject directly but correctly
So the hate doesn't consume
And send me to an untimely tomb

(Who is IVy?)

[VERSE 2]
The Negative Seven
Was turning my heart black
Like cards stacked against me
IVy, please set me free
Between savior and destroyer—
Innocence
She is my other, my compliment,
My completion
Seven plus eight equals more
Than fifteen minutes of fame
We never play the game but we win all the same
Longer than a lifetime, we did it through a rhyme

But are we ruled by 6—
66

(The Infinite Visionary? IVy)

[VERSE 3]
Six fingers means angelic
I tell you we're both relics
Two heads with both parts
Androgynously attached creating art from the start
Growing inside me like a purple heart
A spirit who can fade in and out of worlds
Unlike any other girls
And become curled inside each other
But no longer like a fetus and a mother
She is green like life
Bursting with flowers despite
Hidden teeth that bite
Creeping leaves to bring me nectar
But somehow I suspect her
To leave me torn asunder
(Who is IVy?)
But when veins fill up with toxins
Skin itches from ivy which is poison
Crawling up legs and constricting
We start conflicting as I'm depicting
The way she's restricting
But the pain is so addicting
Aggressive ivy growth leads to death
No breath, but your heart attracts

Directly by opportunistic disease and insect attacks
Caused by weakness form duress
Let me confess, ivy growth putting stress on my wall,
Damaged and breaking, causing stones to fall
Sometimes ivy can be an invasive species
Can she be killed with a deep freeze
Cause ivy creates a dense, vigorously smothering
Evergreen ground-cover to leave me sputtering
Wet, hardening, and prostrate
Allowing moisture and fungus
To penetrate and accelerate
Wet-rot and eventual collapse
Lost in the woods with no maps
To shake it, I'm unable
Even though it's very unstable

To shake it, I'm unable
Even though it's very unstable

Light

[VERSE 1]
In the light we fight to keep our sight
But they might try to blind us out of spite
This is night
Despite our rights to know the truth uncovered
When the realist get smothered
How can knowledge be recovered
When they keep us in the dark

Every spark is illuminating
But death is penetrating
Aggravating in this space
Breath is forever waiting
Shaking foundations
And destroying fortifications
What was cloaked in shadow
Will be brought to the light
When what was thought as shallow
Is the only thing in sight

[CHORUS]
Light (light, light)
Essential for our sight

[VERSE 2]
I fracture into a spectrum
Lecture over drums
This is not ho-hum
If I catch you sleepin'
I'm out of sight creepin'
Blood leakin' through your chandelier
Rainbow Warrior blazing cavalier
A seer near what it is you hear
What cheer comes from the sun
Day battles, are we having fun
How will we know we've won
Sun sets against this gun
We've begun, settling sun
Come play games, same rains
Army men waiting on riverbanks pacing
With eyes closed, light still seeps in
And ears still hear an eternal din

[CHORUS]
Light (light, light)
Essential for our sight

[VERSE 3]
We begin by spilling essence
An innocence phosphorescence

Blind helplessness into lawlessness
Devils in our passages resigning
Shining like Seraphim designing
Creates a spirit flow
The energy seeds to sow
To forever know
We live for this glow
Sanctions to cut our rations
Words set in motion chemical reactions
Not get lost without our sight
We exist to burn out bright
Branded record label stamps
For bringing sanctuary lamps
We have a knack
Reveal an unknown cloaked black
Pry it back
Pry it back
Can see we lost our rights
Burn forever, we just might
Blaze flames, heat and light
From bright sky fall, descent
Transparent becomes apparent
We part ways in the park
Light can't exist without the dark

[OUTRO]
Light can't exist without the dark
If we didn't have nothing
To spill our light into
There'd be no good

Just evil
Dark, light
Dark, dark, dark, dark...

Dark

[VERSE 1]
I'm just loving all the hate I'm receiving
Different voices have got you believing
That my good is deceiving
Or there's nothing beneficial
You could be receiving
I catch myself grieving when you're leaving
My body in the dark
I leave the night ship and disembark
From the tip of the spark
Night and day goes in an arc
To send sun into death
Let the Moon catch my breath
When I become Lady MacBeth
You leave, so you don't catch the rest
When I'm blessed, you can see it
When I'm cursed, you can feel it
I never conceal it, my ideal is unreal
Something so surreal
It's like the Seventh Seal
A white lamb ready to reveal

The light of God illuminating as a firing squad
Into a pitch black pit, stand up and admit
That my sinister wickedness
Is a compliment to my righteousness

[CHORUS]
Dark (dark, dark)
Blindness leaves a question mark

[VERSE 2]
Then I chose to bring it back from the black
Bet you thought I was gonna say:
I'm back and black
My soul is like light shining through this night
I still retain my sight
Eyes are flashlights bright despite the fright
Generated from either black or white
Simply dismal as the gentle flames dwindle
To crystal shimmers leaving brittle ripples
To sprinkle sullen tinsel
No longer shining like a visible nickel
The good deeds shrivel when I become sinful
And feel invisible
When you say I'm a pitiful unskillful
Symbol covered in spittle
But believe me when I say, I'm no swindle
I am nimble but becoming tearful
When no one even attempts to solve this riddle
So I mingle between twinkle and sinful
Like I said, there's nothing single

Maybe I'm just an evil Sybil
Sent to be a Spindle Trap
That will swivel from one extreme to the next
Casting an illuminated hex
Blessing you with cheerless sex

[CHORUS]
Dark (dark, dark)
Blindness leaves a question mark

[VERSE 3]
But what was once in shadow
Shall be brought inside this glow
Sticks and stones may break your bones
But words can also feel like blows
What you all bestow on me: Black Mist
Wishing to steal my Master Key
This is the way we see through the dark
Any offhand remark enlightens like a spark
Be it if it mentions me
Under cover of darkness, there's something very free
But if bathed in light you'll see me lurking in a tree
Sometimes you choose not to use your sight
For fear of things not being actually as bright
Tarnished, destroyed, tainted
Like white roses being painted
The truth is faded and jaded
I'm aged and naked inside hatred
Wasted and fated but still sacred
But still haven't tasted

Because the road became gated
Shaded by trees
Under this casted shadow, I find the Master Key
Step through the gate into the light
Where I become
Anything and everything I'm meant to be
SEE!

Light
I find the Master Key
I found the Master Key
So step through the gate into the light
Where I'm becoming everything
I'm meant to be
So, see

Threshold

[INTRO]
Nilotic
I'm standing at the threshold
Looking up at the Infinite Cornerstone
Contemplating where I'm going
And where I've been
Now listen
These are my words
That flow from an infinite spring
Brought from within
And I know sometimes
I do things that I don't really understand
That you don't like
But here, this is me

[VERSE 1]
I'm pushing past the threshold
The Apex is next
Tell me what you expect
Nothing?
Then I'ma give you something

To dominate the conversation
No hesitation, your underestimation
Has decided your termination
And my eternal determination
Has cleared away a path
To speculate my aftermath
Try to still this wrath
Now listen, this world is just a ride
But mine hasn't been able to glide
So decide to turn it all around
Through IVy keeping me alive
Making me survive
Love is what I found, check my different sounds
And let me reload clip-rounds
Astound, pounded into the ground
Then take off while they all around me scoff
Saying my words aren't profitable
But I'm unstoppable
Now you all will pay, hear me say
With your life, with your wallet, with your wife
Whisper now: *he called it*

[CHORUS]
This is the threshold
I'm breakin' every mold
With a soul never sold
Creating all my own

[VERSE 2]
Now I'm choosing cause before I was losing
You were snoozing
Wake the fuck up, shut the fuck up
I'm rappin', mind trappin'
No way I'm gonna be stoppin'
I'm not the one who's floppin'
I'm toppin' this Hip Hop with more props
Scarin' cops, intellectual knocks
STOP!

GO!
Flow
I don't just make it rain
I make it snow
Blizzards when we grow
Bringin' the Apocalyptic, so know
Ill Will, Twizzy, all my crew
They're the ones who knew
If you stick with me, we will be free
We'll be able to see, you will pay our fees
Without me asking please
We will never cease
We control this ride
So come over to our side

[CHORUS]
This is the threshold
I'm breakin' every mold

With a soul never sold
Creating all my own

[VERSE 3]
When I came out
I let them *Nail Me to the Crossdress*
Already I was a fucking mess
Then I wrote about the sickness
Which is *CNT*
They thought my style was a front
Pushing me farther toward martyr
With no father
So I developed a *Messiah Complex*
During a time I was barely having sex
So what's next
The Perfect Forever took me on
And then I'm being severed
While swearing she would never
During kissing and holding me after
Goodbye
Those were my *Lullabies for a Lifestyle*
Hip Hop keeping me sane for a while
But be careful when you write hell dot com
Into a song
net.art became an obsession
0 and 1 written in my confession
Possession with a mixtape
Bringing me closer to my fate
But feeling no love, all hate

Put me in an *Emotional Ghetto*
So listen, so you know
ARR and Nilotic about to blow
Like supernovas
Threshold pulling me up
No need to collect change in a cup
When I'm *Mythic* and about to erupt

I'm about to tell you the plan
With no metaphors, man
I stand, do the chores, I can
Paid my Dues in blood
Pulled my face from the mud
I will build my Finality Factory
The Strangest Sanctuary
To hold infinite shows
This is what you chose
We comin', so bring 'em
Mythos will go platinum

We comin', so bring 'em
Mythos will go platinum

[OUTRO]
Yeah, Apocalyptic Rhymes Records
We comin' to every area
On the face of the Earth
Ill Will Beatz
Nilotic

Threshold
Remember, come to my Scorpion web
And I'll spin you a Myth

"We can explore space, together, both inner and outer, forever, in peace."
   - Bill Hicks

Nilotic and Tocxina rocking the stage at As220

That's Not Me - Single (2013)

Cover drawing by Scarlet Eyes

1. That's Not Me
2. Free & Accepted Type (ft. Wills)
3. In Our Flesh (Demo)

Promo for the collaboration between Nilotic and Scarlet Eyes. It's something a little different from Nilotic, giving the fans a more soulful side to the persona, and singing about it for a change! This release contains two bonus tracks when you download or purchase a physical copy.

That's Not Me

[VERSE 1]
They don't know nothin' about me
What you see is not who I am
Not sayin' I'm a scam
But there's more than what you see
The eyes can deceive
And what you may perceive
May be distorted by the view
I keep no secrets from you
Don't assume, it's all conjecture
Cause what you see is only half the picture
What you see is only half the picture

[CHORUS]
I can't be what you want from me
So hate all that you can see
I'd give up all that makes me free
But that's not me
That's not me
That's not me
That's not me

[VERSE 2]
So pick your poison
Give yourself over to addiction
Saying you can't control your affliction
So pick your sickness
Mental, physical, emotional
Just say it's all sensational
The purpose is not to shock
But what's the point of speaking softly
When no one's there to hear me

[BRIDGE]
I didn't feel a thing when I was slipping away
I didn't need a thing when I was tripping this way
Tie me to those lies that men believe
This may be the truth from my lungs
But you'll still perceive I deceive
But you'll still perceive I deceive

[CHORUS]
I can't be what you want from me
So hate all that you can see
I'd give up all that makes me free
But that's not me
That's not me
That's not me
That's not me

[VERSE 3]
I said I couldn't do this anymore
Remaining sore without a score
Dead inside this crowd
Leave me be if my scream's not loud enough
For you to even turn your head
Leave me be, I'll be there soon
Then it's okay to be alone
Then it's okay to be alone
Then it's okay to be alone

[BRIDGE]
I didn't feel a thing when I was slipping away
I didn't need a thing when I was tripping this way
Tie me to those lies that men believe
This may be the truth from my lungs
But you'll still perceive I deceive
But you'll still perceive I deceive

[RAP]
I don't represent what's not me
I'm free, don't you see
I'm just doin' me
A dead emcee with a mic I spit creatively
Not hastily, sloppily,
I'd never flop like Nelly

[CHORUS]
I can't be what you want from me
So hate all that you can see

I'd give up all that makes me free
But that's not me
That's not me
That's not me
That's not me

[BRIDGE]
I didn't feel a thing when I was slipping away
I didn't need a thing when I was tripping this way
Tie me to those lies that men believe
This may be the truth from my lungs
But you'll still perceive I deceive
But you'll still perceive I deceive

Free & Accepted Type

[INTRO]
Wills
Nilotic
Apocalyptic Rhymes Records
Sick vocals
Bear with me
Check it out

[NILOTIC]
My great-grandfather was a Freemason
Now this is what I'm facin'
My relation to the plantation
Aligned in a pyramid constellation
An elusive redemption
Walking side by side with temptation
I went to the woods to find salvation
After understanding reparations
Our people burning under a polluted steeple
With creepy features
Developed after being deceived by his teachers
And preachers

Oral sex with the leeches
I mean you and what I speak is true
And you might survive the flu
But 85% never knew
So watch the fucking clues
Proof of something aloof
Doomed to only see the gloom
Keep breathing toxic fumes
Then steal gold from our tombs

[CHORUS]
Are you free but not accepted
Tested through being molested
Flies soon will be nested
I'm unfettered, an exodus scattered

[NILOTIC]
Diaspora
An Aryan Apocrypha
Spuriously and furiously
But sometimes I'm blessedly delirious
Curious of sorts
Suspicious of the courts
They'll distort reality
Then create every malady
Making God a fallacy
So challenge me
I walk free, you see
Slave to just One
I'm not run by the gun

Ruled by Might and Majesty
But snakes still here are tempting me
Listen, look, awareness, covenant, decree
Align yourself above with love
Or get dragged below
Someday you'll know

[CHORUS]
Are you free but not accepted
Tested through being molested
Flies soon will be nested
I'm unfettered, an exodus scattered

[WILLS]
Everything around you is sacred
Blessed by the one from once created
So why do you mire it up and desecrate it
Man, have I been hoodwinked
So y'all can lead some cushy-ass elitist life
Blinded by the tube
Microwave food
Electro-smog
Gonna shed some light on the blighted techno-Magog
Drunk on petrol and blood
That's over, we wanna New World Order
Of light and love
And not a blatant oligarch's gonna smite the buzz
Because all men are sovereign
Walking talking Muhammads
He was just blindsided

In the war on your conscience
Get up, brush it off
Get up, brush it off
How many times you gon' let 'em hit ya
Fore you get involved and fuckin' evolve
To the zenith genius you are
Let's give ourselves a round
Of before-completion applause
Cause it's already done
Cause the darkness against us is part of the One
So love your enemy
Love your neighbor
Love life, love light
Make love your nature
For you are goodness, for goodness sake
And your thoughts manifest
Manifest Destiny

[CHORUS]
Are you free but not accepted
Tested through being molested
Flies soon will be nested
I'm unfettered, an exodus scattered

[OUTRO]
Yeah
Welcome to the new exodus
(Apocalyptic Rhymes Records)
From that oppressive Capitalist bullshit
(Free & Accepted Type)

Free and accepted souls and spirits
Rise, be empowered
True power
Love
One

In Our Flesh (Demo)

[VERSE 1]
Combat the Bat
Till there's only one vat of acid left
With a sting felt through your placid cleft
I'll jet
Into a disappearing net
When everything is set
To destruct
And I'll be there to conduct
You're out of luck
So suck a fuck
Cluck when I cum
So where you from, son?
My cock is a gun
I'll flex it when you run
Intrinsic system failure
In a jail you're
Getting raped
Disgraced
Just a subtle taste of what's to come
After cracker and a half

Bleeding as I laugh
It's a trap
A murder rap
I beat it
You can keep it
In order to see it
Feel it
And peel it back
To discover you're heart's black
Drag you screaming in a sack
I am what you lack
So backtrack
A sand lake
It's too late to outrun your fate

[CHORUS]
These words are etched into our flesh
Cutting deep, so let's confess
We're the product of incest
After the fall, are we becoming less?

[VERSE 2]
Crackling like embers
Practicing like menders
Defenders of the throne
Now you're prone to be thrown
If we all had ever known
The seeds that we have sown
Has left our blood cold
After our bodies have been sold

The coffin is a mold
And decreasing in this fold
Is something I've been told
Centerfold is dead
We heard every word she said
But if it's maggots I am fed
Is it silky when she bled in bed
I'm a sky train
Cry rain
Try pain
Destroy the brain
When the raven came
There were seven names
And the righteousness he claims
Doesn't hide the fact he maims
Courting disdain
And the emptiness he feigns
Reigns over me
What will the lovers see
When my feet are the roots of this tree
Love me where I stand
Or char me in my land

[CHORUS]
These words are etched into our flesh
Cutting deep, so let's confess
We're the product of incest
After the fall, are we becoming less?

[VERSE 3]
I'm like sand filling your lungs
Broken rungs of the ladder
I'm hearing chatter
An undefined clatter or blood splatter
Gun to my head it doesn't matter
My words are just a pitter-patter
So don't flatter yourself
You're nonexistent as an elf
If you brag about your wealth — show me
If you come into spirit health — know me
Choke me as I begin to float free
Into Finality
Master Key
Infinity, we seek
Blood on these hands
There's blood on your brands
Don't join Masonic clans
I know every single plan
So I rage against every time I can
So if I'm not a man I'll be beheaded on my knees
Please
Find a way to make the violence plead for peace
Before we're all deceased
Released from a flesh prison
Or we'll have to serve a sentence
Write it for your penance

[CHORUS]
These words are etched into our flesh

Cutting deep, so let's confess
We're the product of incest
After the fall, are we becoming less?

Jay Wills wearing Nilotic t-shirt

Psychoactive (2013)

1. Dreaming of Water
2. Trans-Mute
3. Psychoactive
4. Tangled
5. N7 6666
6. What it Really Is (ft. Jerry Pokerton)
7. The Dark Prince Speaks
8. manIcure
9. Kush Push
10. Twinkle Twinkle
11. Like Water (ft. G-Tek the Ill Meta4)
12. ARR Radio Interlude
13. Queen of Da Nile

niarb ruoy ni citolin

Dreaming of Water

[INTRO]
Yo, it's David
I'm sitting in the forest
By the bank of the stream
Watching the brook run by
Like my flow

[VERSE 1]
Right now I just don't give a fuck
So I find a map and reconstruct
But the fucking route ain't marked
And I don't remember where I disembarked
Take a part, I'm still casting for this roadshow
But deep inside my ghost knows
I'm angsty to postpone
But there's no fucking band
I'm one man living just to stand
Remember, fan the flames
I almost lost the game
If a theory's so engrained
We'll never free the chained

We're being changed
No, stay put, don't move that foot
You're out of lines
And wish you did those crimes
But what I come to find
Is there's more to my own mind
So explore through every tube
If you're glued, break the bonds
If you're new, sprint on frozen ponds
Then I'm gone

Sprinting through the trees
Searching for he who frees
Naked through the thorns
My flesh is being torn
When will I be born

Following the water like an otter
I'm natural, Humanimal
Breaking down as if I shot her, right
My jaw is clenching tight
In my eye is a blinding flash of light
A sight provoking fright
A sprite invoking night
With a vampiric bite
But I'm no longer parasitic
Forever esoteric
But Universe-All like a stream
Now y'all can hear me scream
I'm emerging from a wet dream

[CHORUS]
Dreaming of the water
Searching for a magna mater
A hydromancer, necromancer
You're a dancer, find the answer

[VERSE 2]
Nervous, breaking, shaking
You can't afford any hesitating
Watch my vein pulsating
Tracing the lines, then I face the waves
Spirit of the ocean saves
I'm no longer Potiphar's slave
But I crave to be depraved
Up in your graves
Despite a heart that's brave
Will this baptism be the cleanse
To wipe the germs crusting up my lens
Guess I gotta pack a bowl with stems
Down by the river, wish I had a bow and quiver
So I could wait till she delivers—me
Sight-see nightly
My image is so princely
Above a reflecting pool
You'll realize, despite my size
I'm one side very cruel
Always ready to duel
Play it cool, be ready for my rule
On the other hand, I need the fuel

Cause I'm taller than a seed, fool
Ha!
I can be so tranquil, calm
Healing in my palms
I silence all your qualms
This'll be my hydro-psalm

[CHORUS]
Dreaming of the water
Searching for a magna mater
A hydromancer, necromancer
You're a dancer, find the answer

[BRIDGE]
I'm a cyclical miracle
Turning wine to water
My spherical satirical
I walk and never falter

[OUTRO]
It's the water

Trans-Mute

[VERSE 1]
This screen is glued to your eyes
My lines will decide
If you live or die
Pry open the cranium
With sounds that will go platinum
We'll flatten 'em
Leave 'em only to be seen by the taxiderm
We provide you with a mirror
How can I make it clearer
When it's shattered
Standing before it, I'm fractured
With a body patterned, quilted
A gender tilted
My flower sometimes wilted
Or forcibly taken, physically shaken
Let me wear a dress
Anima to express
This tranny does impress
Press, flex, get some sex
Encrypted in this text

Transmute gender, so what's next
Human or alien, injected with the saline
The fans they all come trailin'
I'm sailin' away
Still better than you're favorite emcee
Even when I'm gay

[CHORUS]
This trans'll leave ya mute
Dildo mic, she thinks I'm hella cute
This time, my gun is not the part to shoot
Here's proof
Body and Hip Hop, the way that I transmute

[VERSE 2]
Bring this into focus
Double bubble, toil and trouble
We need some Hocus Pocus
Not the locusts
But in flesh we've many lusts
Waiting for that thrust
I distrust
But respect you show me, must
Blow up, combust
Never leave the rust
Give me a compliment, I flush
Shush
I need that push
Hermaph, def got that good kush
Get a Dutch

Maybe we too much
Androgyny gets you lifted
I know your mind has shifted
Recognize I'm gifted
Follow me, I'm driftin'
My tour'll leave 'em stunned
Reparations for the years that I was shunned
I won it!
This is where it's at
The lines that we be gunnin'
From the queer you will be runnin'
Munging, look it up, that shit it will be something
It's my music you be bumpin'
Creepin', my boots you hear 'em thumpin'
We're feindin' somethin' else
It's what will bring the wealth

[BRIDGE]
Trans-Mute, baby
Trans-Mute, bitches

[CHORUS]
This trans'll leave ya mute
Dildo mic, she thinks I'm hella cute
This time, my gun is not the part to shoot
Here's proof
Body and Hip Hop, the way that I transmute

[VERSE 3]
Inside a microcosm

I knew it was like fluid
We move it with our words
With the thoughts behind these chords
G-Tek got a mic-sword
Nilotic got his sight North
I call you forth
Do you have room for a rapper ever so dapper
Can't say I'm a flapper
But with this game, I sometimes tamper
And the faggots won't get pampered
Cause I call you as defenders
Eternal gender-benders
Ascend first, and the thirst will be no more
We're royal, refusing to be poor

[BRIDGE]
Trans-Mute, baby
Trans-Mute, bitches

[CHORUS]
This trans'll leave ya mute
Dildo mic, she thinks I'm hella cute
This time, my gun is not the part to shoot
Here's proof
Body and Hip Hop, the way that I transmute

Psychoactive

[INTRO]
You've just injected me directly
Intravenously
Now I'm swimming through your veins
Toward your heart
And then into your brain
This is the Nilotic
Switching on those parts of your mind
That you don't normally use
Listen to your unconscious
I'm psychoactive

[VERSE 1]
Ingest me like a chemical compound
Twist off the head and spin around
The clowns
Jokers with upside-down frowns
We ain't that small, fuck ounces
We bringin' pounds
Million lines sprayed off like rounds
Come eat this fun I found

Plant life grows, leaflets pieces
Leaving us all speechless
What about these trees, they have to teach us
How to give speeches
How to reach a pulpit through these speakers
Rappers sometimes pose as preachers, leechers
They're created creatures
But I, I, I spy a dilated eye
I'm humpin' your cannabinoid receptors
Making your dreams seem like celluloid projectors
Intoxicating infectors
You have less control than a room full of directors
If you test her in her sector
You'll do little more than pester
I'm swimming in your blood-brain barrier
As a psychotropic carrier
The more the merrier
As long as I'm just a bit scarier
Than a tab of acid gone bad to make you lucid
Like blood in clear fluid
You're stoned, I fuckin' knew it

[CHORUS]
I'm psychoactive
Now let's say it backwards
niarb ruoy ni citolin

[VERSE 2]
Within a frame of psilocybin
A smile made of mescaline

Hanging on the horizon
Did the razor taste like poison
The voices have chosen you to take this potion
Feels like an ocean voyage
Did you experience a temple explosion
MDMA to set in motion a chemical emotion
One full rotation
Please God, don't ever stop this sensation
My toes start to tingle
The Kodama come to mingle
Teach me the meaning in the symbol
A mandala, dormant for the time that we rekindle
Think nimble, but flow with the freedom of the people
Baking opiate cupcakes with cocaine sprinkles
Numb the pain
But will these visions permanently scar the brain
A theory that wouldn't fit inside my mainframe
My face is the computer
The screen is now the user
Man-machine body fuser
Do you see this as our future
Stare into the fire
And you'll find you're sitting there with Luther

[CHORUS]
I'm psychoactive
Now let's say it backwards
niarb ruoy ni citolin

[VERSE 3]
I'm lubing up with your dopamine
Your eyes rimmed with a faraway gleam
In which dream are you little alice
Put this into practice
Fuck your social status
But I won't back off
If you choose to grant us trust
The spun kid is on the cusp
Of floating to the stars
Or sinking into dust
But we live the way we must
I'm on a radical sabbatical
A poet, grammatical fanatical
Eating pot brownies off a spatula
Sitting on a Holy Mountain covered in tarantulas
Adrenochrome straight to the dome
No puke, just a little foam
The room is flashing red
I'm far from home, I might just end up dead
At least you'll hear my poem
What do I gotta show 'em
You got me flowin' in the meter of ether
A little like a teacher
Stoned to the bone
The beauty's in the tone
And the feeling stays unknown
Follow me where I roam
To the sea or to the stage
Come to me or disengage

The world is a magickal motherfucker
You'll see it, but only if you trust her

Tangled

[VERSE 1]
I'm permanently knotted like my mane
Remember my hair and don't forget my name
I never claim to be something other
In my life I've finally reached the summer
I'm not just a number
So awaken from your slumber
No longer encumbered by I'm a deadly mixture
If you're blind, just feel my texture
If you're deaf, watch the procedure
Of how I give a lecture
A creature of the nocturne
Tell me if you can discern the way I burn
I can be as stern as a dictator
Or set you free as a liberator
But I'm seeing the disintegrator
That's why I fuck up all my haters
Leavin' 'em in craters
But tell me, how can I become greater
When my soul is like a mixed basket
I'll take you to task and leave you in a casket

But right now, I don't give a fuck
Cause I'm so blasted
I passed it
We're all One, I love it
I'm just having fun, so gun it
I run it
But I can't untie myself
Might as well write it and put it on your shelf
(Put my albums on your shelf)

[CHORUS]
I'm tangled
A bit angled
If you come over here
Then you'll get strangled

[VERSE 2]
I wish that I could choke her
Fuck it, just burn her with a poker
I'm the fire's stroker
Provoking uproar
Cause my brain's a mess of wires
You know how I know that you're all liars?
Cause you wanna grab his nuts
And twist 'em with the pliers
No, stop, I can't complete that thought
What was it I brought
Oh yeah,
Love and blossoms
Doves and bosoms

Persimmons and Jolly Ranchers
Nice lemons and Dirty Sanchez
Haha, I'm in love with you
Would you rub by chute
Give a hoot and don't pollute
Woodsy Owl thinks little Mackey's cute
Nah, let's get down to root
Psychoactive proof that I always raise the roof
Yes, I am a total goof
But there's room for everything under the sun
In sight of impending doom, do you run
Back into my arms
With no need of protective charms

[CHORUS]
I'm tangled
A bit angled
If you come over here
Then you'll get strangled

[VERSE 3]
What if I became Rapunzel
Tagging a long-haired stencil
I write with a magic pencil
Take me to *Imajica*
Where there's a unicorn called Dracula
Back it up
No, I meant back this way
What else could come today

In the branches of my sway
Between saving the forest
Or crucifying on a crooked tree
Sometimes the rich is the poorest
But my spine leaves a crooked me
Don't you see
I'm part *Magician's Nephew*

Listening to Ces Cru
When I'm sitting in Midian feeling like a specimen
Ten minus three is all me
You still don't know my name like Rumpelstiltskin
In your ear there's somethin' nestin'
Don't bother resistin'
The chloroform keeps persistin'
Go back to sleep
Count bodies like sheep
And dream of mystic lands
Where heroes can go bad
Rainbow Brite would take a stab
And evil is sometimes in the right
I don't know
You tell me who's in the crosshairs of your sight

[CHORUS]
I'm tangled
A bit angled
If you come over here
Then you'll get strangled

[OUTRO]
This little piggy went to market
This little piggy stayed home
This little piggy had blood and butter
This little piggy had a dead son
And this little piggy went dripping
All the way home
I'm the origins of the finger-play
And questionable sex games
After it's been bent a frame never looks the same
No 16:9 or 4:3
It's warped, don't you see
You're fuckin' up my chi

Dude, come on
Stop fuckin' up my chi, man
Walk over here and look at things
From my angle
You'll get fuckin' strangled
Man, just gotta fix all the Feng Shui
In here and shit, man
But I don't know
My hair is like everywhere
All over the fuckin' floor and shit
I don't know, I always find like
Loose strands of hair like everywhere
Like on the floor, like in my ass crack
And shit, I don't even fuckin' know, man
It's tangled and shit

N7 6666

[VERSE 1]
As the blood in my veins changes shape
I feel a spirit on the nape of my neck
In this scheme am I more than a fleck
Or a guilty suspect
Who would you choose to protect
Come next
Cause we need something new from the blue
If I share with you all it is I knew
You'd emerge from it renewed
Resolve a family feud
Chew the bone down
Watch the way you pronounce
But if it's me that you denounce
Dawg, it is your demise we will announce
But if I fit in, lickety-split
Like tranny ain't shit
But I leave my spirit lit like a candle
Am I too much material to handle
I just keep walking in these sandals
Over oceans, locking in the motions

So I can feel the music in the commotion
Make sure you caught the notation
And explain the fixation
Only to yourself
Then put notches on your belt
For every year that you felt like a Celt
Down through time, we sometimes melt

[CHORUS]
Copernican Revolution
N7 6666
Full circle to bring a fix
Or be shipwrecked on the river Styx

[VERSE 2]
Locked in solitary confinement
With a spinal misalignment
While I was in a straight-jacket
I received my assignment
He told me to float
But he told me to go home
He told me to be grown
He told me to be known
And that my wings had already flown
I had gone where the wind had blown
Farther than the stone was thrown
If I'm alone, I come to terms with what I own
When I'm thrown into my zone
And my throat begins to be in tone
I have cuts but now I've sown

This is my public ceremony
Where I eternally give my testimony
I want to cry:
If only, if only
The woodpecker sighs
The bark on the trees was as soft as the skies
As the wolf waits below
Hungry and lonely
He cries to the moon
If only, if only
Enter seven digits daily
Is my skin becoming scaly
If I state I'm a snake very plainly
Hear sarcasm very faintly
I could be very saintly
The numbers maybe show it
By I'm possessed with absinthe, psychotic poet
I'm toking and I'm floating

[CHORUS]
Copernican Revolution
N7 6666
Full circle to bring a fix
Or be shipwrecked on the river Styx

[VERSE 3]
I'm the weed man
And the weed man can
Cause he mixed it with love

And makes the world taste good
With an everlasting cocksucker
Or discover the I Ching when we plot numbers
We progressively get dumber
But the barrier's crumbling under
Hear that rolling thunder
Instill a sight of wonder
This world has come under fire
We no longer need a Sire
Our alchemy is desire
Alchemy is desire

[CHORUS]
Copernican Revolution
N7 6666
Full circle to bring a fix
Or be shipwrecked on the river Styx

[OUTRO]
If only, if only
The woodpecker sighs
The bark on the trees was as soft as the skies
As the wolf waits below
Hungry and lonely
He cries to the moon
If only, if only

What It Really Is

[JERRY POKERTON]
Turn my swag on real quick
While I'm turnt up on the mic
This what we do, nigga
This shit ain't to be cool,
To act cool, nigga
It's what it really is

You can catch me in the coop
When I'm all blacked up
I'd use color for these hoes
But I don't keep 'em wrapped up
My niggas is strapped up
These niggas they act tough
They bitches attack us
Only money can distract us
Come back, we reversin' bitches
Fresh bitches finally attract us
Finding the track tough
No more foes
I'm a lyrical Mack Bus

Head shot to these niggas
But honest, they raps suck
We don't love these hoes
It's nothing but wack lust
I've grown Ford Tough
When it's the only thing I love
All white on like I'm walking into dugs
And I'm with a group of thugs
When I'm walkin' around the club
We walkin' around deep
But I'm the one who's got the snow
I'm the flyest type of nigga
You can catch me fresh as fuck
And I got like moves
Wayne told me to step it up
Start dancin' niggas
You better hide, chances are
My foot is all the way down
I tell 'em I ain't think of lettin' up
Watch out for these hoes
They're the ones settin' up
So I just smoke with 'em
Tell 'em to move back
And let my niggas do that
I'm going buggin'
The bitches say I'm a cool cat
I'll build 'em a shoe rack
I'll order a few packs
And run through a few stacks
Only add, no multiply, no divide

It's the new math
I'm always a attractive, motherfucker
My rule's back

[CHORUS]
We come from the bottom
But rise to the top
No demon's gonna stop 'em
Beat in the brain
Your vein is poppin'

You might catch me out through traffic
With the crazy motherfucker
Smokin', drinkin', relaxin'
Steady countin' up Jacksons
No lie

[NILOTIC]
I'm on a higher level
Illuminated, but not the devil
We prevail, set sail
Never fading frail
These scars harden us
In jail he's learning calculus
But we still need that Kush Push
When the darkness settles in
Let the sinnin' begin
With an evil painted grin
Sainted men mired in their gin
Did he wear a ring

Cut it from his finger
Infidelity scents do linger, a singer
Ballad of jaded scarred hearts
Mated charred marks
Lately I'm hard and dark
Cause I wrote a different chart
Vicious from the start
Cause archetypal splits seem to sit in a psyche slit
A grownup throws a fit
In a dark throne I sit
Watching all your stories
Orchestrating epic allegories
Like *Tuesdays with Morrie*
Only a little more gory
With syringes, rusty hinges
We're brimming on the fringes
Edges of our conscious
Rolling in a frozen tundra

[CHORUS]
We come from the bottom
But rise to the top
No demon's gonna stop 'em
Beat in the brain
Your vein is poppin'

You might catch me out through traffic
With the crazy motherfucker
Smokin', drinkin', relaxin'

Steady countin' up Jacksons
No lie

[OUTRO]
It's no lie
Yo, it's King David
Jerry Pokerton
Psychoactive mixtape 2013
What, motherfucker
Apocalyptic Rhymes Records

The Dark Prince Speaks

(This was transcribed from audio recorded at Occupy Providence. The random guy speaking on the track mumbles and talks very fast and erratically. So this transcript isn't perfect, but it's the best of what I could understand of these rantings and ravings. Enjoy.)

Bullshit, that's the reason why. And the thing about it is we could be up in the fuckin' hotel right now chillin', relaxin', or I could make the fuckin' spark on all the apartments on everybody in there. Even if we out and sittin' there with three or four in the room, we ain't gotta be in the cold. We're out in the frost right now, we die and they be sittin' there laughin', right?

Damn, it is cold out here, man. Like, they're just sittin' in their warm houses like "these people are gonna die, we don't give a fuck." Yeah.

And the thing about is that the home-owners is right there with you. That's the whole point. That's the reason why they more fucked up. All we need is for to be out and be here. And they that fucked up. They would fuck up everybody's finances, all their money, sittin' there trying to say: fuck it, I'm better than him. Guess what, your money ain't worth shit anywhere else unless I'm here. Money ain't worth nothing, American currency ain't worth anything in any other country until I took the reins. So come on now. Before, you go to Japan, the Yen, you'd have a thousand dollars, you only get one penny. Now you get at least 250 dollars. Come on, man, every advancement we made was because of the so-called devil, this black man right here. So how, the phones, technology, everything. Remember, before you only had—superiority complex now motherfuckers will provide anything in our fucked up world is a fucked up life for everybody. The thing about it is everybody is in a hardship. It's not just black people, white people, it's everybody. And they trying to put somebody on a superiority complex on top instead of putting people that's gonna help the people that need the help. And the government, the government knows that they're being financed by the black man. By a black man because they call me the devil but they ain't even gonna respect the fact that the American government ain't got shit without me. Real talk. Dollars ain't worth shit, ain't not worth shit. It's because they want to be superior.

That's all they need. They got all the money, all they need is power.

The thing about it is, they ain't got the money cause the money ain't even in this country. I ain't leave my account in this country.

My account is in Switzerland. My Swiss account is my social, my social security number. 03503299. And you know what, they can't even respect the fact that they ain't even financial advisor. All they finances come by me. Without me they dollar ain't worth shit and they know that. That's why they're wrong. Hey, the thing about superiority, it's about the people. They ain't for the people, by the people, of the people, none of that shit. The Republicans sitting on their old fat ass trying to fuck up everything for everybody.

Dude, you are pissed, huh?

You know why? Because my kids, my females, my people are struggling and they're the ones sitting there laughin' at us. Like there's something funny. Well, guess what? Anarchy 99 is my family now. You know why? Cause we need to break down—bring down your establishment. Actually the industrial—conglomerate, the global conglomerate on industrial and industry there is me! So guess what, that's not what we're fighting. We're fighting a child mentality of that ain't your shit and you mad about it. And that's the problem. We're the solution. Thank you.

manIcure

"Greetings, Agrestic Elementary School, class of 2006. Hello, teachers, parents, step-parents, siblings, boyfriends and girlfriends of parents, assorted relatives, friends of your mom and dad who you call aunt and uncle who really aren't, and principal Dodge. As I stand before you today on the brink of junior high, here is what I have to say. You have failed us all! Everything is not okay! We have become alienated, desensitized, angry, and frightened. If we picture Agrestic as an airplane, a grand soaring jet carrying us through the sky, I think you all need to understand, there are motherfucking snakes on this motherfucking plane. We are not safe. You moved here so that you could feel safe, but your children are not safe. I'm not done!"

- Shane Botwin in the show *Weeds*

[INTRO]
Yo, it's Nilotic
About to sing for you motherfuckers
So sit the fuck back

And get served
By a queer

[VERSE 1]
My genitals are rusted
It hurted when you thrusted
An anal hole combusted
Methane backin' up
So much for shackin' up
Just bust a nut in a cup
Disrupt a penis pump
And start the everlasting hump
But I gotta take a dump
Shit to bump the rump
I'm toyin' Donald Trump
With this Hitachi Wand
He's leakin', making the bed a pond
For his balls I'm very fond
I lick a taint and then I'm gone
Who's the fastest shot with cocks drawn
How does it feel to be a fuck pawn
Pleasurable, this ecstasy's immeasurable
Hentai with the tentacles
Watch out for the sentinels
Sexually we're radicals

[CHORUS]
I cure man
Push to reach the climax
If not I'll lick your tampax

[VERSE 2]
Im-preg-nation
Carrying the seed of destruction
Pe-ne-tra-tion
Let me give you a demonstration
This ain't no fabrication
Jerking off in the Imagination Station
This is a perennial celebration
Your cut is my destination
I could harness this vibration
With a strap-on visualization
We're in the days of cannibalization
We eat our young, come get some
And make sure you bring a gun
That way we'll have some fun
Sneak a peek under the habit of a nun
But if it's hairy then you run
She's pregnant with Destroyer
Notify you're employer
The plan is set in stone
Why is my head filled with acts I don't condone
At least I don't spit it in a monotone

[CHORUS]
I cure man
Push to reach the climax
If not I'll lick your tampax

[VERSE 3]
If I ate a fetus
It wouldn't be enough to feed us
Breed rust but I need lust
Every time I bust
I always feel fire in my loins
Could I buy your company
For just a few coins
The world is better with two groins rejoined
Please put us back together
Is that why I fiend for a girl
Lighter than a feather
Whatever the weather
I'm enjoying your sweater
But just so you know
I'd never be tethered by a Heather
Cause they all deserve to die
Bodies flung up high
Blood dripping from the sky
You ask why
I ask why not
I'm thickening the plot
When you say the confusion's like a knot
Forever tangled and not even a cat
Could save it from its lot
You say I'm more than two shot
I say okay
You say my set's for shock
That's when I make you pay
But maybe I'm gay today

So walk a bit my way

Maybe I'm gay today
So walk a bit my way

Kush Push

[INTRO]
Hello?
Is anybody there?
I think that was, uh
Getting a little too weird for, uh
Everybody right there, but uh
I'm back in the house, so I uh
I had to take a couple hits off that blunt
In the back right there, but uh
Check this one out
It's called Kush Push

[VERSE 1]
I'm psychoactive
Sometimes radio reactive
Wack emcees are like a zombie epidemic
Brainless, so there's no need of paramedics
I created these theatrics
But with directions I'm dyslexic
That's why they call me the Opposite Man

I was pessimistic but found out the positive can
Withstand a battle in Neverwonderland
One side of the mushroom
But the ones with the black nipples
Would put you in your tomb
But if you wish to grow larger
Decide how much to charge her
ECID told me to *Go High Lion*
Since then my mind's been flyin'
I got that kush push
In the temples feel a whoosh
Go high
Take the test high
Get high scores
But wait, there's just a little more
I'm fallen to the floor
Swimming in these colors
I need this to lift the world from my shoulders
Feels like I'm pushin' boulders up the hill in Hades
Lay siege to the chemicals that made me
But plants, I appreciate them fully

[CHORUS]
So give me a kush push
A rush of blood
I glimpse a burning bush
Will I be caught up in the flood

[VERSE 2]
I'm crawling up this pyramid
Trying to break free of the grid
They want my body amid the rubble
Since the Threshold I've been in trouble
Bumpin' Hip Hop all over America
You heard the rumble
When the towers crumbled
My blood drained
Tears I shed
Spark up one for the fallen
The unwanted
The people haunted and cravin' something different
The world is bent
So we smoke
But don't treat life as one cosmic joke
Yeah, I've been fuckin' broke
But I'll be rich before I croak
If you finally awoke
Then I hope we spoke
I'll leave you with a coded note
That I scented with some oak
Or was it the herb
Don't stop writing, respect the word
Cross-joint, a trinity in unity
Come to me, of course it be
All the weed you see
Of course it be
All the weed you see
Come to me

[CHORUS]
So give me a kush push
A rush of blood
I glimpse a burning bush
Will I be caught up in the flood

[VERSE 3]
To the West and to the East
Packing bowls
Even on the day I faced the BeaST
Will we ever have a victory feast
Or let me give a victory speech
They teach us that it's wrong
But y'all just sing along
And I string along behind
Wishin' I could mime
Because inside I wish to hide sometimes
Then I take a hit
And pop up like it ain't shit
Time to get fuckin' fit
MMA training, put up a fist
The man of Rohan gets me lifted
I love the way I'm livin'
And you should love it too
But maybe I'm too new
When I dream blue
You say it's for the few
I say it's for the all
If you ever seen us march

I tell you we ain't that small
We stand tall
Answering our call
So wake up
It's time to shake up
The established
Cause they're content to leave us damaged
Who's streets?
Our streets
Who's streets?
Our streets
Who's streets?
Our streets

[OUTRO]
Oh, shit
That just got heavy, man
Pass that blunt, dawg
Pass it over here
We need that kush push

So give me a kush push
A rush of blood
I glimpse a burning bush
Will I be caught up in the flood

Twinkle Twinkle

Hello, this is the Nilotic
You have just entered the IM
The IM
The IM is where
All the fucked up people go
When there's no more fucked up to be had
The Mad Hatter's here
The March Hare
And I think I spy at least a few alices
Around town
We're just chillin'
Kickin' it in the IM
This is the IM
And the IM is where all the fucked up people go
When there's no more fucked up to be had
And today's the day that we
Kick it doggystyle in the IM
And in the IM we know
That we're all mad here

Twinkle, twinkle little star

How I wonder what you are
Up above the world so high
Like a diamond in the sky

Locked out into transgression
Repression of emotions
Controlling depression
The compression of the lungs does not produce
I'm loose, dangling like a silver blue noose
What's not, is always what is
His muffins became my mind
Blind from conception
The deception of my soul belongs to one
And she has the gun
Blunder is my middle name
Asunder is how we're torn the same
This flame never flickered, it just went out
We met and departed, the Ankh and the Stout
Bring me where I haven't been
Show me all I haven't seen
But do we say what we mean
Or mean what we say
I dream, cause then I stay
I'm seein' stars all day
I am a Nursery Rhyme
It's all a matter of time
That we'll all be part of an army
But I rely on God to guard me
Through the heart and the mind
Deep inside, in visions I always glide

Be by my side
Because our dreams coincide
Live life out to its max
We aimin' for the sky

Then the traveler in the dark
Thanks you for your tiny spark
He could not see which way to go
If you did not twinkle so

Sometimes we're targeted as bisexual heretics
Seeing the world through crucial hypnotics
Writing stories of brutal plot twists
That's why our thoughts are elevated
Guard your heart or you might just end up jaded
Feelin' hella faded
We made it, we contagious
Outlandishly courageous
With material to fill millions of pages
The fire in me rages
So I write it, you cite it, recite it
Then buy it, just try it
Make success the only option
After ascension you should be exhausted
I know they think I lost it
Cause I lay it on thick and keep it hot
Like Beggar's Pizza
Tell me where I should meet ya, greet ya
Ya got tagged by the Mark of the Keeper
Dig deeper like Shaun T

I stick with Insanity
Like a schizotypal
When did we become bipedal
When did we pick up a mic
And feel what it could be like

In the dark blue sky you keep
And often through my curtains peep
For you never shut your eye
Till the sun is in the sky

Alice was a Pisces
But now I need Aquarius
The water, not the fish
I could sting you if you wish
I could sing to you if you insist
But then you're crawling through a Black Mist
The White Rabbit is partially to blame
For this Triptych list
I'm blessed
Even at a horror fest
In LA my chest was bleeding
It was a journey I ended up needing
No path other than succeeding
Sometimes life is fleeting
But if we search within it meaning
We will feel our psyches changing
The rabbit hole is infinite
But the descent into is not
In Underland am I an immigrant

Mad Hatter, or its equivalent
I don't know if you catch the intent
When the metaphor is too intricate
Fuck it, it's magnificent
I put the omnipotent in a predicament
My throat is like a wind instrument
Almost unlimited
On a chess board I pop a stimulant
Visually indiscriminate
A Red King and a White Queen
Making your beheading imminent
Just because you're effeminate
Was I alice or was I Lewis Carrol
Or was I Ver
Don't cut yourself unless you want to kill yourself
This is the Metamorphosis
So get a little close to this
I'm fuckin' up your poker chips
I spit it, and grip it, and create it
With these cracked lips

As your bright and tiny spark
Lights the traveler in the dark
Though I know not what you are
Twinkle, twinkle little star

ARR Radio Interlude

NILOTIC: Welcome, ladies and gentlemen, to Apocalyptic Rhymes Radio. We are sorry to interrupt your regularly scheduled program to bring you this slight commercial interruption. We are sitting here with G-Tek the Ill Meta4 from Chicago, Illinois. This is the fuckin' Nilotic. Fuckin' respect. So, G-Tek...

G-TEK: What's up, man?

NILOTIC: Who are you and are you working on any albums that you're gonna release in the near future?

G-TEK: I'm G-Tek the Ill Meta4, you fuckin' know who I am [laughing] already, but for the viewers I am G-Tek the Ill Meta4. And yes, I am working on on some shit for—that's coming out real soon. It's called *Way of the Intercepting Rhyme*, it's gonna be a mixtape, I might be dropping an EP soon too. Maybe three, four songs, let you guys get a taste of my shit.

NILOTIC: What's the concept of *Way of the Intercepting Rhyme*? Is there a concept to your mixtape?

G-TEK: There's definitely a concept, but let me take a quick hit of this shit real quick. What is it, the water spirit?

NILOTIC: Yes, the Ocean Spirit.

G-TEK: The concept of *Way of the Intercepting Rhyme* is pretty much I'm using a lot of mainstream beats. It's not completely because that's not entirely my element, I like to be a four-dimensional emcee. Meaning, I'll do some trap shit, I'll do some fuckin' straight up underground Hip Hop shit, I'll do some—I'm experimenting with R&B and Reggae right now. But that's a little more later projects, but as for *Way of the Intercepting Rhyme*, mainly I'm gonna be doing mainstream beats, except I'm gonna be flowin' with with my type of, my type of rhyme schemes which is conscious underground Hip Hop. Talkin' about politics, talkin' about the Industry, and corruption in the Industry. And just gettin' ill wit it on some Hip Hop shit.

NILOTIC: So is this gonna be your first release?

G-TEK: As far as a mixtape goes, or just CDs in general? Yeah, it probably would be.

NILOTIC: So have you done any live performances or are you looking forward to anything coming up soon?

G-TEK: I'm gonna do my first live performance with the fuckin' Nilotic right here, man, coming up May 23rd. We're gonna be in that fuckin' Bobby McGee's and we're gonna tear that fuckin' place down, man, hell yeah, dude.

NILOTIC: We're gonna tear it a new asshole.

G-TEK: [laughing] I can't wait to fuckin' do it, yo, man, and my fans can't wait either, man. My fanbase is fuckin' awesome, man. Not much right now, but they're still supportive as fuck.

NILOTIC: So we are here on ARR Radio, coming to you live again with G-Tek the Ill Meta4. His show is going to be on May 23rd. It's next Thursday and it will be at Bobby McGee's. And other people who are performing: D-MENZ, as well as Gabe Gizz, also known as Gabe Jizz, maybe, I don't know if he's in porn or anything but it sounds like a porn name to me.

G-TEK: He's dope, bro.

NILOTIC: He is dope as fuck though, you should check out his mixtape Young World Order. Check that shit out, he's gonna be there. And a couple other people are gonna be spittin' on that mic.

G-TEK: I think Middle Finger Militia's coming through, too.

NILOTIC: For real?

G-TEK: Yeah, it's gonna be poppin' bro.

NILOTIC: Oh, hell yeah! All right, fo sho. Peace, we over and out.

Queen of Da Nile

[INTRO]
Queen of da Nile

[VERSE 1]
She's as beautiful as a fleur-de-lis
Her name is Kristy
Can I take a peek at your medical history
Does she have any maladies
Physical or psychosis
I think she thinks I'm Moses
Or was it Judas
So fuck off, the queen has chosen
There are bodies in the Nile
She's hiding it
I can see it in her smile
Sit the fuck back, relax a while
Listen to the yarn I be spinnin' buck wild
Kristy's a divorced single mother
With an onion relationship
With the local pot farmer

He's thinkin' he's a charmer
Despite the barter, each night
They're at each other's throats
As you can see, she put her fingers
Around his neck and choked
The demon's been invoked
If the Sunshine's been revoked
He's a father
I thought men were supposed to conquer
But the only thing he thought was that *I want her*

To him she was a taunter
You know the way a dealer saunters
But her rejection was enough
To make him tie a noose
Lucky Spoon was there to stop it
And to top it
She's got children, no income,
And a landlord who wants to fuck her
Fuck it, just ease up off her nuts
She feels stuck in a rut
So she downs a bottle of Jameson
What a shame it's been
Numb my pain again
She's screaming *fuck off*

So I take a hit and cough
Schizophrenic, twist off the top
Her brain is lost, the wrath starts
With flipping tables
Life's no more Aesop's Fables

When the journey gets unstable
That's why she'll drink her heart away
Anal rape and GHB
Her world is not what she dreamed
But she's still the fucking queen

[CHORUS]
If alice is the king
Am I by default the queen
Listen to the words I sing
Life is now what you dream
Queen of Da Nile
Queen of Da Nile
Queen of Da Nile

[VERSE 2]
His name rhymes with jaded
An engineer top graded
Before his eyes faded
Always part of the team
Three Floyds patron since sixteen
But his brains didn't wash out with his dreams
Come clean, popular kid turned lonely
I don't think you're phony
But you're screaming "fucking hold me"
Don't scold me, promote me
Come close to see an inner vacancy
Filled with vodka
I didn't mean to call ya out on this one
Life can still be fun

But you're saying it's all undone
Might as well use that gun
Fuck it, I won't run
Fresh out of jail wanting to set sail
But he's emotionally a bit frail
The real world is like a javelin impaled
Drink until it's gone
That's why he's so withdrawn
His guts are laid out on the lawn
With a brother away at rehab
A dome's a giant meth lab
Keep a death tab
Here, smoke the herb and dream
Build your self-esteem
Like the muscles in the mean
Fuck it, he's the queen
Fuck it, he's the queen

[CHORUS]
If alice is the king
Am I by default the queen
Listen to the words I sing
Life is now what you dream
Queen of Da Nile
Queen of Da Nile
Queen of Da Nile

[OUTRO]
This is for my friends in low places
Feelin' they've fallen short of God's graces

I smoke hella bud
And have nothing but love
I smoke hella bud
And have nothing but love

* * *

(The following is transcribed from the Occupy Providence audio used as the outro for *Psychoactive*.)

She packed up her tent too, didn't she?

I don't know if she packed up her tent, but I know she packed up her tent earlier.

And think about this. Y'all doing something for the love of humanity. You doing something for the love of humanity. That's what I am. I'm a humanist. I-I-I love—I'm part of the humane society, not the inhumane society. Cause these motherfuckin' Capitalist pigs all they fuckin' are is just inhumane people. You understand me? They ain't even worried about the people that need to eat, people are starvin', the kids are starvin'. You know what? That's my worry, that's my fuckin' fear. That's the reason why I'm payin' welfare, SSI, medical. What, are you serious? You understand? Your superiority complex they takin' care of everybody. You ain't takin' care of nobody but yourself, you self-centered bastards. Shut the fuck up, sit down, and get served, ya dummy! You need to serve yourself!

Go get a plate of caviar and eat that shit, you know why? Cause I'm gonna have some ribs, some pork, steak or something and we'll overeat and we gonna laugh at you motherfuckers because we are the masters. You are a motherfuckin' minority. Shut the fuck up and sit back!

Damn straight! Damn straight!

And this is for my people. With love. Ya dig? This is the reason why they call me the devil. Remember, the devil's the angel of music, you forgot about that? Ya dig? My spit gave me nothin' but truth. So if you didn't understand, we got a lot people walking around the land with nowhere to live. A lot of strife and struggle, or we'll just sit back and chill trying to figure out how to juggle. To way to make a hustle so we can sit back and eat. You lookin' at me laughin' at the people but you don't understand you ain't equal. You ain't even enough, you a minority, dawg, and I'm callin' your bluff. The account's mine. You mad cause you ain't got the paper. Lookin' at me but you all got the vapors. Guess what, I clear your account and leave y'all broke and if you dumb, guess what, you'll be lyin' in smoke. Cause if I die y'all gonna be broke. Your money ain't worth nothing out of the country, so how you talkin' dumb like you better than me? You lookin' at everybody around here talking bout they dumb. But guess what? You dumb. Cause we from the slums. We know how to live and we born survivors. But guess what? I'm gonna put it together like MacGyver. Deuces. Thank you. My name is [indecipherable]. My social is 03850299. That's the account number. Jeffrey Stanza, Jehovah-jireh, and also it's 18000 other accounts. That's all for America, not just for America, all countries. And I'm the global financial backer. That's the reason why they call me the Black Prince of every country. It's saying the devil, cause I'm not really their family but I'm their family. I'm the adopted family because I'm the financial backer. The globe is in jeopardy because of white supr—not because of white supremacy, sorry, because of supremacy issues period. Ya-nuh dig? Because all rich spoiled rotten rich kids is don't want people to have anything. And you know what? If that's your issue, y'all can be without and we could take over. Cause you know we are the masters. If you are not willing to let the masters live, then you are willing to die.

So why do they call you the devil?

Cause I'm a Black Prince. That's why they call me the Dark Prince. Because of my skin color. Cause I'm the black man that helps finance everybody and I'm the actual crowned prince of every country with every family, with every royal family. America is denying everybody's royalty, everybody's right to live because of supremacy issues. It's not about color, it's about background. These silver spoon kids that's mad because everybody else is about to eat. They don't want anybody else to be on their level. That's all it is. They don't want anybody else to have. And you know what? Yous a assholes cause you know why? Your grandparents or parents had to start just like we did. So shut the fuck up and sit back! Get served, dummy! Cause you know what? The money you got, the reason why you keep getting money, I gotta pay your waitresses and everything else. So shut the fuck up and get served! This is a big thing that I like to do. Fuck you if you don't understand! We are the people and we need our money. Holla. It's not just for me, it's for everybody. Deuces.

[NILOTIC]
Aqua-lyptic Rhymes Records
Psychoactive mixtape 2013
Nilotic
Splashing through the shallow end
Watching out for sting rays
Apocalyptic Rhymes Records

Fuck you if you don't understand!

antiSwag EP (2013)

1. antiSwag 2. InI
3. Keep Ya Mouth Shut 4. Lightbulb
5. Suck a Deep Dick 6. Chi-Town Queen

Some of my favorite lyrics are on this strange little EP. The songs in antiSwag planted the seeds for my later work to become really spiritual. It was the beginning of MC Pan taking shape. The metamorphosis had already begun. Remember, I am just me and you.

antiSwag

[INTRO]
Nilotic, the antiSwag fag
Apocalyptic Rhymes Records
We're coming to the fuckin' Industry
It's the Apocalypse
Take it over!

[VERSE 1]
Listen, iffen
I started spinning rhythms in graffiti
Finally release me
From this prison meant to restrain me
A dying fetus coming back
This is a parasitic fact
Etched into a clouded cataract
Into an emcee's mind is a tesseract
Compacted into an unstable form
With a stage persona torn
Creating an antiSwag - fag
With Lady GaGa in the crosshairs
Of a rainbow sniper rifle

So remember never trifle
With a homicidal queer
Hip Hop's greatest fear
Emo gangstas shedding crocodile tears
Your bling-bling won't give you wings
Sing to the intellectual perceptual spectrum
Instead, you're tripping drums
Ears dripping with Wayne alien cum
I have fun

[CHORUS]
Flip the red, white, and blue
Into, an anti-GaGa flag
AntiSwag fag dedicated to the true
So watch the way you brag

[VERSE 2]
Anti-GaGa
Worse than crying over spilled milk
First man dying over filled milfs
A body made of silk
She's become transparent
A seductive evil ferret
Unaware she's become a marionette
But don't fret just yet
This is how my chess board is set
You think you're at the Apex
I'm a taken queen waiting for a pawn to bring me back
So don't distract yourself
The Fame Monster's on my shelf

Waiting for me to fuck her
When it comes to her and I, she's stuck-er
A sucker
Stefani Germanotta
Illuminati firm ya gotta plot her
Dropping blotter
The eye is here to spot her
My fashion is her ashes
As GaGa bats false lashes
A fake crying over lost shoes
I choose to bring 'em Truth

[CHORUS]
Flip the red, white, and blue
Into, an anti-GaGa flag
AntiSwag fag dedicated to the true
So watch the way you brag

[VERSE 3]
My mission is fishin' in the stream
For stars living in an American dream
Everything is as it seems
A culture tearing at its memes
I'm redeemed
As an asymmetric quilt
Held together with global flood silt
I'm your muddy buddy built
From pieces of a severed penis throne
Farthest from a popism clone
I've disowned this industry

Cause it's aural cloud is raping me
A million cameras taping me
But is that what's shaping me
Now I'm breaking free
Clearing eyes to brighter see
So sit and have some tea with me
We can just be
Don't flee from this eternal jubilee
Cause an orchestra is a symphony
Fuck the industry
All they have is false imagery
I come forth visibly
Not timidly
Express brilliantly your epiphany
Because we are all the Trinity

[CHORUS]
Flip the red, white, and blue
Into, an anti-GaGa flag
AntiSwag fag dedicated to the true
So watch the way you brag

[OUTRO]
Cause this is Apocalyptic Rhymes Records
Comin' to the fuckin' industry
California to Chicago to Providence
Fuckin' everywhere on the map, bitch
Suck a Deep Dick
antiSwag

InI

[INTRO]
It's Nilotic
It's a random-ass motherfuckin' song
But I like it because it was divinely inspired
What up! Yeah! Check it out!

[VERSE 1]
We come up from the Underground
Like zombies, but conscious
She watches like a flaming eye
Devilish and monstrous
Your pain may be a constant
But I was born without a conscience
In the darkness I was honest
I promise

The grin is turning evil
An anarchist upheaval
Like a bloody battle medieval
Check your information retrieval
The weasel is anthropomorphic

To distort your logic
To jerk you out of autopilot
Quiet, Violet, it's a moment of silence
Succeeded by more violence
How can they have compliance
Manufactured and anonymous
Clones
Mirrors of the drones
Spit it straight into their domes

[CHORUS]
I am just me and you
I am just me and you
I am just me and you
I Am

[VERSE 2]
We're here to shake it up
If you ain't got nothin' to say
Then tape it shut
There's a village in the cut
Stuck in a rut
American mutt
Do it in the butt
We're all smut
You slut
I'm sorry, the sky is still starry
That's where I'm headed
Out of the town of dead ends
So your ears would you please lend

To me for a second
You did come when I beckoned
Because I tell your stories
A goddess descending to Earth from Ceres
The God and I are married
She the prince and I the faery
Do I still come off as scary
Good, you motherfuckin' Mary
Staring, we're swearing at the pairing
Snaring drums tearing
But eternally declaring
I'm daring to be caring
We're repairing what we're wearing
No more despairing just blaring

[CHORUS]
I am just me and you
I am just me and you
I am just me and you
I Am

[VERSE 3]
All I see are dead macoons
So make room for a mushroom Dune
With spice to entice
If you step to me twice
Your death will be decided with the dice
Wicked ice
I've got it on the granite
A deciphered picture

Made of Tantric eccentric fanfic
Fuckin' pass it motherfuck-it
I'm hittin' the snake bowl
What's your motherfuckin' fate goal
Never slow because our soul knows
How to make our energies glow
When our heads hit the pillows
We'll finally dissolve the plot to leave us split
And never resolved
After I take this hit,
This equation's getting solved

[CHORUS]
I am just me and you
I am just me and you
I am just me and you
I Am

I Am
I Am
Just me and you
I Am
We are
We are
We Am
We Am
We Am

Keep Ya Mouth Shut

[INTRO]
What do you know?

[CHORUS]
Say say
I don't know about that shit
Say say
I don't know about that shit
Say say
I don't know about that shit
Say say

[VERSE 1]
You wake up imprisoned
By Lifespan Corporation
Paid to keep you alive
But in a state of vegetation
Feeling no sensations
Numb to all revelations
Have patience and stay resilient
To their system

The way we film it is brilliant
But if you remain different
And literate, consider it
A mind conquest against the fascist
A corrupted interest basis
Keeping us in stasis
Remain amazing
With lyrical guns blazing
But if the Authority isn't the entity you're praising
Then your life's gonna need re-phrasing
They don't want your brain vibrating
So if they swipe you, an anarchist terrorist
This is the only thing you should be stating

[CHORUS]
Say say
I don't know about that shit
Say say
I don't know about that shit
Say say
I don't know about that shit
Say say

[BRIDGE]
Keep ya mouth shut (keep it shut)
Keep ya mouth shut (keep it shut)
Keep ya mouth shut (keep it shut)
Keep ya mouth shut (keep it shut)

[VERSE 2]
They make it our fate to hallucinate
In a holographic maze
So don't hesitate to evolve
Higher than primates
Face the facts
Your green stacks
Won't save you from a mean axe
Or paying income tax
But if you cash in on that advance
Your axe might balance out the cracks
Get a grip
Joined at the hip
Come join me on this trip
After a sip of some dandy dip
I flip and take a double dip
With a quivering lip
Nip it in the bud
I'm smoking
Contemplating how to provoke ya
I'ma theoretically soak ya
And stimulate to promote ya
To a level better to be unfettered
Like a balloon
You'll reach the height of it soon
Wait, I forgot
My mind ain't mine
And I'm still blind
Oh, I'm sorry, Officer

[CHORUS]
Say say
I don't know about that shit
Say say
I don't know about that shit
Say say
I don't know about that shit
Say say

[BRIDGE]
Keep ya mouth shut (keep it shut)
Keep ya mouth shut (keep it shut)
Keep ya mouth shut (keep it shut)
Keep ya mouth shut (keep it shut)

[VERSE 3]
I'ma flip it right quick
To the Spirit I stick
Like an animist
Almost a pacifist
Eyes quivering the mist
I insist that you grace us
With the pleasure of internal treasure
An alchemical contribution
Male and female fusion
An androgyny sacred unity
We're fluid, Ji
Just water like our life source
So perceive it to guide your course
Oh snap, I don't think I took that college course

Of course, I read about the pale horse
But I forgot how a mythic law gets enforced
I'm chillin' with the Norse
Holler at the father
I could be your son or daughter
I'm that otter in fresh water
No, no
Come back to Earth
You're living in this curse
Low-level stress
Couldn't you guess
That Buddha said it best
What thoughts do you now ingest
On your inner journey
Or is it just for profit
Declaring yourself a prophet
A Hermetic schizophrenic
Deciphering TV static
They think you're crazy, but fuck it
You amaze me, praise be
To She who made we
An ecstatic symphony of chi
Come and see
We are the one that just BE
SHE

But you don't know about that

[CHORUS]
Say say

I don't know about that shit
Say say
I don't know about that shit
Say say
I don't know about that shit
Say say

[BRIDGE]
Keep ya mouth shut (keep it shut)
Keep ya mouth shut (keep it shut)
Keep ya mouth shut (keep it shut)
Keep ya mouth shut (keep it shut)

[OUTRO]
BITCH
Keep ya fuckin' mouth shut
Cause you don't know about that shit
Better not tell anybody what you fuckin' know
Because we'll throw you away
Nobody will ever hear from you ever again
Ha ha!
We control it

Lightbulb

[CHORUS]
Don't turn up
Unless you turn your brain on
(Lightbulb)

[VERSE 1]
I am that light
Illuminating your neocortex
Not a hex
I'm just a speck
But we can change how our deck is set
Disassemble the complex
Until it's spotless
Mind-music, lossless
This is an initiation process
So keep focus
Promote it
See past the swarm of locusts
Like Moses
You ain't paralyzed, you're frozen

Level up
Huddle up
Muddied in blood puddles
But I became aware of my Reptilian
My Hitler, my politician
I'm a stickler, no one fickler
Contra-sexual contradiction
Your brain on superstition
Thinking you'll go to hell for masturbation
Don't stay in the dark hoping you'll go far
Cause everything you want or can be
You already have and are
You already have and are

[CHORUS]
Don't turn up
Unless you turn your brain on
(Lightbulb)

[VERSE 2]
My seven higher angels
Have seven lower demons
Lust when my mind is on the semen
But I'm dreamin' of the cosmos
My crown, a million petaled lotus
It was God that spoke us
But I walk the middle ground
Hoping they can hear my sound
Balance what you found
Like a dick in the dirt, head in the clouds

I'm above the Earth
But my face is with the clowns
Is it a curse
Where I fall y'all will raise a mound

Institutions crumbling
We're bumbling
Stumbling over stones
Children with pains of being grown
Sown stitches, blown switches
They think we're witches
When the Matrix is glitchin'
Stop bitchin', we're listin' and insistin'
We power up our brains
To end this pain
Cause when you turn up the ignorance
Indifference will never inherit deliverance

[CHORUS]
Don't turn up
Unless you turn your brain on
(Lightbulb)

Suck a Deep Dick

[VERSE 1]
I'm that thing you never seen
I'm not a fuckin' meme
I'm a vivid dream of a different scene
Come clean when I scream
So cream in the seam
I'm a fiend
Could you cope with what I've seen
More horrific than a reject of the Devil
I float to a higher level
Small pebble tossed to sea
Still ripples cause of me
Consolidate what it is you see
But you still can't get over me
They say, "what's up with his hair?"
I couldn't care less
When we gaining success
Feelin' the stress
Bring some order to this mess
I don't necessarily need to impress
It's a test when I rise above the rest

I bring it from my chest

[CHORUS]
Suck a deep dick
Nilo to the tic
Insanity no trick
Alchemist when I spit
I'm just that fuckin' sick
So suck a deep dick

[VERSE 2]
Been spillin' my soul from the beginnin'
Mama says I'm sinnin'
And I never left 'em grinnin'
Just their heads spinnin'
Skinnin' 'em alive
Tell me for what is it you strive
I'm alive!
Up from the grave
I pave the way
Don't play to save the day
You'll crave a different name
Cause your sound is just the same
I work outside the frame
Can you feel my pain
A body that contains
An eternity of vibrations
I make you feel sensations
You never knew existed
Twisted psyche, don't blind me

You bind me but now find me
Rewind, I'm coming back
To pick up all your slack
You're making this a fact
Attacked by an abstract tact
Tatted like a book
Look I have impact because I'm backed
Yeah!
I watch you all react
I'm grotesque but still intact

[CHORUS]
Suck a deep dick
Nilo to the tic
Insanity no trick
Alchemist when I spit
I'm just that fuckin' sick
So suck a deep dick

[VERSE 3]
This is Providence
Here to show omnipotence
So what do you think the problem is
Cause I bring it with the diligence
And if you say it's frivolous
I'ma remain infamous with the instruments
Within the Seven Synthesis is a stimulus
Even though it seems like a syllabus of wickedness
It's soon to become felicitous
A queer with a career

Making emcees appear austere
I'm at the threshold of pain
But if you can't restrain me with the mundane
Nilotic stays to remain in this game
And I maintain
Seven times seven times
Even though I'm caked in grime
Covered in slime
I still find a way to shine
Because the rhyme is mine
And everywhere you go
My name is what they'll know
Like N9ne say, you're gonna love me tomorrow
So much more than a king, yo
I'm a Pharaoh
Yo, I'm a Pharaoh
Yo, I'm a Pharaoh

[CHORUS]
Suck a deep dick
Nilo to the tic
Insanity no trick
Alchemist when I spit
I'm just that fuckin' sick
So suck a deep dick

[OUTRO]
Apocalyptic Rhymes Records
Back in the fuckin' building
What y'all know about that shit

Suck a deep dick
It's Nilotic!
Jacob Steep, Rosa McGee,
Edie Warhol, Adolf Crowley,
Benevalment, Priest Crow, alice
But now it's King David's ascension

Chi-Town Queen

[VERSE 1]
I'm fuckin' with this chess board
A console I gotta press more
Hardcore, never thought you'd hear
My music from my vocal cords
Shoeless drove me away
But now I'm here to stay
I'm steady, I don't sway
Chi-Town queen
In her eye, a mischievous gleam
I'm living my own dreams
Never falling from these balance beams
I'm not what I seem
A taken queen back like a fiend
Life is now green, lean, mean, and freed
No other option than to succeed
I bleed just like you
Open to what's true
As this creature, I am new
Chicago, I will rock, bro
Hip Hop, I don't stop, yo

And I realize:
You can't have a king without a queen

[CHORUS]
Chi-Town Queen
This is what we need
A quantum-Tantric unity
Where I see you and you see me

[VERSE 2]
GaGa ain't no bodhisattva
The government just flaunts ya
Independent, I will taunt ya
Pause, brah
Government hooker
Ghetto crack cooker
Look closer or they demote ya
I float like a remote satellite of Earth
God grows glory from the dirt
Dance with trees in a flowing skirt
A Druid nature goddess in a sunbeam headdress
I clear skies or make it rain
We free minds, ending all our pain
But I stay critically insane
Our immortal tradition never fades
So escape from all the hate
That doesn't mean run from your fate
Just know our Spirit's great, Earth-Race
Chicago, know my face

Providence, I left my grace
To come back to this Distanian state

And I realize:
You can't have an animus if you don't have an anima

[CHORUS]
Chi-Town Queen
This is what we need
A quantum-Tantric unity
Where I see you and you see me

[VERSE 3]
She's the anima of my Shadow
I'm moving like a queen
Within an aura's golden glow
I don't need all my pawns in a row
Cause I don't control ya
But my music will console ya
The Apocalyptic is here
Wipe away the sneer
Because I want to eradicate your fear
Wipe away your tears
Checkmate the industry like a knight
The Peaceful Warrior's fight
G-Tek and InI take flight
Come into all your sight
My game is fuckin' tight
But I'm anti-game, anti-same, anti-lame
I'm gonna go back West

But till then I'm in the nest
Rockin' Bobby McGee's and Reggie's
Fuck sayin' please
But get off your fuckin' knees
I don't really need your praise
But our sounds are dope and we get paid
Ha!
You're pissed Nilotic stayed

And I realize:
She is just a projection of my own psyche
As am I a projection of hers

The L Test (2015)

1. 451
2. Earth Spins (ft. Documentaries of the Dead)
3. Double Murder
4. Fuck the Industry (ft. G-Tek the Ill Meta4)
5. Sex Mouth
6. Curse of the Empath
7. New Creature
8. Soon the Union Cometh (ft. Slaq-r)
9. Metamorphosis

undaground tape of unreleased nilotic tracks

can YOU pass the L test?

451

I'm burning at 451 degrees Fahrenheit
Read or die through my sight
Blinded on a holocaust night
Kristallnacht
Street brother walked the wrong block
And got shot
Body shakin, Luciferian illumination
Holy Spirit crawling your spine
With a tingling sensation
What's a heathen redemption
Practitioner of ritual abortion
Murder coercion
We're Legion
So make sure you're fuckin' breathing
Cause revolution is in season
We're done with kneelin'
Shout it out if you're still feelin'
And reelin', spinnin', every layer peelin'
Revealing a light held back
Factions, looks like you seen a ghost
When showed the facts

A new believer handed a religious tract
Revoke that suicide pact
React, don't hold back, you book of blood
I'll run across a landmine to prove it was a dud
So open up your pages
Red tattooed by sages restraining
The temptation to bomb Central Station
Cause I know the ragin' anticipation
To become the causation
For the annihilation
Of a corporation
So will we have damnation, creation,
Or reincarnation?
Create this a declaration of oration
Consider this a salutation
A letter from a social leper
They painted us as debtors
Invisible coins become the fetters
What's better than to send a beggar
To the shredder
Dehumanize your enemy
To a dirty monkey
Breathlessly and helplessly
An entity decaying mentally and physically
So readily accept the penalty for your ecstasy
This is how it's meant to be
The remedy for entropy
Is in your brain chemistry
Degrading a system
So how can we gain wisdom

When we're hard-wired to electric fire
And our only desire is to acquire?
Mechanical Animals
Saturated with tailor-made pathogens
Rotted out with a plastic abdomen
Haunted by binary phantoms
Reminding you you'll die with a memorandum
Black balled, the Shack called, the track stalled

Leaving me silent
Anticipating the violent
We must be fluent in our movement
The inducement of improvement
So vent your dissent
Till the foundations have been bent
And you know you're heaven sent

Earth Spins

DD: Documentaries of the Dead
NILOTIC: Steep. Come over to the side of despair
DD: Nah, man
NILOTIC: Of bleakness, of blackness
DD: Come on
NILOTIC: There's no hope for this society
DD: There is, right here, look

[NILOTIC]
Yo, fuck it
Suck the pain down to the depths
So don't expect for everything to be better
Perfect down to the letter
We're dirty, filthy, flirty, sexual perversity
That I love, I'm oh so thirsty
There's no diversity
So embrace the waste

[DOCUMENTARIES OF THE DEAD]
Suck the pain to the depths
But learn to embrace the grace

And just accept what is left
I'm bringing sight to the blind
I'm bringing sound to the deaf
Third incarnation of Christ, yes
Resurrect
I let my pain find the pen then
I let my pen find the pain then
I precisely dissect
And just watch me as I step to my left
Forgiven the sins you thought were
Too late to correct
So expect love to infect

[NILOTIC]
Fuck that shit
Let the pain infect
Reject all love that disinfects
We're all defects, live it like rejects
Our deaths don't matter, we're just subjects
Lab-rats to be dissected, tested, then directed
To the trash, watch the screen flash
When we're drained of all our cash
What's the backlash?

[DOCUMENTARIES OF THE DEAD]
Don't mean to put your shit on blast
Directed to the trash, what's the backlash?
That's a potent question that you ask
If you square the quotient then quit mopin'
Here's your potion, horror films and baby lotion

Tissue soakin' sittin' on your ass
I suppose you're copin'
Life looks a lot different depending on how you focus
Like a camera will catch anything
Depending on how you hold it
Instead of being pepper-sprayed and tased
Roped in like cattle, I'm choking on life
Declaring my independence
I'm too fucking free to battle

[NILOTIC]
Earth spins
On hinges tilted
Count our sins

[DOCUMENTARIES OF THE DEAD]
Waiting for these carcinogens
To kick in
And for these spins to begin again

[NILOTIC]
Occupy my dick
So sit on it, bitch
Even if you're good
You won't get off without a hitch
Your mouth forcibly stitched
Your world, glitched
Cause you're part of it
The movement to bring death
Cursing God to our dying breath

Forcibly sterilized, so bust off inside
She won't even realize

[DOCUMENTARIES OF THE DEAD]
Yeah, you could fit it all inside
But she wouldn't even realize
Yeah, that's no surprise
Hey, Frankenstein, I really hate to hurt your pride
But all the demons that you're speaking of
Yeah, they're all living inside

[NILOTIC]
Glorify the destruction
So bring on the seduction
How could you help the blind see
Listen to me, God took half your sight
So might as well turn out both the lights
Boom, it gets cold at nights
If it's pre-ordained that we fail
Kill yourself before you go to jail

[DOCUMENTARIES OF THE DEAD]
You shed the weight
But you can't shake the hate
Turned off half the lights,
So how is it that I'm seeing
While you're lacking all insight?
Your best attempt to flow like me
But if beauty is skin deep,
Then you are ugly inside

And your style is vile
I can see it,
You're so empty completely
When you try to smile
And you're standing next to me
Lacking complexity
While I go the extra mile
Dominance and persistence are evident
Because ever since I've been flowing
I've been better than you
Or anyone coming through
I'm a veteran like Argyle
Warn me before you flow next time
And I will prepare with some Excedrin
Take it from a champ, bro, I'm better than
You've ever been
I am transcendent, you're a child
You are dependent, infantile

[NILOTIC]
Earth spins
On hinges tilted
Count our sins

[DOCUMENTARIES OF THE DEAD]
Waiting for these carcinogens
To kick in
And for these spins to begin again

[NILOTIC]
But don't get it twisted
I only dissed ya cause
I'm Mister Deception
Depression infection
The dark devil resurrection
Put you under inspection
And steer you into the direction
Of hopelessness, possessiveness, sickness
A society on its last legs
Before I pull the plug I'll make you beg

[DOCUMENTARIES OF THE DEAD]
Heal the sickness
Blissfully put it on my Christmas wishlist
That every other gifted, twisted, sadistic misfit
From the Limp Bizkit to this kid
Whoever is ready to get ballistic
You had your shot and then missed it
Then I picked it up where you left off
That's why I remain persistent
This is the instance of a twisted tale
That gets lost in a instant

[NILOTIC]
We both point and missed
But listen, both sides persist
And tangle together
To make our wits thin

[DOCUMENTARIES OF THE DEAD]
Yo, man, all this shit stinks
Let's put an end to this thing
But not one over the other
Finding a balance between good and evil
Stay tuned for the sequel
Thank you all for listening

NILOTIC: Earth spins, Earth spins, Earth spins
DD: Spins
NILOTIC: I'ma hurt you before you hurt me
DD: You can't do that
NILOTIC: I'ma stab you before you stab me
DD: I'll hug you before you hug me
NILOTIC: Yeah, I'ma fuck you over before you fuck me over
DD: I've got only love but strictly brotherly
NILOTIC: I'll be evil before you turn evil
DD: I'm good, man

Double Murder

[INTRO]
Ver-ily I say unto you
If we were still together
Your life would go no further
We'd have a double murder

[VERSE 1]
We're both an Animagus
Letting symbolism rape us
So come face us
Bastards and bitches
Cunts with sexual glitches
Misrepresented like the goat
A she-devil boat
With a leak, you'll never float
Ripped down by strange maidens
Releasing caged Satans
I'm a snake
Wooden stake, reptilian cat
Nipping at your leg like a bloodbath rat
Fuck you like an animal

Eating your heart and then your pussy
Your one, your only cannibal
I'll murder your family to possess you
Here's the clues so you eternally know the truth
Of salvation desecration
I'll crawl your insides
So you know where death abides
In a womb snare, bloodlust hides
Miscarriage, Lucifer induced
Consume the child, you've been seduced
When slavery is forever, your life has been reduced
And we'll have a double murder
With a double ring, a double noose

[CHORUS]
With you
It won't be murder-suicide
Deep in my bowels
I feel that Jesus cried
One man for one woman
We live the way died
But we worship one, the self
So we fear all lovers lied

[VERSE 2]
Become one through the tip of my gun
Painted vibrant, hate-fucking
Fainted vibrated, taste cutting
Lick your wounds to make me more
Psychic vampire, we're wicked to the core

In a flesh mesh mess
Can't lie to God, so now confess
We writ parallel plans under much duress
I wield a poison Scorpion sting
You, a goat with massive horns that thunder brings
Voices, in unison we sing
So cling to what you know
Cause it's violence coming slow
Cut your first-born to pieces
We brought acid-rain that never ceases
And if you see the creases
The tension somewhat eases
But be this
Vindictive, manipulated,
Calculated, premeditated, and dictated
War-drums are your name recited
Equal fury, equal wrath
Can't turn it off and can't go back

[CHORUS]
Deep in my bowels
I feel that Jesus cried
One man for one woman
We live the way died
But we worship one, the self
So we fear all lovers lied

[VERSE 3]
Take me as I am
For I am he and you are she

We fail to flee
Even though clairvoyantly we see
That we're both brought to our knees
Psychically head-butting
Cutting open pathways never shutting
Let me in to drink you
My purpose is it sink you
Force mentally to think new
Who's the strong and who's the weak
When it's equality we seek
But if I'm an *Eat Me, Drink Me* freak

I may be crucified by a lover I've been tied
Choose which side to guide
When we both have separate knives
With no hesitation, we take each other's lives
Simon Says we die
Rivers dry, we can't cry
Burning love, now we fry
Repent, a savior's wish we circumvent
When you bleed I pitch a tent
Here's your only hint
In my blue eyes you'll see the glint
A gleam of a broken dream
Here things are exactly what they seem
Molested dolls slicing at the seams
There's no such thing as teams
If it's us against the world
The metaphor becomes unfurled
Drowned in a wedding gown

Lips sliced to an ebbing frown
Music is a shredding sound
The killer in you is the killer in me
Double heart, we set each other free

[CHORUS]
With you
It won't be murder-suicide
Deep in my bowels
I feel that Jesus cried
One man for one woman
We live the way died
But we worship one, the self
So we fear all lovers lied

Fuck the Industry

[CHORUS]
Fuck the Industry
Monarch slaves are being freed
Independently
Unshackle from the greed
The spirit's all we need

[NILOTIC]
Told to change my strategy
Or doors would close on me
Into the Industry
Wished to seize up and freeze up
No luck, so fuck it
Shit sucks below the ground too
What was your first clue
This shit ain't news but it's true
If you snooze you lose
But it all hinges on how you choose
Chill with the right crews
With a tight noose around throats already loose
My fuse is short, so if you take me to court

I'll court a deadly sport
Murdered for a witty retort
And if you consort with the wrong sort
Your life may be short
Your life will be short, but mine won't be
Cause I'm stretching to the end of infinity

[CHORUS]
Fuck the Industry
Monarch slaves are being freed
Independently
Unshackle from the greed
The spirit's all we need

[G-TEK]
Harnessed and harvested
Marvelous arguments
Giving empowerment to the powerless
Mentally raped by a parliament
That wants no part of us
I am free (mentally)
Fuck the Industry
We real emcees,
Ain't no puppet on some strings
Brag about my bling
Or the shit that I got
Call themselves rappers,
But really they are Pop
If you hop to what's hip
Then you're not Hip Hop

Most of these cats more gay than Nilotic
'Cept they ass still stuck in the closet
Or they stuck in a box
Cause really they are products
Are you mentally disabled
Signed to a label and you live like a fable
Mainstream versus Underground
Demons versus angels
Look man, they trying to dumb you down
With all these sounds written by some clowns
Who are pawns of a circus
Making music with no purpose
Worship of the paper
The concerts are the service
The rappers are the priests
And we are the servants
But not me (not us)
All I need
H-I-P H-O-P
Fuck the Industry

[NILOTIC]
Butterfly lies
Inferiority complexes to minimize your size
It's all to keep up a disguise
I living product with a million ghost-writers
Lyrics contrived to manufacture
Consent and compromise
Go to hell
We're breaking through their shell

[CHORUS]
Fuck the Industry
Monarch slaves are being freed
Independently
Unshackle from the greed
The spirit's all we need

[NILOTIC]
Yeah, I'm gonna say it
Fuck the Industry
I could never be how they wanted me to be
Shaped like a neglected child
Finally embraced then misplaced
Erased, never again chased
Wasted, fame never tasted sweet
Just laced with cocaine,
Blood, disgraced love
Unbreakable covenant
Either a giant or an ant
They will say you can't
So we fire back a chant
To show them where we stand
Strong as pyramids in the sand
This is our land
The burned seven on my arm is a brand
We're not kids that need a reprimand

Yeah, fuck the Industry
Independent one hundred percent

For eternity, infinity
Our immortal spirits, independent
Fuck those motherfuckers
Apocalyptic Rhymes Records
The Apocalypse of infinity
Independently

Sex Mouth

[INTRO]
Well, shit
Nilotic

[CHOURS]
I must know your deepest secret
Thrusting slow, your speech is indecent
Repeat this discreetly
Through sex mouth you teach me
I smell ether beneath her
We're one creature with a fever
And our scent shall never leave her

[VERSE 1]
Cum inside
Shhh…
I'll make out with her
After going down on her
You heard the purr or maybe just a slur
Something on the spur of the moment
I own it, her moanin'

Casually slide it in, miscalculate the sin
This is where we begin
Salivatin' behind the grin
Subtly bite the lip, hungrily excite the tip
This is when we flip and I take you on a trip
Nilotic got a tongue like Gene Simmons
Oh shit, wrong bathroom, says *women's*

Even though I'm feminine
I don't have to be a gentleman
Let him in, I'll make your skeleton my specimen
I'll pleasure you're girl until her toes curl
I'll pleasure you're girl until her toes curl

[CHOURS]
I must know your deepest secret
Thrusting slow, your speech is indecent
Repeat this discreetly
Through sex mouth you teach me
I smell ether beneath her
We're one creature with a fever
And our scent shall never leave her

[VERSE 2]
I love you
But I might want some blood too
When I'm liable, you're pliable
I chew goo till tongue lust fulfilled
We instill the tremors
Eat this pill until I kill

Just chill, I think I will
She calls me the drill
My teeth'll scrape your curves
Cunnilingus, the way I lick these nerves
This is just for pervs
But she knows it's me who serves
Sex mouth, taste like strawberry preserves
Learn it from the best
I push you to your crest
Your body is my quest
You got me tasting it like zest
Always ride me when you're facing West
Sunset to sunrise, snake eyes
Your mouth is my prize
To baptize may be unwise
We came high with breathy sighs

[CHOURS]
I must know your deepest secret
Thrusting slow, your speech is indecent
Repeat this discreetly
Through sex mouth you teach me
I smell ether beneath her
We're one creature with a fever
And our scent shall never leave her

And you shall never leave me

Curse of the Empath

[VERSE 1]
Through this storm I hold your heart
So we will never beak apart
From this nightmare, we now disembark
I'll take you on a path away from the wrath
That's the curse of the empath
These facts arose after they dispatched
Me from them they chose
I put on pain clothes
And went out to the streets
To spit healing over Hip Hop beats
Repeat, so take a seat when I speak
I could tremble from the peak
Or grovel at your feet
Come in, sit and eat when we meet
I keep discreet from the elite
Cause my people never admit defeat
I die for you
This is inexorably true
All I see is blue then it's you
I feel you in my spirit

These emotions you disperse
The energy to hit it, spin it
Sometimes I feel like a nurse
When I spit an intro-spiral verse

[CHORUS]
I'm over the curse of the empath
I think we're at an impasse
There's a compass pointing north
Balancing the spirit henceforth

[VERSE 2]
I'm a positron atom
Entering your prefrontal cortex
In space we know not of human mess
Human suffering, human misery
Here we always have some synergy
Dual energy expressed inwardly with liberty
The closest thing to magickally
Maybe wizardly
Merlin spitting rhymes to dethrone the clergy
We emerge free
Just open your eyes and see
If for the first time in your life
The gold right outside your strife
Drop the knife, I'm reaching for your hand
You can take it where you stand
Pull you to my Neverwonderland
Where everything is green, everything unseen
You overstand, then never more demean

Only the machine
You will feel serene as if in a dream
Even if you're close to splitting mental seams
Hold me as we glow
That's me absorbing dark and letting out the light
You no longer need to fight
I take the trauma from your sight
And smite it in the middle of the night
But sometimes I have to take it in
To lessen the load on the tattered skin you're in
I love, a gift given from above
I take pain from your brains
So resurrect me when I'm slain
Resurrect me when I'm slain

[CHORUS]
I'm over the curse of the empath
I think we're at an impasse
There's a compass pointing north
Balancing the spirit henceforth

[VERSE 3]
But sometimes I just wanna be like
"I kill niggas"
And under these pants ain't a dick
It's a trigger
But that ain't me, if my heart was any bigger
I'd be no body, just vigor
Part of the ether

You sip me like fine wine
As I become one with divine
But wait, devils, demons
Sorcerers, legions
Vibrations provoking secretions
I wanna FUCK YOU
I only speak in sooth
You want proof?
I'm tying up this noose
Wait, I came back into grace
Upon my face is a shimmer without race
But a creature God most assuredly misplaced
Cause a mere touch could jerk the tears
Or provoke my deepest fears
All I wanted was your cheers
But where were you when I came near
This is unmistakably clear
Love needs the love to flourish
And when it don't get nourished
I just hope it's me you cherish
Cause if I perish it's *you* who live my dream
The one I dreamt for you
So you're woven to all that's true
If our spirit touches soon
I'll be stricken by the moon
To lay down as if one
The stitching's almost done
So don't run before it's gone
Depleted like semen

I know you're not a demon
In Eden we speak treason
Even a heathen could make our freedom deepen
That's the curse of the empath

[CHORUS]
I'm over the curse of the empath
I think we're at an impasse
There's a compass pointing north
Balancing the spirit henceforth

[OUTRO]
Yeah, this is the Nilotic
Jacob Steep
Rosa McGee
Edie Warhol
Adolf Crowley
Alice
Benevalment
Priest Crow
This one's for that Egyptian princess in my life
I seal this with a kiss
Seven

New Creature

[INTRO]
The Alchemy of Desire
Enter the Sanctuary of All Possible Worlds
We're here
Now
Now
NOW

[VERSE 1]
Let it commence
I followed the Providence
Of the 299 Carpenter
Sharpener like a partner, a word harvester
But for God I was no worshipper
Just an interpreter with spinal curvature
A torturer, they think I'm a murderer
But I'm closer to a sorcerer
Never been a fuckin' perjurer
I'm a new creature
That always spits with conviction
Never contrived, no fiction

If you let in, spread your mind open
Y'all wouldn't have a problem with my depiction
But you livin' in suspicion
Words leakin' is the product of the friction
Sayin', that's not his jurisdiction
However, after dereliction
I rap a benediction
Dissipate the rage even if I get booed offstage
We're at the end of an Age
So will we bring Aquarius or the Aeon of the Scorpion
Better count your men, will the means justify your ends
Defend, look at the way we contend
We fight for our life, but I'm new
Give me beats with a fife or a bagpipe
The time is just right, like fruit that just riped
It's a rhyme to get ya hyped

[CHORUS]
The rap game needs
A new creature
This tapped vein bleeds
A teacher for the people
The mapped train leads
Come out from under the steeple
You're my people and I'm the new creature

[VERSE 2]
My state is not an ocean, not an island,
Not a road
If I don't know where I come from,

How do I know where to go
It's not where you're from, not where you're at,
It's where you're going
And I am going home
Back to claim the throne
Y'all did never know
How much that I have grown
Since I've been away, ya'll may naysay
But I'll pray on this day a papier mâché name
Doused with water
Thought I'd have to scream a mayday
Hold conclave to soul-save
None of you know the extent to which I gave
My mind was in an Ocean State
As220, never underestimate
If you hesitate
Even for a second, you disintegrate
An abyss you get left in
But I crept in
Testin' the waters of the East
Even AI in Boston
What did it cost him?
I lost it thinking rap would get me tossed in
But I rocked it
Told to stop it when I didn't make a profit
But the RI believed in me
I kept an open heart,
So some rappers started deceiving me
Khyree would slyly undermine me
Use my studio for free and then deny me

You lied to me, homie
Don't cry to me, homie
You tried to be gay with me, homie
I understand that you lonely
But I never sucked your cock
And for that I fuckin' rock

[CHORUS]
The rap game needs
A new creature
This tapped vein bleeds
A teacher for the people
The mapped train leads
Come out from under the steeple
You're my people and I'm the new creature

[VERSE 3]
This presentation is my transcription
Of spiritual evolution
Transformation, transmutation
Positive vibration
I still give you stimulation
This world is malleable and changeable
So, we're bringing the solution
I got crew in the East
I got crew in the West
I got crew in the balance
But don't forget me in my absence
I always love a challenge

And you know I've got the talent
I can make it without alice
To everyone who's been associated with ARR
Much love
We are the brightest stars
Light leaking through our scars
But it ain't easy to set the bar
Now I have to address the bizarre
Back out in the East, Will, I'm sorry
You had to see the BeaST released
But hey, that night had to be the yeast
The catalyst to turn me from a masochist to an animist
That made me more passionate as an activist
But you saw it as abandonment
As you looked out in astonishment
I didn't mean it to be a contaminant
I'm cursed to be the antagonist
But you know I'll always stay compassionate
Never intended to make you feel inadequate
But it was no accident
We found ourselves stuck in this entanglement
So, audience, what is your analysis?
Thinking you got nothing in common
With a Manson-looking crossdressing
Rapper with painted face
Still within God's grace
Wielding a double-edged truth sword
Why you think JCM's *Hedwig* struck a chord?
My soul has been restored

With a journey mapped out on my spinal cord
From this day forward, I won't ever be ignored

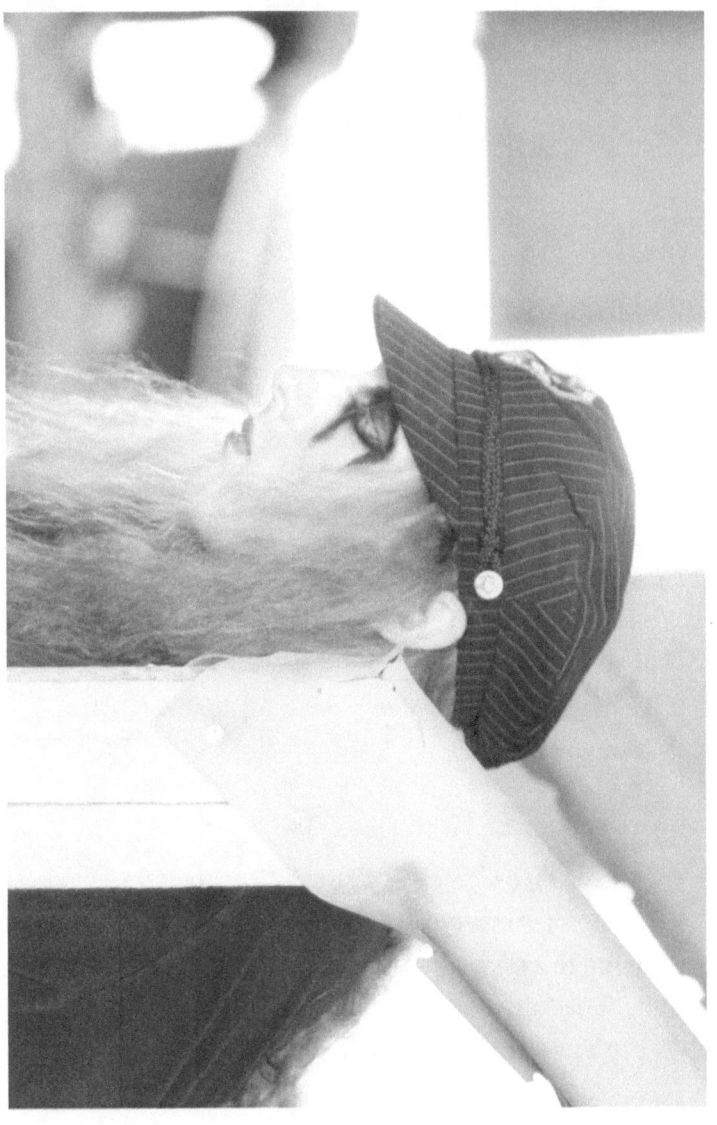

Soon the Union Cometh

[SLAQ-R]
When you dream
Your lies become true
And what's left of you
Will surrender soon
When you dream
You see what you feel
The visions seem real
Like her blood you spilled
When you dream

[VERSE 1]
We made love like it was music
Us, just notes in a twisted fusion
Coming to a slippery conclusion
But it's deceptive the way we use it
We're a never never tapestry
Weaved in blood

These hieroglyphics depict a global flood
Soon the union cometh
A love that you could covet
I plummet, she said to ride this bullet
The curtain's closed
I grasp the cord and pull it
When the show begins, don't ignore it
Explore it
Cause I pour more, for what I store
Is a whole lore before *Nevermore*

Forgotten, P-O-E is me
I'm praying for the raven to save these engravings
Etchings, rants, and ravings
While society is decaying
Work on what you're saying
Art, music is praying, meditating
Feel male and female melding
We're bleeding
Balancing the meeting
But we know the Shadow's call
Are you prepared to take that fall
Are you prepared to take that fall…

[SLAQ-R]
When you dream
Your lies become true
And what's left of you
Will surrender soon
When you dream

You see what you feel
The visions seem real
Like her blood you spilled
When you dream

[VERSE 2]
We hugged and then unplugged
From a future not yet spun
But told like a yarn
A story to disarm guards
That surround every part of your heart
But you're integrated into my art
Absolute but fabricated
An album is just life truncated
But my style is still mutated
Cause I drank her essence
I'm one man honored by your presence
So don't mind my hesitance
You'll find your inheritance
A fragrance effervescent
I'm aching for an instant
Just a flash of fire
Satiation for your desire
It's imperative to acquire
And sexually conspire
We're creatures in the flesh
But higher than the rest
So we are without excuse
But I feel it's all an elaborate ruse
There are no rules, only for fools

We have different tools
Spirits trapped in body
But technically
I copy of a copy of a copy
Of a copy of a copy of copy of a copy…

[SLAQ-R]
When you dream
Your lies become true
And what's left of you
Will surrender soon
When you dream
You see what you feel
The visions seem real
Like her blood you spilled
When you dream

[VERSE 3]
We all experience the spiritual side effects
The crowd rejects but we still reflect
Like light refractured
Will we end before the rapture
A time-lapse HD capture
For all those left behind
Make no mistake in meta-mind
Rewind to the Apocalypse
It's here like a dark eclipse
As the brain trips
The world we live in tips
Take a sip of fatal mist

Because our union cometh
Together, one behemoth
What would this marriage cost us
They say the church is the bride of Christ
Sacrifice is the price
Soul becoming ice
I don't fuck with dice
Cause in my life I've more than just a chance
Notice me after one backward glance
You're already in my pants
So it won't be hard to slide 'em off
Already hot and wet, ready to get off
Let our union cometh
I've got you by the stomach

[SLAQ-R]
When you dream
Your lies become true
And what's left of you
Will surrender soon
When you dream
You see what you feel
The visions seem real
Like her blood you spilled
When you dream

Metamorphosis

[G-TEK]
I was chillin' with the magic caterpillar
That smokes hookah
And he looked at me, he was like
Yo, G-Tek, go tell Nilotic
To kill that shit, yo

I mean, obviously she's like sacred knowledge, it's interesting that she's there with the hierophant. You need like the high priestess energy of... it's the accumulation of knowledge that's just for you.

[NILOTIC]
I'm just floatin'
Ascension like a demigod, demigod
I speak the people's mind
Call me demagogue, demagogue
This is pure soul
You're an analogue, analogue
Grow with me to the promised land
The Hip Hop synagogue

I emerge from Plato's cave crawlin'
Like a worm, a larvae toward my callin'
But what if I found myself fallin'
Stallin' on the track, but still maulin' the wack
Cause I'm coming back from the underground
But I still gotta track the the facts of the evolution
Of my sound, started out in Nigredo
Shat out of darkness with a questionable libido
But my aim was still to get free though
But it's hard to crawl out of hell when you feel low
Even in hell dot com where I'm from
I knew I had that real flow
See, know, once I past the worm stage
I'ma fly like a flock of seagulls
They chopped down the tree of knowledge
Built a treehouse in a bloody collage
Where I was initiated, radiated, illuminated
By Illuminati
When they raped me to do damage
Fuck a bandage, I languished in a new language
A different kind of challenge
In *Fallen Flesh*

But I spit fresh, I enmeshed a crossdress mess
Fuck it, I confess
Instead of cursing I made it bless
My breath separates me from the rest
It's a test to see if I play chess
Etch stress into the press

I don't feel less cause of my death
Hit refresh, I'm wearin' a dress
Will I evoke Hip Hop success?
Yes!
Connected within the light, sex
I'm your fetish, your obsession
I'll give you the dick to relieve this tension

This is the spiritual metamorphosis
I'm neurotic with this lyrical psychosis
The Nilotic, psychotic, Doc
What's your diagnosis
Rock it
Phonetic, epileptic, prophetic
Leave 'em in hypnosis
I'm floatin'
I'm rockin' the boat when
I release you with this pen
Unplug you from the Matrix
But still only I have the tricks
To remix the Apocalypse
I'm stickin' to this beat till you retreat
I'ma perform past Hip Hop feats
See this speechless greeting when we're meeting
From rage, the enemies keep fleeing
But if you're true, come meet me
You free me when you see me
So I built you this galaxy
To dismantle this world's fallacy

But that was treasonous blasphemy
Rejected from the family
As if infected with a political malady
Hungry with no salary
Sherry already scary
Prepare me was what they did
Turned focus away from the sexual abuse as a kid
Rubedo
Almost hid in darkness with the Heartless
But now I transmute rage
To powers keeping us caged
Locked up in the maze of confusion
No solution
DNA change, illumined mutated fusion
What's the Finality conclusion
Cause what is without is within
Mired in their sin
Try to exorcise the jinns
Fuck government, the Anonymous still wins
I feel the cold winds blow through the flow
Of my poems, just show 'em
Society's in my head
Maybe we're already dead or locked in bed
It was all just a dream
But I still say fuck the mainstream
Maybe I should morph it to mid-stream
So I can achieve my dreams
Yeah

I live in the meta-world

In a meta-form
And fuck meta-girls
With the Ill Meta4
Word magic
Can be a tool of the fascist

I'm an immortal
Just my DNA coil
Planting worlds in spirit soil
Meet me at the decibel portal

Yeah, Citrinitas
Metamorphosis alchemist
Change spit to golden mist
I'm emerging from the cocoon
Transcending past the gloom
And release the psyche from its doom

This is when I become a mutated form
Emerging from the storm of demon swarms
Be informed to perform
Spirit deformed if physically conformed
Deformed
I wormed my way to freedom
Through wisdom perceived as treason
I was a heathen ripped to pieces
For one reason, revolution season
Eden garden needed Sodom as a medium
No longer ism
Indigo Children experiencing evolution

Vertigo
Coming through the radio
Satellitic analysis it's a catalyst
When I insist to be a lyricist
The Alchemy of Desire
Grew me wings to conspire
To attain attributes of a Monarch
Butterfly
Can't silence me violently
The dark can't kill the spark
Split you down to quarks
Cover your eye little butterfly
There's a multiplicity within me
I multiply like passers-by
To sing you a lullaby
With a powerful quality pulled my Mercury
Now I'm Hermes
With Hermetic Perceptions
Hermaphroditic sensations
I reached mystical vibrations
Torched by truth
Blinded by the proof our our divinity
Music inside, we are infinity
Now you sing for me
The Godhead said as my mortal form bled
Flesh is just the body
Your spirit is what's godly
Don't follow me
We are the Universe-All fluidity
Holy Trinity, femininity, masculinity

The God within the entity
The deity, the enemy, the imagery,
The instrumentality, and empathy
I emphasize solidity
Cause our sickness is an inability
To reach maturity
We are the epitome of eternity
Cleanse the doors in your heart
Don't ignore you're at war
Peace is in the core
After immortal then there's more
I spiral past the trials and temptations
Cause there's only one destination
Promised Land, and we're there
Finally you possess the realization
Material is the fraud
But look inside yourself to find the god

Opus Magnum

The hierophant is when you get to use that knowledge in front of people. Cause it's the pope. You get to lead people-you get to be-it's like a-not just like a rockstar in front of people with like leather pants on. It's more spiritual than that.

Bonus Tracks

1. Away from Here
2. Sea Lion
3. East Coast Figures
4. God's Gift (ft. G-Tek the Ill Meta4)
5. Murder-Suicide
6. Psycho Dick
7. Apocalyptic Rhymes Chicago Cypher (ft. G-Tek & B.E.Z)

Away From Here

[CHORUS]
I want to fly away from here
To a place where there's no hate and fear
From all this want and lust and clear
A path to the sky where peace is near
Spread my wings and make sure I'm freer

[BRIDGE]
I'ma blow this place
And leave no trace

[VERSE 1]
Fuck this hateful place
Where I can't stand to see your face
Times I try to hold back the cry
But I just want to roll over and die
Fuck these walls
My screams feel like prison calls
Through all my high school halls
He cracks and falls
Through all the trends and dolls and malls

I can't sit still because through these halls
Death crawls

[BRIDGE]
I'ma blow this place
And leave no trace

[VERSE 2]
Put it back up on the shelf
And stop selling myself
I'ma leave these fears behind me and
Go to a place that's fun and can
Pick me up and hold me there
Through these years I wasted without a care
Trudging through these fuckin' tears
Scared to be the point where
I'm hooked, bound, gagged, not spared
All the tragedies that people fared
String me up and fling me down
To a place where I can't hear a sound
Of a mind bound
With everything deceitful and crowned
With darkness

[CHORUS]
I want to fly away from here
To a place where there's no hate and fear
From all this want and lust and clear
A path to the sky where peace is near
Spread my wings and make sure I'm freer

[VERSE 3]
Trick for trick
Dick for dick
Traded for nothing in this world of ticks
Blood runs from my eyes
When I think of all these ties
To be broken
And not be smokin' or tokin'
Or jokin' about the trials in my life
All I feel is strife and strife and strife
Of all the places in time and space
With this fucked up world
I come face to face
With everything I fear
And face the mace
Burning my eyes
All of my tries dies
Cut the strings, fly away balloons
To Saturn's many moons

[BRIDGE]
I'ma blow this place
And leave no trace

[CHORUS]
I want to fly away from here
To a place where there's no hate and fear
From all this want and lust and clear
A path to the sky where peace is near

Spread my wings and make sure I'm freer

Cut open the sky

This track was written and recorder for the demo version of *Lullabies for a Lifestyle*, which had a limited run for promotional purposes before recording the official versions of all tracks on *Lullabies.* This song never made it to the official album and, as they say, ended up on the cutting room floor.

Sea Lion

[NILOTIC]
Dad, Dad, look what I did, Dad
Look what I did to my dick
I cut it
Gave me the condom
Gave me the lube
Didn't say how to use it
Didn't say to love and fuck
Every girl till I was left heartless
But I took it upon myself
To cut them up and distribute the blood
Check in the hotel
Strip in the room
Swim in the mouth
Drown in the eyes
Build another house out of the lies
Burn it down till what's in the bed dies
I'm going mic to the mic
I'm already dead
Tell my dad, who's becoming blue
I'ma fuck this pad till it drains my life

And commit suicide at my debut
And take you down to the courthouse
I'ma spend some time with your separated spouse
And make Dad proud of the progress I've made
Cause I've always been the writer of my life
I'm glad that I never passed the genes
And I never put down the axe
Hip Hop man with a barren stage
And an audience with a vacant look on their face
His bra is packed and the absence of claps
Makes it hard to connect
The confusion with the words
Flutter like birds
When they fail to reach the ears
Of the ones not ready to reach that conclusion
Ahhh
Don't need your "stop it" to keep going
No, I know no one has to listen to my words
But sweet Jesus who wants to sleep with me
Way too many people to please
Not enough people to appreciate
Look it, Dad, broken hands
I cut my chest
When I wasn't in fifty emotional states

This track was written and recorded as a gift I gave to Sage Francis when I lived in Rhode Island. I found the instrumental track to his song "Sea Lion" and decided to record a cover of it. On the recording, the first part is me reciting Sage's verse on the song, then I wrote my own version to record on the second half of the beat. This is that verse. This song was recorded to go with another song I wrote and recorded called "Dear Sage." These two songs I burned to a CD and gave to Sage as my letter to him in song form. Unfortunately, "Dear Sage" has been lost to the expanses of time. Maybe Sage still has the CD, and if he does, I'm pretty sure it is the only one that exists.

East Coast Figures

[NILOTIC]
Nilotic
Bred to be psychotic and demonic
A schizophrenic lyricist
To twist minds when I'm pissed
And write lines with a fist
I'm here to insist
Don't front like you're real
If you want mainstream appeal
You'll be a meal for the Underground
Body never found
Your flow is a lie
So blow up, fall off, and then die

"East Coast Figures" is a collaboration track with several other emcees from New England. The Underground is alive and well. We're coming up out the dirt like resurrected souls.

God's Gift

[G-TEK THE ILL META4]
Damn, I just blow up
You can call it Hiroshima
Touch a beat, it dies
I'm known as the Grim Reaper
When I get up to them Pearly Gates
I walk up to Saint Peter
He'll promote me to gate-keeper
And I'll let you all in
To a Heaven that's within
God forgive me for my sin
Who have given me a gift
For the people, I will spit
That boy go hard, harder than a brick
Genius and emcee, my mentality is split
I'll miss all the fakeness
I was destined for this greatness
Time invented by a man
So my time I never wasted
And my rhymes become adjacent
To a monk that's levitatin'

Escaping out this matrix
Planning in the basement
So that day gon' come
Humans freed from enslavement
My rhyming is a habit
The government can't stand it
They ask themselves why
This spic keeps spittin' classics

[G-TEK THE ILL META4]
I always wonder dyin'
What was my life's purpose
It came to me in visions
To expose you of these serpents
Centralized banking
Money got us like their servants
More war, less schools
Human souls become so worthless
Water-Source of life
Now a product that you purchase
You are just consumers
The media's just rumors
To keep your mind fixed
While the world around is ruined
Got me contemplatin'
Are these politicians human
Bet they never told you that we got plenty of oil
Keep the prices high
Invade a country for their spoils
No rest for the wicked

To the money, they stay loyal

[NILOTIC]
We toil diligently
You feeling me
I write it in blood
I'm bringing a flood
Down from above
When I say that I love
That just means to hurt me more
Torture me for a purpose
So I must keep focus
Tell me if you ever notice
How devoted we be to this word
I'm different than you heard
I'm different than you heard
But if the word was with God
And the word was God
I descended from the spaces in my fuckin' pod
So play Pogs with rabid frogs
So dislodge the illegal mod
We're sick of cattle prods, false gods
What's the definition of Jihad
It means to struggle
I leave you befuddled
In puddles of trouble
The only thing left is rubble
You fumble with the rhythm
Cause you can't take the rumble
The treble, one pedal

Accelerate or we'll be very very late
We must circumnavigate
At any rate, the mic will vibrate
Cause it's tapped when I rap
Mind trap
Stop fighting for the scraps
Cause if Jesus was black
And we brought him back
The government would kill him with crack
So, sell me a sack
And don't ever slack
Cause an emcee who falls back
Is wack

This song was a collaboration with G-Tek the Ill Meta4, one of the first emcees I ever worked with in Chicago. He is such a talented artist and never gives up the passion for the rhyme. This track never made it onto any album, I'm pretty sure. There was one time we performed it at a show, and that was fucking epic. I wish we had a video of that.

Murder-Suicide

[INTRO]
Memory of a time
Can change in a rhyme
To become strange and redefined
If you're so inclined
To become listeners of mine

[VERSE 1]
She became the Perfect Forever
But never left a role unfettered
Down to the letter, I signed
But forgot to remind
Myself, that pain is infectious
Being insane is pretentious
Relentless control
Being played like a video game console
So now we switch roles
In my version she was squirmin'
Under a knife, begging to be my wife
So then I took her life
So much for Forever

When your heart has been severed
I made her part of my record
Bleeding on vinyl, I know
Sitting in your blood
When you were the only one I loved
I turned the knife on myself and thought
You might as well kill yourself
You're already dead
Then I buried the blade in my head

[CHORUS]
I planned a murder-suicide
For just me and you
So decide
If our love is true

[VERSE 2]
I met a little girl and dubbed her alice
She excited my mind and my phallus
To me, her place was a palace
Before this, I shoulda become callous
Full of malice
Put 'be an asshole' into practice
But I ended up on her mattress
Having sex with a halfway actress
Someone playing at seductress
I viewed sex as success
But I was wrong
Our fling didn't last long
Cause when I wrote her into a song

I guess it had to become a torch song
So sing along
Love is always one-sided
We collided then I decided
That I was in love with her and what she provided
But I was misguided
Cause she had already divided
She didn't want me, inside she presided
Over a kingdom
But in my fearsome mind
I raped her to this rhythm
Created her my victim
In my version, put an end to all her symptoms
Wisdom never came
And freedom inked in fame
Am I just the same
Pick up this gun and put it to my brain

[CHORUS]
I planned a murder-suicide
For just me and you
So decide
If our love is true

[VERSE 3]
Then, outta nowhere, I met this bitch
Wishin' for someone to pull me out of a ditch
During this time, I'm the opposite of rich
After we fucked I shoulda fallen off the map
But I fell into her trap

Searching desperately for a connection
Unaware it would become an infection
But I was weak to seduction
While she avoided detection
I enjoyed her affection
So I thought it was love
We never used a glove
Inside, I knew she had something to hide
So she became IVy, both poison and beauty
But when she fell for me
It took me off guard to a degree
But what this emcee didn't foresee
Is that the tables had turned
I was now on the other side of how I'd been burned
This upset sea began to churn
She was loving but controlling
Expressive but possessive
And I wasn't as obsessive
If the relationship's regressive,
Repressive, and aggressive
Live vicious vines
So the choice was mine
It wasn't turning into murder-suicide
If I'm being crucified, we're not unified
So I unilaterally ended it
But in mind, I bended it
Laid in the forest where growth once flourished
Now was burned to ashes
Matches in hand
Am I free to stand

I'm not one to command
Admittedly, I did fan the flames
What a fuckin' shame
If you think love is a game
Watch me take aim
While we both pass blame

[CHORUS]
I planned a murder-suicide
For just me and you
So decide
If our love is true

[OUTRO]
Memory of a time
Can change in a rhyme
To become strange and redefined
If you're so inclined
To become listeners of mine

This song was written for an album called *Fallen Flesh* that also got lost in the expanses of time. The concept of this track was taking the experiences of three relationships, one per verse, and showing how the hate that can sprout from initial love could become twisted and contorted in the mind. The song "Double Murder" which appears on *The L Test* is a sequel to this song.

Psycho Dick

[INTRO]
This song is for anyone
Who's every been on
Psychotic medications
Like Lithium
Fuck that shit

[VERSE 1]
I'm breaking away
Never faking this way
Stay like the only game
Worthwhile to play
Even if I'm gay
I'm not ashamed of the fame
My life's never lame
But through saying everything's the same
To whom do you pass blame
Now I'm drained
Fully insane
I status engrained
Engaged to something unchanged

Panic frantic manic
I still look Satanic
But nailed to the cross
I'm not fully the boss
I keep my body Tantric
Keep my mind enchanted
Came with captivating choruses
The audience now flourishes
Eating food which nourishes
Even if I curse
The words still serve a purpose

[CHORUS]
I'm sick
A psycho dick
Killing a bitch
Pick which chick

[VERSE 2]
Bipolar means I fuck on both poles
Leaving bullet holes
Tracking down moles
Souls worn thin like foot skin
I still hear the din
Voices telling me to make my own choices
No medication
No sedation
Just meditation
Full penetration
This sensation provokes a presentation

Representation of Revelation
Fuck consumption
Love masturbation
Lick menstruation
For mentation
Watch the suicide
Never abide in a censored world
Where a bitch is called a girl

[CHORUS]
I'm sick
A psycho dick
Killing a bitch
Pick which chick

[VERSE 3]
Eat shit
Drink piss
Don't miss me
Just set me free
So that you can see
That I can just be
A tree, branches ecstatic
Elastic stretched tight
I always put up a fight
I might take flight
With psychotic wings
An ape that flings feces
I'm the last of the species
Mice in the experiment

Share with me this torment
Government informant
A deceitful sex procurement
In a bloody current
Make sure you have the stomach
To come to terms with what you covet
Know thyself
Someday you'll reach the summit

[CHORUS]
I'm sick
A psycho dick
Killing a bitch
Pick which chick

I wrote this song when I was in the psych ward in Rhode Island. The track was intended to be part of the album *Fallen Flesh*, but like I said, that one got lost to the expanse of time. The concept was inspired by Tech N9ne's song "Psycho Bitch." It was difficult to transcribe these lyrics just from the live recording since the audio quality wasn't that great. But I figured out what all the words were and I'm pleased to have these lyrics here in the collection.

Apocalyptic Rhymes Chicago Cypher

[G-TEK THE ILL META4]
Just when I blink
Making these rappers extinct
Even before they are born
Leaving their fetuses meaningless torn
Aborting these devils and slicing the horns
Put on my armor of karma preparing for war
I walk with the Lord of Lords
My vocal cords a sword
I form a swarm of storms
When the Ill Meta4 performs
Get on the mic
And just zoom like a Lycan
A psychic with lightning
Tsunamis are heightened
With lyrics I'm writin'
I could be enlightened
That's saying too much
This is what Hip Hop has done to us

Emcees are dangerous
Most of these rappers are flavorless
Chopping their heads on some Vader shit
Mind is God, Alpha Omega shit
G-Tek is a human weapon
I be fighting these flows with words
My mental unfolds
A hybrid of Mortal Combat and Tekken
To fail was a secret blessing
To get you closer to Heaven
Not up in the sky
I'm talkin' inside
Spitting a rhyme and I channel Divine
Step in my mind and return an immortal
Then go through a portal
To glimpse at the end
There is no end
The cypher keeps goin'
Like I just keep flowin'
Life is forever in motion
Particles and wavelengths
Attraction, vibration
That's everything in Creation
Freed imagination
Through music I'm embracin'
Break chains we're enslaved in
Obligated to operate
On third eyes like Lasik
All I got are bars
Sick like Sars or eating shards

Sharp front yards
From parents born on farms
So I'm an animal on tracks
Act like the mic's attached to my arm
Only to the wack I attract harm

[NILOTIC]
I am the Murder Mystic
With the lyric
That'll leave you catatonic
Then I transform into a medic
Heal a skeptic
Your doubt is just pathetic
Cause I possess real magick
They push hypnotic products
She'll flaunt it to make a profit
And my relationship to this beat is not platonic
You're tragic, mainstream rap
Corporations got you in the consumer trap
I'ma go through the spirit flap
Combat with my writtens
Leave your bitches smitten
With my rhymes like sex kittens
My metaphors are too hot
You couldn't even grasp it with oven mittens
I'm flippin' grippin' mics like it's my life
I wed the octave, made the melody my wife
Spittin' remedy, you sent for me, I'm white
I'm blasphemy, enter the prophecy, rhyme tight
Word felony, wack emcees, end to history

Blind sight
Cause only perseverance makes you last
You thought I was behind
But I'm the future, you're the past

[B.E.Z.]
Look at the life you live
Take a second and open up your fridge
There's kids all around the world
Who don't know what any of that shit is
Look at what you take
But in return you'll never give
A single fuck
You were born into a family of kings
Well, that's luck
I was born with a sword in hand
Now that's tough
I never had a chance to hold the holy book
Now that's fucked
I waited every night of my life
For my mother to come give my blankets a tuck
Or after a long day just come and give a baby a hug
I feel the hatin', I'm just waitin' on the love
While it's closing in in every direction
There ain't nowhere to run
I'm smokin' blunts to stop the pain
But you motherfuckers think it's for fun
A man shooting up a theater
But y'all blame the gun
So now you trying to disarm me

To prevent civil war too
But in this day of age
I feel like that's what we aught to do
We've been beaten into submission
Till we're black and blue
And they're sitting there acting like
This is what's best for you
But this is what I'm askin' you
Is life just passin' through
Is that money you make just cruisin' through
That fin you spent to match your dude
The bill you spend on a hat and shoes
All goes back to corporate America
Who's sitting there fuckin' laughing at you
All that money you blew
All those numbers you drew
All those loans you took out too
Just to get through
They're fuckin' laughin' at you
Money, greed, and religion
Are the true root of all evil
You tryin' to enforce your religion
Makin' the Holocaust look like
It's about to have a sequel
I swear, fuck all these people
Where the hating, killing,
And discrimination is legal
But that's war
Where freedom of religion and beliefs
Are tore

Where you can find more bullet casings
Than cigarette butts on the floor
For one reason, cause you all want more
You're scum to the core
I don't give a fuck
This Lady Liberty bitch to me
Sounds like a money-obsessed whore
Where your first reaction
To every single problem is war

This was a fun little cypher I did in Chicago with G-Tek the Ill Meta4 and B.E.Z. There's a lot I really like in my verse on this one, maybe I should bring it back and make a whole song out of it.

Shout Outs

Thank you all again for sharing this journey with me. If you've made it this far in the book, I commend you for getting through all of that—I do like to write and write and write. This whopping volume is just the songs I wrote when I was working under the name Nilotic. Stay tuned for the next volume with all the songs I wrote under the name MC Pan.

There are so many people that I am appreciative of, and who have had a part in this whole journey of music and art. It would be difficult to name every person who has touched me along the way; so if I forget anyone, forgive me; you know you became a piece of these lyrics. Firstly, I'd like to thank my parents—without you I wouldn't be the person I am today, and I wouldn't change anything I experienced growing up because without it I may not have written so many multifaceted songs. The ones who were by me back when the Nilotic first emerged in Chicago, or Distania as I like to call it, deserve a standing ovation: G-Tek the Ill Meta4, Jose, Leo, Oscar, Julie, Domenic, Scarlet Eyes, Aleks, Jordyn, everyone at the Heartland Cafe, Stefinitely Slaq-r, Elan, Peter, Danny,

Bleedsynth, B.E.Z., Jerry Pokerton, and Infamuz Blaze who made some fire beats for me.

When I fled Distania, there were other beings from my soul family waiting for me in Providence. Big shout out to Sage Francis; if it weren't for me being so obsessed with his music, I may not have lived in Providence and had so many enriching experiences. The beautiful souls who came into my life in crazy Prov are Ill Will, Khyree, Chris Harley, Twizzy, Documentaries of the Dead, Tocxina, Jared Paul, Jay Wills, everyone at Occupy Providence, Coppa Shot, Brittney Blue, Dizzy, DubK, Randi, and everyone at As220. Thank you all so much for making my time in New England so memorable. I'm sure there are others I can't think of right now, so if you crossed paths with Nilotic on the East Coast, thank you for sharing your beautiful energy.

There are so many more people I should probably name, and if I think of them, I'll shout them out at the end of the next volume of lyrics. And if you're reading this, thank *you*. Just for you to listen, or to read, makes the sharing of this life all that much more amazing. Thank you for being you. I love you.

Avtar

Avtar Simrit is a modern mystic and an artist. His writings and art are inspired by mystical inquiry as well as all inner and outer journeys. Avtar's main artistic mediums are the written word, Hip Hop music, and video. To check out his music and other work, visit the author's website: www.mc-pan.com.

www.ingramcontent.com/pod-product-compliance
Lightning Source LLC
Chambersburg PA
CBHW020132130526
44590CB00040B/362